D0636924

B.C.H.E. – LIBRARY
DISCARD
00030424

PANORAMA
1842–1865

The world of the early Victorians
as seen through the eyes of the
Illustrated London News

Selected by
LEONARD DE VRIES

Foreword *by* Arthur Bryant
Introduction *by* W. H. Smith
Text abridged by
Ursula Robertshaw

JOHN MURRAY *Albemarle Street* LONDON

EDITORIAL NOTE

Throughout this volume the text is taken directly from the original issues of the *Illustrated London News*.

It has been difficult to reproduce some of the illustrations because the original wood blocks were destroyed during the First World War with the exception of those published in the first issue, and the original copies of the *Illustrated London News* were not always in a good condition. Despite this difficulty, several of these illustrations have been included on account of their historic and dramatic value.

Thanks are due to many for help and advice but in particular to Ursula Robertshaw for carrying out the necessary abridgements with the assistance of Charles Bricker; to Ilford Ltd in connection with the illustrations; to the University Library of Amsterdam; but, above all, to the Editor and staff of the *Illustrated London News* for all their willing and invaluable co-operation.

Designed by Joost van de Woestijne
and printed in Holland by the Ysel Press, Deventer
from type set in Great Britain
by William Clowes and Sons Ltd, London and Beccles

FOREWORD

BY

ARTHUR BRYANT

It is sixty years since I used to lie on the floor of my father's library, turning over the pages and drinking in the pictures of the vast bound Victorian volumes of the *Illustrated London News*. Thirty years have passed since I became a regular contributor to that journal and thirty-five since I first began to write for it. Yet even the tremendous changes that have happened in the world since then have been no more than a fraction of all that has been faithfully and vividly mirrored in the paper's pages since—a generation only removed from Waterloo—its first issue appeared on May 14th 1842.

Viewed in their entirety the bound volumes of the *Illustrated London News* constitute what is probably the most important single pictorial source for the social history of any age or country. I can think of no other from which the social historian of the Victorian age and our own revolutionary century can draw so much. Here is a living contemporary picture, drawn from week to week, of the life of Britain and the British people and of every country throughout the world with which they were associated in that long span of time. From the crowded indexes of its volumes one can see how true this is; there can be few places on earth that have not figured at one time or another in its pictures and letterpress. For in Victorian and Edwardian days the events depicted in its woodcuts, drawings and photographs were elucidated by long, detailed and first-hand commentaries. I recall how some years ago my old friend, Jack Lawson, the Durham miners' leader, sent me an account he had written of an explosion in a Staffordshire colliery that had made a tremendous impact on him in his boyhood. By taking down the relevant volume of the *Illustrated London News*, I was able to supplement his memories with a wealth of detail, both pictorial and descriptive, about this tragic occurrence—one which few but he could remember and which, so far as I am aware, figures in no modern history.

In a book describing English life in the Victorian age, I wrote that to turn over the pages of the early volumes of the *Illustrated London News* was to experience a social revolution. For its first volume pictures an England that, apart from the capital, was still predominantly rural—a land of cathedral spires embowered in trees, of country towns and market-places peopled with gaitered farmers, squires and smocked peasants. Where the manufacturing districts appear, they do so as a savage *terra incognita*, with rough unpaved roads, grim gaol-like factories and men and women of sullen and brutish appearance. "Even here," I wrote, "one feels that the country has only been occupied by a horde of nomad invaders; on the outskirts of Manchester there were still sloping wooded valleys with girls keeping sheep a stone's throw from the flat slate roofs and tall smoking chimneys." Yet by the end of the 'forties the background mirrored by the *Illustrated London News* has completely changed. "The stress is now on paved streets, vast Gothic town-halls, the latest machinery, above all the railroad. The iron horse, with its towering, belching funnel and long load of coaches, plunging through culvert and riding viaduct, spans the land, eliminating distance. The England of Winchester, Canterbury and Chester was already a thing of the past. The England of smoking Rotherham and Hull and colonial Crewe had arrived." And in that first volume for 1842 there is told, in picture and letterpress, week by week and with an urgency to be found nowhere else, the tragic tale of the rising of the starving workers of the manufacturing districts that looked, for a few nightmare weeks, as though it was going to culminate in an English revolution. Far more than the abortive and much publicised Chartist demonstrations of six years later it was the real crisis of the "hungry 'forties", causing Carlyle to write of the industrial north as "a dingy prison-house of rebellion, rancour and black mutinous discontent", and Tennyson to pen his ominous prediction:

> Slowly comes a hungry people, as a lion creeping nigher
> Glares at one that nods and winks behind a slowly-dying fire.

It is all there, set down in woodcut and print, in that wonderful first volume of the *Illustrated London News*.

Of the energy, enterprise and courage of the remarkable man who conceived and founded the world's first illustrated newspaper, Herbert Ingram of Boston, others have written in the pages that follow. But I cannot refrain from paying a tribute to his grandson, the late Sir Bruce Ingram, who took over the paper—then in some difficulties—in the closing months of Queen Victoria's reign and continued to edit it until his death in the winter of 1962/3. Like the paper he controlled—a national institution, and, under his direction, Britain's chief export journal in two world wars—he bridged with his working life an immense gulf of time without giving, even in his 'eighties, the slightest indication that he belonged any more to the past than the present. To the end he remained as enthusiastic and youthful as he was unassuming and dedicated to his beloved journal, an inspiration to all who worked for him. How he would have rejoiced in this book!

CONTENTS

The dates refer to the issues of the *Illustrated London News*.

A wonderful pictorial pageant of history began when the world's first illustrated newspaper proclaimed, "Here we make our bow, determined to keep continually before the eye of the world a living and moving panorama of all its activities and influences".

The panorama opened with the first issue of *The Illustrated London News* published on Whit Saturday, May 14th, 1842, containing as its principal feature two pages of pictures illustrating the Magnificent Fancy Dress Ball given by Queen Victoria at Buckingham Palace only two days before publication.

News of a disastrous fire at Hamburg which broke out on May 5th was brought to London by the steamship *Caledonia* when she anchored off the Tower of London during the evening of May 10th. The big fire was red-hot news—just the very thing for the first issue, so an artist hurried to the British Museum, borrowed a print of Hamburg, re-drew it on to a wood-block and added smoke, flames and sightseers. Then the picture was engraved and, accompanied by a full descriptive text, made a dramatic feature for the ILN's first front page.

The sixteen pages of the first issue had plenty of up-to-date news items in addition to the thirty engravings of various sizes. The letterpress included a Parliamentary Report; a Dreadful Railway accident near Paris; an Awful Steamboat Explosion in America; War in Afghanistan; The Bal Masque at Buckingham Palace; Royal Academy Exhibition; Cases heard at the Central Criminal Court; Horticulture; Everybody's Column; Paris Fashions; and three pages of small advertisements. The leading article began, "We commence our political course by a distinct avowal of an unconquerable aversion to the very name of 'Party'...". An engraving across the foot of the last page depicted a crocodile of two hundred men with ILN billboards above their shoulders announcing the advent "of this important publication".

ILLUSTRATIONS OF NEWS EVENTS

Illustrations of news events had been published in newspapers from time to time before the ILN's advent but not as a regular feature. The *Weekly Chronicle*, which fostered sensational pictures, went to town in 1837 when Hannah Brown was murdered by James Greenacre, whose trial at Newgate with its many gruesome details provided ample material for engravings in six consecutive issues. When Queen Victoria aged nineteen was crowned in 1838 the *Observer* published a somewhat crude engraving of the scene in Westminster Abbey; and two years later when she married Albert, later Prince Consort, the same paper contained a picture which had been engraved by Orrin Smith who later was to work for the ILN.

Those and other sundry illustrations were scanned eagerly by a young man, Herbert Ingram, who sold papers at his shop in Nottingham. Born of poor parents near the Market Place in Boston, Lincolnshire, in May 1811, Ingram subsequently attended the local elementary school and at the age of fourteen became apprenticed to Joseph Clarke, owner of a printing business in Boston.

Young Ingram's apprenticeship ended in 1832, and at the age of twenty-one he journeyed down to London where he worked in the printing trade for about two years, becoming familiar with the contents of the chief newspapers and making contact with many useful people in and about Fleet Street.

In the meantime his sister had married Nathaniel Cooke, with whom in 1834 he set up a partnership in a printing business which also sold newspapers and books at its premises in Chapel Bar, Nottingham. During the next few years Ingram became increasingly aware of the fact that many additional copies of the London newspapers were sold whenever they contained a picture of a topical event. Thousands of extra copies of the *Weekly Chronicle* were demanded when the public were eager to read all about the Greenacre murder and to see pictures of the accused man, his house at Camberwell and items more sordid.

Ingram dreamed of the day when he could launch his very own newspaper—a paper with plenty of pictures to illustrate the current news—but he knew that a lot of money would be needed for that purpose.

Although the business of Ingram and Cooke had become profitable, there was not enough capital to spare for the launching and running of an illustrated newspaper, but the partners had a useful sideline which could be developed. They sold a patent medicine—an early Victorian custom often indulged in by printers. The medicine, Parr's Life Pills, sold by the partners was favoured by thousands of people who bought them in boxes of different sizes costing 1s. 1½d., 2s. 9d., or 11s. for a "family box". The printing side of the firm came in useful for supplying the large number of illustrated pamphlets which were given away to advertise the medicine: "The Life and Times of Old Parr who lived to be one hundred and fifty-two years old, with remarks on Health and the means for Prolonging Life,—to be had gratis of all Agents". One agent wrote, "Please to send me one hundred dozen boxes small, and twenty dozen large as my stock is again low. I perceive my sale since a year ago has been 18,308 boxes".

The increase of this business encouraged Ingram and Cooke to operate from London and premises were acquired in Crane Court, Fleet Street, next door to Number Ten, where Palmer and Clayton's had their steam driven printing machine.

Plans for launching the illustrated newspaper were now being organised and Ingram became friendly with a young man named Henry Vizetelly who, with his elder brother, had an engraving and publishing business near to Crane Court. Vizetelly, a wood engraver, was already associated with others who engraved illustrations for books, and he knew many versatile artists including A. Crowquill, Kenny Meadows, "Phiz", and Leech, who were making drawings for *Punch*, then only recently founded in July 1841.

Based on Ingram's own ideas and Vizetelly's recommendations and suggestions, a million copies of a prospectus for "No. 1 of A NEW WEEKLY JOURNAL" were printed and distributed to the public in March 1842. "Entitled The ILLUSTRATED LONDON NEWS, Price Sixpence. Containing Thirty Engravings Every Week of the Most Interesting Events of the Day, in Addition to Forty-Eight Columns of News. Engagements have been made with Artists of Ability in Every Important Town in England and in Paris and other places on the Continent".

To ensure continuity of readership Ingram astutely dangled a free gift before the eyes of the many thousands of people who had been influenced by the prospectus, "To Subscribers who buy *The Illustrated London News* regularly each week for six months a copy of the splendid Colosseum Print of London will be presented". That Colosseum Print was to be one of Herbert Ingram's most brilliant ideas.

Palmer and Clayton were engaged to print the contents of the ILN at 10 Crane Court, and to publish it at Clayton's newsagent's shop at 320 Strand, on the north side of the church, St. Mary-le-Strand.

PREPARING THE FIRST NUMBER

Accommodation for the editorial department was made available at No. 10 and, as an editor was needed, Vizetelly introduced an experienced journalist, F. W. N. Bayley, aged thirty-four and the author of *Comic Nursery Tales*, *A New Tale of a Tub* and *Little Red Riding Hood*. A reviewer wrote of Bayley, "His verse is flowing and easy; rhymes seem to be his natural language, and his stories are evidently dashed off rapidly by a masterhand". Although Bayley was named as Editor there is no doubt he was only responsible for organising the descriptive text. Vizetelly, under Ingram's direction, was chiefly concerned with the engravings, and there is some evidence that Ingram's boyhood friend, Mark Lemon, lent a helping hand when he was not too busy editing *Punch*. No information, however, is available concerning Nathaniel Cooke's activities on the first issue. It may be he stayed up in

Nottingham to keep an eye on the Ingram and Cooke premises in that city.

The pictorial heading and title for ILN's front page had already been chosen by Ingram and engraved—St. Paul's Cathedral and the multi-flagged barges of the City of London Companies escorting the Lord Mayor's State Barge along the Thames to Westminster Hall. The engraving was made at Stephen Sly's wood-engraving firm and is signed S. Sly—a signature which frequently appears on ILN wood-blocks.

SATURDAY, MAY 14TH, 1842

Immediately after the first announcement of the forthcoming Fancy Dress Ball at Buckingham Palace, Ingram hurried down to the Blackheath home of John Gilbert, a young artist, nearly twenty-five years of age. Gilbert had become adept at drawing pictures direct on to the smooth surface of wood-blocks so that an engraver's work could begin immediately. He undertook to work for Ingram and arrangements were made to deliver eight pieces of box-wood to him with various news-cuttings describing the guests who would be attending the Ball and the historic costumes they would wear. The artist, after reading the details, was to use his fertile imagination and with a pencil draw the picture lines on the wood blocks which would then be taken back to London for engraving.

The date of the Ball was Thursday, May 12th, just before the Whitsun weekend, and Ingram realised that John Gilbert's double page of eight pictures of young Queen Victoria as Queen Philippa, escorted by the Prince Consort robed as Edward III and their numerous titled guests all in historic costumes, would make a strong topical feature. He therefore decided that Saturday, May 14th, was the appropriate day for his illustrated newspaper to spring to life.

The paper, on which the ILN was to be printed, had been ordered from Spalding and Hodge of Drury Lane, and they had to deliver it by horse and cart to Somerset House in the Strand where a Revenue official lifted the corner of each sheet and stamped it with the words "NEWSPAPER. ONE PENNY" around a design which included a crown and the ILN's name. The paper then had to be carted back to Crane Court for printing. In addition to the penny tax, the white paper itself was taxed and eighteen pence had to be paid for every advertisement published in a newspaper.

Activity at 10 Crane Court increased. Compositors were setting type, proofs were being read and corrected, engraved wood-blocks were accumulating, newspapers were being scanned for the latest happenings at home and abroad, and at long last came Saturday morning, May 14th, a mild day in Spring, temperature seventy, birds singing, omnibuses, hackney cabs, and drays all with horses clip-clopping over the cobble stones of Fleet Street—a wonderful day!

Inside 10 Crane Court the piston-rod of Palmer and Clayton's steam engine hee-hawed up and down to make a big fly-wheel rotate adjacent to the recess in the wall; governor-balls spun round to control the engine's speed; the engineer looked at the pressure-gauge and shovelled more coal into the boiler's stokehole; the printing machine manipulated its cogs, cranks and rollers, and as the printed sheets came hot off the press they were stacked and loaded quickly onto carts and galloped along Fleet Street, past Fetter Lane, through the old Temple Bar, past St. Clement Danes Church, down the Strand until alongside St. Mary-le-Strand the vehicles pulled up at No. 320 where Joseph Clayton in his paper-shop received the very first batches of the newly born *Illustrated London News* and sold them in quires to the eager crowd of newsvendors, who hurried off to their own shops in all parts of London and elsewhere.

The sale of the ILN's first issue exceeded 26,000 copies "which might have been doubled could we have anticipated the demand" but they made up for that omission during the next few weeks by reprinting it three times. Subsequent issues remained steady with an average of 24,000 weekly until a second Royal occasion presented itself in September when Queen Victoria went up to Scotland in the Royal Yacht on a fortnight's tour with Prince Albert.

Ebenezer Landells—"our distinguished artist"—aged thirty-four, was commissioned by the ILN to record the various incidents of the tour, and no fewer than fifty-six engravings were published in five consecutive issues with the result that sales continued to increase week by week until they reached 66,000 by the end of December, by which time the readers were eagerly awaiting publication of the Colosseum Print of London, as promised in the Prospectus "for all our subscribers of six months".

THE COLOSSEUM PRINT

Herbert Ingram believed that photography, first announced to the world in 1839, could be of use to his illustrated newspaper and he had in mind the publication of the giant view of London photographed from the top of the Duke of York's column, 124 feet high. Official permission was granted for photographs to be taken from its summit and Antoine Claudet, with his daguerreotype camera, climbed the twisting steps inside the monument. At the dizzy top he set up his apparatus and exposed a sequence of views of London, looking north, and another sequence looking south.

After development, the daguerreotype plates of silvery metal were laid side by side in two rows one above the other to make a lay-out of the picture which was to be printed on paper four feet four inches wide and nearly three feet high, but first an artist, C. F. Sargent, using a pencil, had to draw the photographic detail onto the smooth surface of the biggest wood-block ever made. It was composed of sixty pieces of box-wood joined tightly together "without line, speck or flaw" and then sent to Ebenezer Landell's engraving firm where he and his staff of eighteen assistants worked day and night for two months on the largest engraving ever executed. While it was being completed, the ILN moved into its own premises at 198 Strand, a big shop at the corner of Milford Lane facing St. Clement Danes Church. The ground floor was used as the publishing office, and on the three floors above four rooms accommodated the editorial and advertisement offices and an engraving studio. Two rooms were lived in by the new publisher, William Little, whose sister Ann was engaged to be married to Herbert Ingram.

By the end of the year, the great Colosseum View of London in 1842 had been engraved, stereotyped and printed by Palmer and Clayton at 10 Crane Court, and this famous picture was supplied in company with the ILN issue of 7 January 1843.

The print was a huge success and exciting scenes were witnessed at 198 Strand where crowds of newsmen shouted their demands to be served. At one period the staff were so tired that the premises had to be closed while the men rested.

THE FIRST ILLUSTRATED NEWSPAPER

By then *The Illustrated London News* had been well and truly established as the world's first illustrated newspaper—the forerunner of the French *L'Illustration* and *Le Monde Illustre;* Germany's *Illustrierte Zeitung;* Amsterdam's *Hollandsche Illustratie;* America's *Leslie's Weekly* and *Harper's Weekly; The Graphic; The Sphere* and scores of other well-known weekly and daily picture papers including in recent years *Life* and *Paris Match*.

But what of Herbert Ingram himself? Men who worked with him said he was short, broad-shouldered, dark complexioned, untidy and careless of appearance, but with fine intelligent eyes, a genial smile, kind-hearted and generous. If you wished to see him at 198 Strand you had to fight your way step by step through a howling mob of news-boys and men waiting for their supplies of the ILN. Arriving at the stairs, you went up to the first floor and joined a motley crowd of authors, artists, engravers and personal friends of Ingram. He was full of excellent ideas, determined to carry them through at all costs and would silence objections with a vigorous thump of his fist on the table. His pluck and enthusiasm were infectious and everyone worked with a will to get the paper out in time. Artists and engravers often worked sixteen hours a day, and sometimes thirty-six hours at a stretch with only a few snatches for meals, and an occasional half-hour's rest on the floor.

Other occupants of the editorial room were the Editor, F. W. N. Bayley—a portly figure with long ringlets of black hair—and John Timbs. Very few details are available about Bayley's activities, which were mostly literary no doubt, but he was lucky in having John Timbs as the "working editor", who, busy with scissors and paste, remained oblivious to the noisy buzz of conversation within, and the sound of traffic, people and bells (of St. Clements) outside in the Strand. Timbs had previously been editor of the *Mirror* and author of the books: *Curiosities of London* and *Year-Book of Facts*, and a critic had said of him that "he is a man of nice discernment who knows where to look for good things and to make the best of them".

Bayley disappeared from the scene early in 1846, and Timbs, with three assistants named Carlton, Clyatt and Wade, kept the editorial flag flying until 1852 when Ingram invited Dr. Charles Mackay, ex-editor of the *Glasgow Argus* and a forceful writer on foreign politics, to take the lead at ILN. He served there until 1859 and was followed by John Lash Latey, already on the staff, who remained responsible chiefly on the literary side of the paper until 1890.

Others who wrote for the ILN in its early days included Peter Cunningham, Douglas

Jerrold, Mark Lemon and Shirley Brooks. In addition to John Gilbert, artists included Henry Anelay, Alfred Crowquill, Birket Foster, H. G. Hine and Kenny Meadows—among a host of others whose pictures appeared during the ensuing years.

Wood engravers working for the ILN included Ebenezer Landells (1808–1860), and William Harvey (1796–1866) each having been pupils of the famous Thomas Bewick (1753–1828). Landells, artist and engraver, had a large staff of assistants and pupils and the signature "Landells" in small letters appears below many of the engravings. Pictures signed "S. Sly" were engraved by members of Stephen Sly's firm in Bouverie Street, just off Fleet Street.

One of the reasons for moving the ILN to 198 Strand was to get accommodation where its own staff engravers could work—"We shall be able to keep our wood engraving department further in advance by the retention of permanent artists ready at a moment's notice for the contingencies of every public event".

Wood for the engravings came from the box tree whose close-grained trunk grew to about seven inches in diameter. Slices sawn across the trunk had the bark removed and were cut into rectangles, the edges squared up and the surface made smooth for the artist's pencil. These blocks, about five inches wide, were then available for engraving.

THE ENGRAVER'S ART

When an illustration was to occupy a page, or double-page or even a larger space, the small blocks were drilled and channelled underneath for the insertion of brass bolts and nuts which gripped the pieces of wood together "without line, speck or flaw", thus making a printing surface of the size required. If a large illustration had been drawn on the surface of six blocks bolted together, the pieces could be unbolted and distributed to six engravers and when their work was finished the pieces would be bolted up again, thus saving much time.

How did these remarkable craftsmen, the wood engravers, work? The block, which was steadied by the thumb and fingers of the left hand, lay on top of a leather bag filled with sand. During daylight hours, the bag rested on a bench close to a window, but at night, an oil or gas lamp provided illumination. The engraver's head, with a watchmaker's magnifying glass clipped to one eye, would be bent down near to the block while the thumb and fingers of the right hand gently pushed the sharp front edge of the cutting tool—the graver—to shave away narrow slivers of wood so as to leave whites and tints between the darker lines of the picture.

If we look through a magnifying glass at these magnificent wood-cuts, we must marvel at the skill and patience of those wood engravers and regret that such artistic craftsmanship is now almost lost for ever.

PHOTOGRAPHY AND WOOD ENGRAVING

Photography, as a direct aid to the wood engraver, began to be used after Scott Archer's collodion process had been published in 1851. Hitherto, daguerreotypes had been traced and pencilled on the wood-block, but usually the printed results lacked photographic realism. The collodion process yielded a photographic image of an artist's drawing on the surface of the box-wood and thus the engraver could do his work without the delay and expense of having a pencilled drawing made on the wood. Some of the engravings published in the ILN of the Great Exhibition of 1851, and of the Crystal Palace at Sydenham during 1853–54, have a very "photographic" appearance. Photography "on the wood" continued to be used until the end of the 'eighties when the halftone and line processes came into general use for the rapid production of illustrations.

During the Great Exhibition in Hyde Park, circulation figures of the ILN rose to 130,000 a week, and to 200,000 in 1855 when five of its artists were covering the Crimean War. One of them, J. A. Crowe, wrote: "I had a hard day of it when a shell burst in my tent. I got outside in time to see a cannon-shot bowl through the place where I was sitting just before. Artillery fire became too hot for me and I walked to the rear with shells bursting about me for at least ten minutes. I have never had such narrow escapes of life as on that day."

Photographs of Crimean War scenes were taken by Roger Fenton who had a horse-drawn "photographic van" for use as a dark-room and to hold his cameras, glass plates, dishes, chemicals and tanks of water. He photographed over three hundred war scenes and military portraits, and some of them, including the van, were reproduced in the ILN.

PROGRESS AND PROSPERITY

Early in the ILN's career, a competitor appeared—the *Pictorial Times* which started, after witnessing the ILN's rise to fame, in March 1843, with the help of Henry Vizetelly. It lasted for a while until it was bought up by Herbert Ingram who combined its title with another acquisition of his, the *Lady's Newspaper*.

Opposition became more serious in 1855, during the Crimean War period, when Vizetelly and a publisher, David Bogue, started the *Illustrated Times* in June, price threepence—the ILN's price was fivepence. The success of the *Illustrated Times* met with Ingram's disapproval until in 1859 he bought it for several thousand pounds, with Vizetelly remaining as Editor under its new proprietor who had, since 1856, become Member of Parliament for Boston, Lincolnshire.

With the increased circulation and prosperity of the ILN, expansion of its premises became necessary and 9 Milford Lane, behind and communicating with 198 Strand, was acquired for the installation of the ILN's own printing machinery; and two machines, "with a power to produce nearly four times the present circulation" (over 60,000), were ordered in 1843, to be made by Middleton of Southwark.

At a later date, a "Four-Feeder Vertical Machine" which had been bought for four thousand pounds from Applegarth, came into use and could be seen printing copies of the ILN in the Machinery Section of the Great Exhibition, 1851. The machine was subsequently offered for sale at four hundred pounds when the space it occupied was needed for more modern equipment.

Additional working space was acquired from time to time and by 1860 Milford House, and several other buildings in Milford Lane, were buzzing with machinery and employees coping with the huge demand but, sadly, it was in that year that the founder, Herbert Ingram, died while on a tour in Canada and America. After visiting Montreal and the Niagara Falls, he had gone to Chicago with his eldest son, Herbert, aged fifteen, and on the night of September 7th they were among the several hundred passengers on the steamship *Lady Elgin*, which was touring Lake Michigan. While music and dancing was being enjoyed on board, there was a sudden crash, the ship lurched, rammed on the port side near the paddle wheel by the schooner *Augusta*, and sank thirty minutes later. Herbert Ingram, aged forty-nine, and his son were among the hundreds drowned. A statue to his memory stands near St. Botolph's Church in Boston, Lincolnshire.

His widow, Ann, became sole proprietress of the ILN and her interests were managed by its Printer and Publisher, George C. Leighton, in company with a friend of the family, Mr. Thomas Parry. John Lash Latey continued as Editor, ably supported by Mason Jackson, the Art Editor. Jackson's own experience as an artist and wood engraver enabled him to get the finest results from staff artists and engravers while exciting and important events were taking place during the 'sixties, in particular the American Civil War which broke out when the Confederates shelled Fort Sumter in April 1861. Frank Vizetelly, ILN's special artist and a brother of Henry, contributed a large number of vivid sketches of the bitter four-year conflict between North and South.

Other subjects of outstanding interest were the death of the Prince Consort in December 1861, the International Exhibition of 1862 at South Kensington, and the Marriage of the Prince of Wales to Princess Alexandra of Denmark in March 1863, when the ILN's circulation soared to over three hundred thousand copies. There was Garibaldi's visit to London in 1864; the completion of the Atlantic Cable in 1866; and the Great International Exhibition in Paris, opened by Emperor Napoleon III and the Empress in May 1867—the month and year which completed a quarter of a century's history in pictures recorded in *The Illustrated London News* which will celebrate its 125th anniversary in May, 1967.

W. H. Smith

[Mr. W. H. Smith began his career in the publishing office of *The Illustrated London News* at 198 Strand, a week before his thirteenth birthday in 1897. Later, he joined the editorial staff and subsequently became assistant editor and chief of the art department. His interest in the early history started while he was engaged on all-night fire guard duties at ILN's premises during the last war.]

No. 1.] FOR THE WEEK ENDING SATURDAY, MAY 14, 1842. [SIXPENCE.

[FIFTH REPRINT.]

OUR ADDRESS

In presenting the first number of the ILLUSTRATED LONDON NEWS to the British public, we would fain make a graceful entrée into the wide and grand arena, which will henceforth contain so many actors for our benefit, and so many spectators of our career. We do not produce this illustrated newspaper without some vanity, much ambition, and a fond belief that we shall be pardoned the presumption of the first quality by realizing the aspirations of the last. We have watched with admiration and enthusiasm the progress of illustrative art and the vast revolution which it has wrought in the world of publication. It has converted blocks into wisdom, and given wings and spirit to ponderous and senseless wood. It has adorned, gilded, reflected, and interpreted nearly every form of thought. Art—as now fostered in the department of wood engraving—has become the bride of literature, and there is now no staying the advance of this art into all the departments of our social system.

So now, when we find the art accepted in all its elements and welcomed by every branch of reading, when we see the spirit of the times everywhere associating with it, we do hold it as triumphant that WE are, by the publication of this very newspaper, launching the giant vessel of illustration into a channel the broadest and the widest that it has ever dared to stem. We bound at once over the billows of a new ocean—we take the world of newspapers by storm, and flaunt a banner on which the words "ILLUSTRATED NEWS" become symbols of a fresher purpose, and a more enlarged design.

The public will have henceforth under their glance, and within their grasp, the very form and presence of events as they transpire; and whatever the broad and palpable delineations of wood engraving can achieve, will now be brought to bear upon every subject which attracts the attention of mankind. Begin with the highest region of newspaper literature—the Political. If we are strong in the creed that we adopt, how may we lend muscle, bone and sinew to the tone taken and the cause espoused, by bringing to bear upon our opinions a whole battery of vigorous illustration. Regard the homely illustration which nearly every public measure will afford:—your Poor-laws—your Corn-laws—your Factory-bills—your Income-taxes—your Houses of Legislature—your police-offices—your courts of law—you can have them broadly before you, with points of force, of ridicule, of character, or of crime.

In the world of diplomacy, in the architecture of foreign policy, we can give you every trick of the great Babel that other empires are seeking to level or to raise. No estafette,—no telegraph—no steam-winged vessel—no overland-mail, shall bring intelligence to our shores that shall not be sifted with industry, and illustrated with skill in the columns of this journal. In literature, too, and in the field of fine arts—but let the future speak, and let us clip promise in the wing. We have perhaps said enough, without condescending to the littleness of too much detail, to mark the general outline of our design.

Here we make our bow, determined to pursue our great experiment with boldness; to keep continually before the eye of the world a living and moving panorama of all its actions and influences; and to withold from society no point that its literature can furnish or its art adorn, so long as the genius of that literature, and the spirit of that art, can be brought within the reach and compass, of the Editors of the ILLUSTRATED LONDON NEWS!

View of the Conflagration of the City of Hamburgh.—(*See next page*)

DESTRUCTION OF THE CITY OF HAMBURGH BY FIRE

By the arrival of the boat Caledonia, news has been brought of an immense conflagration which took place on Tuesday morning, [May 5, 1842] at one o'clock in the city of Hamburgh. The district in which the fire broke out consists entirely of wood tenements, chiefly of five and six stories high, and covering an area of ground of about thirty to forty acres. The whole of the buildings on this large space have been totally consumed to the number of more than 1000. The fire was thought to have originated in the street known as the Stein Twite, in the warehouse of a Jew, named Cohen, a cigar manufacturer, and who, upon good grounds, has been taken up on suspicion as the incendiary. The wind at the time blew a stout north-wester, causing the flames rapidly to spread.

A body of one thousand Prussians were immediately marched into the town, and waggons and ammunition were brought down the Elbe to blow up the houses, and to stop the conflagration, yet the fire seemed to increase. The principal houses and hotels, and all the best shops, with their costly property, have not a wrack left. The whole presents a mass of ruins fallen into the dykes which intersected the streets. Upwards of 100 lives have fallen a prey. Owing to the inadequacy of the engines, little could be effected, and the strenuous efforts of the people themselves were of no avail. At the time of its occurrence no water was procurable, owing to the tide being low, so that the street canals were dry.

The loss is at present incalculable, and business cannot be thought of nor even entertained for days to come. There is scarcely a family in the place which has not suffered in some way or other. The conduct of the people is most admirable; quiet, docile, and orderly, but with deep despair and agony displayed on many a countenance, as their existence vanishes before them in flame. The last two days have witnessed continual departures to the country of carts, carriages, barrows, people loaded with furniture, and all they could save of their property. The fields around Hamburgh are covered with furniture and household ware. Whole families, old and delicate women, little children, and the sick have no covering but the canopy of heaven. They are seated in the surrounding villages and the fields, and the utmost misery that can be imagined prevails. They are sleeping thus—rain has at last come, but only now to add to their afflictions. There is no lodging now to be had anywhere for love or money. The loss of property may be estimated, at the least, at from 2,000,000l to 2,500,000l of British money.

Accounts were received on Thursday, stating that the fire had been got under, and that no apprehensions were any longer entertained for what remained of the city.

AN ANTIDOTE FOR THE SLAVE-TRADE

We submit to the amputation of a limb for the sake of life; we hang a man for the benefit of society; we remit punishment, for the sake of truth, when evidence is furnished against accomplices. The appliances for obtaining and rendering justice must be coincident with its demands. For national crimes there must be national remedies. Those nations that dare the world's scorn deserve the world's execration, and when humanity bleeds it behoves the humane to act with energy. The slave-trade is now indelibly branded by civilized Europe as infamous in those nations that allow it iniquitous towards man, and a wicked defiance of the Almighty.

There are no guilty deeds without guilty men. The hardened piratical crew of a slaver are not the only, nor indeed the chief sinners. The breeders and owners of slaves; the builders, owners and equippers of slave-ships; the rascal dealers in our race, the bargainers for blood upon the coast, the marketing buyers in America, Cuba, Brazil; the inhuman taskmasters in each exacting, not only sweat from the brow, but blood from the flesh. These are the beings that Europe execrates.

The sailor on a slave-ship is not so criminal as the owner of the cargo and owner of the ship. He seeks bread—his employers gold, through the sacrifice of blood. The sailors now employed in that trade feel that they are in desperate course; many of them, if they could and had the inducement, would quit it to-morrow. Now, every British port in the British colonies offers an asylum for any kidnapped African, and restores him to his natural freedom; and it may be hoped that, ere long, all other countries, not excepting those who still uphold slavery, will also become such asylums.

Can an inducement be offered for the crews of these slave-ships to carry the slaves into one of these ports, instead of taking them to countries where they would be bought and sold as slaves? If the different colonies can now subscribe to pay the passages for free immigrants, and of free negroes, to the colonies, it would answer as well to subscribe to meet a reasonable gratuity to the crews of slavers, and accomplish thereby the captives' freedom.

The cry from the colonies is for free combined labour, because the manumitted blacks work now mostly for their own account, and chiefly in occupations hitherto neglected. Free emigration cannot be resorted to in any sufficient degree from Europe to tropical climes, nor is it desirable; and spontaneous emigration from Africa is prevented by the convulsions in which that country is kept through the slave-trade.

Now, if we combine a remedy for the honest demands and necessities of a drooping agriculture, and, at the same time, apply a final cure to the evils of Africa; and if the interest of humanity can be combined with those of the planters, not only of the West Indian, but of the very shareholders of Brazil and Cuba, whose existence is periled by further importation of slaves, why should we hesitate to do it?

By these means self-interest would be made to act as a useful assistant in the cause of humanity. The greater risk for the owners of slave-trading vessels to lose their property by the turning of their crews against them, would deter them from embarking in such hazardous speculations.

The "ILLUSTRATED LONDON NEWS," *Published every Saturday. Thirty Engravings. Price Sixpence.*

The above engraving represents the public announcement of this Paper on Friday last. Two hundred men paraded the streets of London to proclaim the advent of this important publication.

LONDON: *Printed by* R. PALMER *(at the office of Palmer & Clayton) 10 Crane-court; and published by* J. CLAYTON, *at 320, Strand. Saturday, May 14, 1842.*

Shortly after the return of Prince Albert to Buckingham Palace on Monday afternoon, May 30 [1842], her Majesty, accompanied by his Royal Highness, proceeded in an open carriage and four horses, preceded by outriders, for her accustomed drive in Hyde Park, the royal equerries accompanying the *cortège* on horseback. On her Majesty's return about ten minutes past six o'clock down Constitution-hill, a young man was observed to advance towards the road along which the royal *cortège* was passing, and upon the carriage approaching the spot at which he stood, he was seen by police-constable Tounce to advance within three yards of it, and at the same instant take from his waistcoat pocket a pistol. Tounce instantly rushed towards him for the purpose of knocking it out of his hand, seeing that it was aimed at her Majesty, but at the moment he seized him the pistol went off without injuring any person. The royal carriage continued its course towards Buckingham Palace, and the prisoner, who did not appear to be more than 20 years of age, was conveyed to the lodge adjoining, where he was searched by the inspector on duty, who found in his pockets a bullet and some powder, as well as the pistol, which was still warm, and affording convincing proof of its recent discharge. The prisoner was driven to Gardiners-lane station-house, where he was questioned, but he refused to give his name, or make any statement.

Then he was conducted to the Home Office, but he still refused to give either his name or residence, or make any admission; but a youth who had happened to be in the park at the moment of the apprehension, recognized him to be a person of the name of Francis, whose father resided at No. 100 Titchfield-street. It was stated that he exactly answered the description of the person who made an attempt to assassinate her Majesty in the park on Sunday evening. We were not inclined to credit this story of a previous attempt, but, on enquiry, we find that it was too true, but as her Majesty was not aware of it, the circumstance was not allowed to transpire. Upon this occasion, however, both her Majesty and Prince Albert were perfectly aware of the attempt, and in fact perceived the pistol flash. Her Majesty, however, displayed her usual presence of mind, and did not betray the least symptom of alarm.

Intelligence of the desperate attempt flew like wild-fire throughout the metropolis; and in a very short time the various members of the Royal family, as well as several of the foreign ambassadors and large numbers of the nobility, hastened to the palace to congratulate the Queen and Prince Albert on their providential deliverance; and throughout the evening a dense concourse of persons of all classes surrounded the gates of the palace, all of whom appeared to be animated by one feeling of abhorrence of the individual who had thus made the regicidal attempt.

Let us hope that the late sad event, while it has excited so much painful feeling in every quarter, will yet, in the demonstrations of loyalty to her Majesty which it has been the means of calling forth, prove to our sovereign how deeply implanted are feelings of reverence and affection for her person in the hearts of the vast body of her people.

THE FASHIONS

Rue de la Chausse d'Antin, Paris. June 1842

Dear Mr Editor,—The ladies are delighted with the new bonnets, yet I fear the most eloquent description will fail to inspire those feelings of enthusiastic admiration in the female heart, which the possession only of these seductive objects are capable of doing. One in particular, is worn for dress—the *chapeau de paille de riz;* the interior trimming being of a double *ruche*, and on the exterior, long, pendant, white plumes, descending transversely forwards, drop gracefully over the shoulders. The bonnets most *à la mode* for the promenade are those formed in *tulle* of various tints; the *voillette en tulle* in pale rose being fastened on the side by a clasp of artificial flowers.

The *Pélerines cardinales* become multiplied to such an extent that the *extravagantes* possess eight or ten. They are now to be found in all dimensions; those in English lace are greatly admired, but the *dentelles Louis Quatorze* are really MOST splendid.

Such are, dear Mr. Editor, a few of the latest revolutions in our *modes*, not omitting to mention that the pretty scarfs are now considered almost indispensable—Au plaisir, Monsieur, JULIE.

THE QUEEN'S FIRST TRIP BY RAILWAY

On Monday June 13 [1842], the Queen and Prince Albert, for the first time, returned from their sojourn at Windsor Castle by way of the Great Western Railway. Preparations on an extensive scale were ordered for the transit of the Royal pair from Slough to the Paddington terminus, which were carried out with the greatest secrecy. Immediately after a quarter past ten o'clock, the Royal train started from Paddington for Slough, which station it reached shortly before eleven o'clock. Previous to the departure from Paddington, the Royal saloon, the fittings of which are upon a most elegant and magnificent scale, were tastefully improved by bouquets of rare flowers arranged within the carriage.

At Slough the Royal party were conducted to the splendid apartments at the station designed for the reception of royalty, but her Majesty proceeded to the line, and examined the Royal Saloon, inquiring very minutely into the whole of the arrangements.

Precisely at twenty-five minutes past twelve o'clock the Royal special train entered the Paddington terminus, having performed the distance in twenty-five minutes, and on her Majesty alighting she was received with the most deafening demonstrations of loyalty and affection we have ever experienced.

THE QUEEN'S DRAWING ROOM

Her Majesty's last Drawing Room for the season was held yesterday at St. James's Palace.

Our engraving may furnish our fair readers with an idea—though, of course, only a faint one—of the immediate ceremonial of reception—but of all the details of this brilliant conclusion to a series of dazzling court assemblies, we refer to our column of Court and Fashionable News.

DEATH OF A MISER—SINGULAR AFFAIR

A few days since a Mr. R. H. Laurie, who is supposed to have been an officer in the army, died in the back-room on the second floor of the house No. 21 High-street, St. Giles's, in a state of apparent destitution, so much so, that it was deemed advisable to hold an inquest on his remains. He had been missed some days by the people living in the house, and his room door being found fastened, it was broken open, and he was found a corpse. At the inquest held before Mr. Wakley, M.P., his death being found to arise from natural causes, a verdict accordingly was returned; but at the same time the witnesses who were examined said, they had no doubt he was possessed of a considerable fortune, as they had often seen bank notes in his possession. They further stated that he was averse to all society, and had been frequently heard to say that he had done with man, woman, and child, and that he neither wished to visit anyone, or be visited. He had occupied the room, for which he paid 2s. 6d. per week, two years, during which time no person had called upon him. He would never allow any one to enter his apartment. The parochial authorities used all their endeavours to find out his relations, if he had any; and no one having made any inquiry after him, Cole and Harvey, two of the beadles of the parish, attended by another person, examined the room, and found bonds and documents relating to money in the funds to nearly 1000l. Who is entitled to the property is unknown.

THE DISTURBANCES IN THE MANUFACTURING DISTRICTS

We have [August 1842] to record the disastrous occurrence of a turn-out of manufacturing labourers in and about Manchester, which must be regarded with sorrow by wise and thoughtful men. It would appear that the sudden and turbulent display of congregated thousands, leaving their daily employment—marching upon mills, forcing willing and unwilling alike to join them and, in a moment, paralysing the whole activity of the natural enterprise of their neighbourhood,—arose, in the first instance, from a reduction of wages in one quarter, given almost without notice, and taken by the men as the omen of a general intention on the part of the masters everywhere else. At once, with a desperation of purpose, they gathered in half-starved thousands, resolved to abjure work, unless they can have "a fair day's pay for a fair day's labour"; and partly with riot, partly with invective, partly with threat, plunged the sober population into fear, and created anxieties, natural to these troublous times, from one end to the other of the land.

All the manufacturing districts have been up in arms; at Preston the insurgents were fired upon, and some of them wounded mortally. At Stockport, where there are upwards of 20,000 persons out of employment who have no resources but those of plunder and beggary, a large body of rioters broke open and pillaged the workhouses of food and clothing, and mobs robbed the provision shops. Troops, guards, and artillery have been poured in upon the shocking scene of insurrection; and there seems to have been a spreading organization of a most formidable and disciplined character. The fact that troops had been ordered off to the disturbed districts soon became publicly known, and produced an intense feeling of alarm and excitement in the mind of individuals generally.

The anti-corn-law leaguer and the chartist are, we fear, responsible for these agitations—responsible, as we think, to their Queen, their country, and their God. We are no partisans; we do not oppose, abstractedly for their peculiar doctrines, either the chartist or the anti-corn-law leaguer; we leave all political opinion, however violent, its fair play; but we despise the infamous diplomacy which would make its game out of the miseries of the people. Nothing can more excite our indignant rebuke than the revolutionary villain or the quack preacher of politics, who says, "I have a charter to achieve here, or a corn-law to repeal there, and, now that the people are starving and in tatters, I will convert their rags into banners of rebellion, and their hunger into the sign of blood." Yet this, we believe, is the course that *was* pursued, furnishing the key to all the riots and seditions that disturbed the land.

Preston—Attack on the Military.

Every way we lament the dismal occurrences that have transpired, from which, because they are destitute of social peace and order, even the justification of injury is taken away. Heaven knows that our cause is with the poor, and strongly have we reasoned and remonstrated on their behalf; but we set up JUSTICE and HUMANITY as our household gods, and for neither rich nor poor will we despoil their altars. There is no justice, there is no humanity, in the late revolts; and although we rest their blame and guilt more upon the inciters than the enactors of the crime, yet we will not take the part of the latter because we execrate the former.

Further particulars of the disturbances.

Reports stated that immense bodies of rioters from Wigan, Chorley, and the district of the collieries, some making them as numerous as 15,000, armed with axes, spades, bludgeons, &c., were on their way to Preston. It was reported that a large cotton factory at Bamberbridge was partially destroyed by the mob. From the church steeple and the North Union Railway bridge, which commanded extensive views of the various roads to Preston, it was soon ascertained that the mob were in a body on their road towards the town of Chorley. However, the police and military were all brought together, and took up their station near Walton-bridge, the police being in the turnpike road, and the Rifles on each side concealed behind the hedges. About three o'clock in the afternoon a mob of about 1000 persons, chiefly armed with iron truncheons, reached Walton, passed through the village, and were about entering the town, when the police force attempted to prevent them, and in consequence a battle commenced. Several of the police were severely wounded, one of whom had two fingers nearly severed from his hand by a blow with an iron bar. It soon became evident that the police force would be defeated, and the appearance of the mob became so alarming that orders were given to the military, who instantly burst through the hedges on each side of the road, and presented a bold front to the mob. The sudden appearance of the Rifles spread consternation and dismay in the ranks of the insurgents, who fled in all directions.

Attack on the Workhouse at Stockport.

The more remarkable features of the proceedings at Stockport were the extortion of money from mill-owners as well as shopkeepers, and an attack on the New Union Workhouse, Shaw-heath, where the mob forced an entrance and immediately commenced to help themselves to bread and money. Information of this was conveyed to the authorities, and they hastened to the spot with the constables, and infantry, and captured about forty of the rioters.

CRICKET MATCH

On Monday July 18 [1942] an interesting match took place at Lord's Grounds, wherein the relative merits of the fast and slow systems of bowling were tried by eight gentlemen and players with three bowlers on the new system, and the same number with three slow bowlers. The same event has been contested on four previous occasions, and the match excited considerable interest. The fast bowlers were Alfred Mynn, Esq., — Redgate, and — Dean, with E. Bayley, William Felix, R. W. Keate, and F. Thackeray Esqrs, Box, Butler, Dorrington, and Guy, against Lillywhite, Hillier, and Nixon, with the Hon. R. Grimston, R. Kynaston, and — Anson, Esqrs, with G. Lee, Hammond, Pilch, and Wenman, on the old systems. The first innings only was completed on each side, when the wickets were struck—the result being in favour of the fast bowlers by 115 runs, to 89. Of the players on the swift bowling side, Box secured 35 runs, and W. Felix, Esq., 23; whilst the Hon. R. Grimston scored 41 runs, and carried his bat out, at the conclusion of the innings of the opposing party. The match was concluded on Tuesday, the fast bowlers coming off victorious by a majority of 47 runs on the two innings. The numbers scored by the players on the new, or over-hand system, was 194, while their opponents scored only 147.

AT THE SURREY THEATRE we have not only "singing" but "acting" for the million. Donizetti's opera of the *Love Spell*, or Bellini's opera of *La Somnambula*, with Shakespeare's tragedy of *Macbeth*, and all for the small charge of "sixpence"! The operas are played with the strongest cast of English singers in London; and if we cannot pay so high a compliment to the tragedy, we should recollect that, although they are not "the tragedians of the city", they are now held in high estimation on the other side of the water.

SOMERSET HOUSE STAMP OFFICE

Somerset House Stamp Office—The Illustrated London Newspaper unloading

Somerset House!—what takes your journal
 there,
(The anxious reader naturally axes
With very fairest of polite digressions)—
Somerset House!—the house of stamps and
 taxes?
To which we answer in a tone as fair,—
'Tis for such merchandise that we go there—
To buy up *stamps* before we sell *impressions*!

The process this—as first important dodge,
We seek the firm of Spalding and of Hodge,
And purchase paper there—
Ream upon *ream*, enough to make you stare,
Until in one grand solid pile it seems
As big as the Cathedral built of *Rheims*,
With which we do—what you of course desire
To know, and very naturally in-*quire*!

Well, then, we put a portion in a cart,
And give our man another cart to start
A *carte-blanche*, bless your heart!
Away he goes at once, and never tarries:
Meanwhile his laden dobbin little knows
Between the *shafts* (or how his heart 'twould
 please,)
That by and by such *shafts* of wit as these
Will surely lighten all the load he carries!
When loads are *thundering* heavy, labour-
 heightening,
'Tis strange what penchant horses have for
 lightening!

Arrived at Somerset House, our cart gives not
Its freight a *somerset* upon the spot,
But is unladen there—
Taken down steps, and placed to get the air
In an official area of the nation.
Yes, all our reams go sliding down below,
In all of which there's nothing wrong, you know,
If *station-ary* suits an *area station*;
Although we should be done uncommon brown,
If rain came on, and it got *wetted down*!

Then by and bye—
It under shelter goes,
With load on load the groaning porters tramp,
Till Government, with a distinctive *die*,
Alters the *colour* of its worth, Heav'n knows,
And makes it of a very different *stamp*!
They print it *red*, by process quick and clever;
But when *we* print it, 'tis more *read than ever*!

Next, they return our paper, that well earns
A right to boast of those same stamp returns,
Which prove,—and not a doubt the fact en-
 cumbers,—
That although young, we've learned to "lisp
 in numbers;"
While any little gentle castigation
That we receive but aids *our circulation*!
For let our brethren *cut* us as they may,
'Tis clear we still have better *cuts* than they!

Well—so we print with all our might and main—
Our steam gets up in Palmer's Court of Crane,
The willing engine deftly rolls along,
While *blankets* turn our *sheets* off throng on
 throng:
In *trucks* the reams, fast as they come to hand,
Are wheeled into our office in the Strand;
And who that among hand-loom weavers dwell,
Ere saw *truck system ever work so well*?
Then comes the business of the day—to sell!
Though publisher counts on with all his speed,
Our sale grows unaccountable indeed;
While all the newsmen—of our varied charms
Have quite enough of *folding* to their arms.
So numbers fly, until we grow too stint;
THE ILLUSTRATED NEWS is out of print!
Ho! rush to Palmer, then! bid him endeavour
Perpetual motion! Print away for ever!

THAMES TUNNEL.—The annexed representation of the entrance to the Thames Tunnel we offer to the notice of our readers less in the form of an illustration of its subject than as a specimen of the new system of surface-printing, of which Mr. Palmer, of Newgate-street, is now experimentalizing a more general introduction.

Scene from the ballet of "Alma". (See next page.)

Agnes and Laura reading their lessons in public.

LONDON SOCIETY FOR TEACHING THE BLIND TO READ

On Monday February 20 [1842] a meeting of the friends of this Society was held at the London Tavern, Bishopsgate-street. The secretary read the report, from which it appears that the benefits of the Society had been conferred on 29 boarders of the establishment, besides upwards of 50 day scholars. It also alluded to the great superiority of teaching adopted by this Society, which enabled the children, and even adults, to read with ease and facility, and which had been introduced into Egypt by a Mr. and Mrs. Leider, who came to England for the purpose of obtaining a knowledge of it, the prevalence of blindness in Egypt rendering such a work of mercy of the greatest importance. The whole of the Gospels of the New Testament, the Book of Psalms, the Book of Genesis, and several other books, had been printed by the Society; and a few select hymns had already been embossed by one of the boys, which afforded an expectation that several inmates may ultimately become compositors, and thus be put in possession of a perfectly new method of earning a comfortable subsistence.

The Chairman in a long and eloquent speech, enforced the claims of the Society upon public sympathy. The appearance of the poor blind children before them was a proof of the helplessness of their conditions. The children were called upon to read various chapters in the Old and New Testaments, and the facility with which they turned to any particular portion of the Scripture selected excited the admiration of all present. Two Chinese children, "Agnes" and "Laura", were objects of great interest, and read their appointed lessons with English emphasis and discretion. Attempts were made to confuse them by presenting to their touch books of a different character from those to which they had been used, but the hoax was in every case promptly detected, and, after a moment's explanation, their names and characters were readily announced.

The system of tuition followed by this society is the one invented by the late Mr. Lucas of Castle-street, Bristol, in 1834; its principles are simple, natural, and easy of acquisition. Abandoning all previous methods, a modification of stenographic characters is employed, together with a system of contractions, which, while they more readily informed, actually *refreshed* the delicate sense of touch. This is now called the "Britannic Universal Alphabet for the Blind". It is composed of four straight lines and four semicircles, compounded with a sort of crotchet-head; these form thirteen simple characters, and thirteen formed from the roots of these with a crotchet-head to each. There are ten double letters from the same roots, distinguished also by the crotchet-head; these also represent the nine figures and the cypher, whether used as numerals or ordinals. In all thirty-six characters are employed.

The manner in which the characters of Mr.

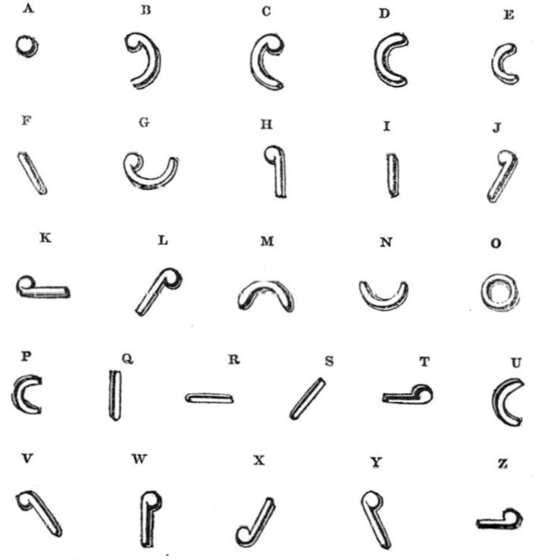

The Britannic Universal Alphabet for the Blind.

Lucas are used may be seen in the following Psalm, only that the extract is given in Roman letters instead of using the stenographic characters.

PSALM THE 100TH

Mak a joyf nois u t L all y lands.
Serv t L w gladn, cm bf his prsnc w singi.
Kno y that t L he hs G; it is he tht hath made us, a nt we ours: we r hs ppl a t shep f hs pastur.
Entr n hs gats w thanksgivi a n hs corts w prais: be thankf u hm, a blss hs nam.
For the L is good; hs mrci s e lasti; a hs mrci ndurth to all gnrsahns.

It will be observed that the repetition of numerous letters are avoided; particles are represented, in most instances, by the initial letter, and when a word, having been once mentioned, recurs immediately or frequently, it is represented by its initial letter also.

The Society recommend that teachers of the blind may be usefully employed in writing and embossing lessons, sums, or even music, for their use. This is done by means of a hard black-lead pencil, or by a style, upon stiff paper, or on thin metal. It may be necessary to remark here, that the letters of the alphabet by which the blind are first taught should be nearly twice as large as those by which their lessons are embossed.

THE BALLET OF 'ALMA'

We have here a scene from the grand serio-comic ballet of 'Alma', a pure Adelphi gem of dancing, devilry, and melo-drama—a sort of compound of Fitzball and Satan—reality and romance, with beautiful leading lines, spectre lovers, ducal halls, palaces of revelry and arabesque dances, waltzes of fascination, Satanic courts, galopades of all the characters of the infernal regions, and, as the great climax of wonder, THE STORM OF FIRE!

Mr. Paul Bedford, in the respectable *rôle* of *Lucifer* himself is unlikely to find his *match;* Madame Proche Giubelei, is not the *Alma Venus genetrix* of Byron, but the heroine *Alma* herself; Mrs. H. P. Grattan is *Tinderina*, and susceptible to the *sparks;* and last, not least, Wieland the magical is master of the slippery night.

Can we not insinuate here a portrait of this same Wieland? the best melo-dramatic devil on the stage: the most fertile body-twister and limb-disposer of all the body-corporate of jumpers and clowns; the living episode of elasticity and indiarubber. Oh yes, he can squeeze in anywhere, and therefore he will squeeze in here! But no! we cannot catch him yet. Either he has cut the wood-engraver, or the wood-engraver has not *cut* him; in either case the light of his countenance is reserved for future illumination.

THE FASHIONS

Rue de la Chaussee d'Antin, Paris. July 1842

Mon cher Monsieur,—The gallantry of your sex declares that of all things in creation woman is the loveliest; but from henceforth none of us will be unwilling to share the palm of beauty with the really charming flowers which our ever-inventive *artistes* have recently produced—flowers that never will suffer that evanescence which destroys the beauty and brilliance of Flora's choicest *parterres.* The *bouquette de camails* which blooms today in its native loveliness, on the morrow, no longer possessing its freshness and attraction, is heedlessly cast aside; but the flowers of which I write when arranged with *goût* upon a summer ball-dress of *organdie* or *barege,* will last a whole season, and attract by their freshness, beauty, and novelty, an endless throng of admirers. They are worn in wreaths, to border the flounces and ends of short sleeves, the most elegant being the blossoms of reseda, geranium, and myosotis. The flowers of the *coiffure* should correspond with those of the dress. Robes are being worn considerably fuller, and the most prevailing skirts are made to consist of four or five large tucks; the first commencing six or eight inches from the waist, and each succeeding one increasing considerably in size to the bottom of the dress. Au plaisir, mon cher Monsieur,

FELICE.

PHOTOGRAPHIC PORTRAITS IN COLOUR.—Yesterday we had an opportunity of witnessing this new and important discovery, and truly glad are we in being able to say, the great objection to this method of producing portraits is at length removed; hitherto the portraits of aged persons only were really striking, their peculiar expression depending less upon colour than upon light and shade. Now may be seen at either of Mr. Beard's establishments, portraits, striking as life, of young and old, each exhibiting the peculiar complexion of age and health, and which alone was necessary to render this wonderful process equal to the original idea of its still more wonderful discoverer, Mons. Daguerre, that is permanently fixing upon the face of a mirror the colour and character of its reflected objects.

THE SEA-PARACHUTE OR LIFE-UMBRELLA

Sir,—The admirably written comments on the "British contrivances for saving shipwrecked and drowning persons" have earned for you every good and thinking man's cordial thanks, and I am proud to proffer you the poor tribute of my acknowledgement. If, sir, there were more men in the field of humanity with your Samaritan-like sentiments, we should have fewer occasions for exercising our sympathy and succour; and believing it to be a duty we owe to each other to interchange our thoughts upon points of public utility, I take upon myself to submit what I conceive to be a new and available aid on occasions of shipwreck. In nine cases out of ten a lee-shore is the scene of death and destruction; this I lay down as my postulate. Now we are all old enough to recollect the buoyant properties of a parachute, since they were publicly demonstrated only a few years since by a safe descent from a balloon. Upon this parachute principle I propose to construct ship-umbrellas; and, setting out, as I have done, with the hypothesis that the vessel in distress is on a lee-shore, I question not for a moment but that a ready-made, or even hastily rigged, article of the description in question would safely convey a man from the ship to the shore, and thus afford the facile opportunity of rescuing the crew, by cradle or otherwise.

I am not, it may be charitably supposed, insane enough to attach any value to this sea-parachute in cases where the wind is not, or nearly so, dead on shore; but I confidently repeat, that nine-tenths of the ship-wrecks that anually befall us are deducible to a lee-shore, and for my melancholy data I instance the recent casualties on the sea-board of England and France.

In brief, then, a tough stick, with a duck, or light canvas, top (if slightly tarred so much the better), and with braces radiating to a grummet, from the end of which (stick) about half a fathom of rope should depend with a short strong piece of wood to sit on, might be made (where no "vessel of mercy" is at hand) the simple instrument of preservation.

The sketch exhibits the construction of the proposed machine, and the circumstances under which it would be used. CALEB.

THAMES TUNNEL OPENED, MARCH 25, 1843

This great work has been watched with anxiety throughout Continental Europe, and had not modern ingenuity extended "the wonders of the world" to seventy times seven, the Thames Tunnel would long rank as the eighth wonder; for this bold attempt to effect a communication between the shores of a wide and deep river, without any interruption to its navigation, has had, and probably will have, no parallel for many ages.

In 1823, Mr. (now Sir M. I.) Brunel, completed a design, which received the sanction of many gentlemen of rank and science, among whom was the Duke of Wellington. The spot between Rotherhithe and Wapping selected is, perhaps, the only one between London Bridge and Greenwich where such a roadway could have been attempted without interfering essentially with some of the great mercantile establishments on both sides of the river. Early in 1824 a company was formed for executing the Tunnel, Mr. Brunel being appointed the engineer; and he began, in March 1825, by preparing for a shaft 50 feet in diameter, which he commenced at 150 feet from the Rotherhithe bank of the river. This he effected by constructing, on the surface of the ground, a brickwork cylinder of the above diameter, 42 feet in height and 3 feet thick. Over this he set up the steam-engine for pumping out the water, and for raising the earth to be taken from within the cylinder, which he then sunk *en masse* into the ground. By this means he passed through a bed of gravel and sand, 26 feet deep, full of land-water, and, in fact, quicksand, in which drift-makers formerly had been obliged to suspend their work. When the shaft was sunk to its present depth of 65 feet, another shaft, of 25 feet diameter, was sunk still lower, till, at the depth of 80 feet, the ground suddenly gave way, sinking several feet.

The shaft and reservoir completed, the horizontal excavation was commenced at the depth of 63 feet, 38 feet in breadth, and 22½ feet in height. It was to be defended by strong walls, and to have room within for a double archway, each 15 feet high, and wide enough for a single carriage-way and footpath. The mode in which this great excavation was accomplished was by means of a powerful apparatus termed a *shield*, consisting of twelve great frames, lying close to each other like as many volumes on the shelf of a book-case, and divided into three stages or stories, thus presenting 36 chambers of cells, each for one workman, and open to the rear, but closed in the front with moveable boards. The front was placed against the earth to be removed, and the workman, having removed one board, excavated the earth behind it to the depth directed, and placed the board against the new surface exposed. The board was then in advance of the cell, and was kept in its place by props; and having thus proceeded with all the boards, each cell was advanced by two screws, one at its head and the other at its foot, which, resting against the finished brickwork and turned, impelled it forward into the vacant space. The other set of divisions then advanced. As the miners worked at one end of the cell, so the bricklayers formed at the other the top, sides and bottom. There were completed—

In 1836	117 feet
In 1837	28 feet
In 1838	80 feet
In 1839	194 feet
In 1840, in two months,	76 feet

leaving only 60 feet to complete.

The opening ceremony was on Saturday last. At the Rotherhithe shaft two marquees were erected, flags were hoisted, bells were rung, and the entire scene was a demonstration of triumph. At four o'clock a signal gun was fired, and the procession started from the directors' marquee down the staircase, along the western archway of the Tunnel, and, on arriving at the shaft at Wapping, the procession ascended and crossed the landing, and then returned by the eastern archway to Rotherhithe. Sir I. Brunel, in his passage through the Tunnel, was cheered with heartfelt enthusiasm.

Rotherhithe entrance to the Tunnel.

The great circular shafts are now provided with handsome staircases for foot-passengers —that at Rotherhithe being shown in the engraving. The carriage-ways have yet to be constructed: each will consist of an immense spiral road, 200 feet in diameter, winding twice round a circular excavation, 57 feet deep, in order to reach the proper level; the road itself being forty feet wide, and the descent very moderate. The cost of the Tunnel has been about £614,000, very much more than was at first contemplated. Since Saturday the Tunnel has been open to foot-passengers at 1d each, and many thousands have already cheerfully paid the toll.

The Marquesas Islanders

The Marquesas Islanders

These new subjects, or allies, of Louis Philippe are graphically sketched by a correspondent of the *Times*, who says, "Having lately smoked a cigar with his naked Majesty King Yutete, who is a fat, good-natured savage, and having visited the entire group of islands, I can assure you and your French readers, that as to soil, harbours, situation and appropriateness for either occupation or immigration, the Marquesas are the most worthless cluster of islands in the Pacific Ocean."

As the Marquesas are to be the scene of the last French colonization farce, we give from the best authority sketches of the natives—fine muscular fellows, but miserably ignorant. The group displays their gods, with two figures holding out, as peace offering to their Gallican friends, the staple produce of their country, pigs and *rats*. Long may Louis Philippe live to reign over his new subjects!

THE EXHIBITION OF THE ROYAL ACADEMY

The Royal Academy opened its doors on Monday [May 8, 1843], and some thousands of persons have ere this gratified their *prestige* for the pictorial by a ramble within its "walls of art." We have lounged our hour with the common crowd, and must confess that we make our report with very decided disappointment. The exhibition is hardly good—certainly not great. The pictures generally are of mediocre class, and the *coup d'oeil* is anything but imposing. The gems of the Gallery are some of the best tributes of never-failing names; but these we go seeking out and dwelling over as it were episodically, as they are scattered like little islands of genius amid seas of common-place. There is no grand and imposing *ensemble*—the eye is not arrested here, dazzled there, fixed anywhere, by prominent indications of mind-mastery. Oh, but you have a wide ocean of portraiture! Yes, you may glance at one broad side of the great room, and glut your fancy with as much tailoring and millinery and as little flesh and blood as ever were gathered within gilt framing. You have a few rare exceptions of beauty creeping up into light, and these you catch eagerly, and thank their painters for arresting your attention from the crowd of chalk faces in the fashions of the day. Alas! When will the patronage of the Academy be so industriously directed and so well bestowed that the *trade* in Art will be less evident, and its loftier spirit be more developed before the world? When will imposing and undenied beauty become not its exception but its rule?

Let us now glance at a few of the subjects which seemed most to attract the notice of the public. These are chiefly by Landseer, Stanfield, Roberts, Creswick, Etty, Eastlake, Howard, Marton, Turner, M'Clise; and a few more recorded favourites; some, however, only favourites of the cliques.

Landseer's pictures are indeed glorious copies from the natural world. Look at the noble boy, with his sweet ingenuous face, mounted on that living pony, and as bright and animated as all the other forms of life around. Look at the dogs, the game, and see how they are painted, how they speak! Or turn to those horses brought to drink at that transparent water—that crystal, that seems to shine and move within its depths. *There* is genius for you, if you will!

Now run away to Turner—presto—from sober beauty to sparkling insanity. Here is a man who has a mania for painting atmospheres—who brings you before his canvas, and makes you sneeze with the dust of powdered rainbows. It is pitiable to see art so deformed into madness. And yet, see how much force of colour this artist can bring into sun and water; how he can rear temples in the gold that glitters from the sky, and make vessels sparkle with the ore on sail and prow as they career over the dancing wavelets. He is an inscrutable person that erratic Mr. Turner.

How eloquent is Roberts this year! What calm, classic grandeur folds its chastened poetry around his pictures! How he revels in a fine noble simplicity of art! Behold his ruins—the falling column, the broken temple, the marble shining in decay. Roberts is the greatest painter of his time.

Etty, as usual, revels in nudity; he only clothes his forms in beauty, and leaves them totally divested of garments which might fold modestly around them too. No doubt, however, that there is much poetry in this painter's art.

Stanfield must not be omitted from the list of those whom we love to praise. His pictures are delicious—his only fault a certain occasional chilliness.

Most beautiful is Creswick—his fresh trees are green as memory—his sweet natural landscapes look as if they were brought bodily from their country homes, and registered "in fair epitome" upon "the painter's page."

Let these general remarks serve to indicate to our readers where they may best go first in the Exhibition.

THE STATUE OF NELSON IN TRAFALGAR SQUARE

Exhibition of the Nelson Statue at Charing Cross. Illustration below: Nelson's Column

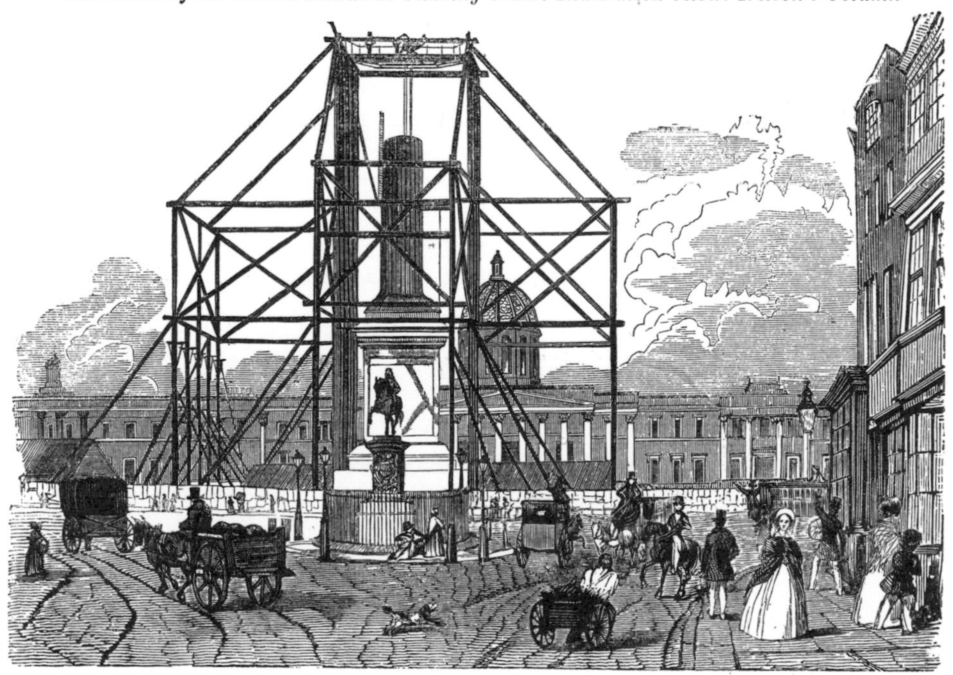

The statue of Nelson—the hero of Trafalgar—having been completed, has been for a short space made visible to the public from a nearer point of view than many of them are destined to have of it in future. It has been exhibited on the surface of *terra firma*, previous to its elevation to the summit of the column, henceforth Nelson's Column, in Trafalgar Square—a locality which, were it not for the common-place character of the front of the National Gallery would become the finest open space in the metropolis. The exhibition is not only a well-advised concession to public curiosity, but an advantage to the artist, being a means of making familiar to the people the talent of one of our best sculptors. Those who have seen his "Nelson"—colossal in size—the features true to nature—a portrait in stone, not an idealism of a hero—the costume, that of an English Admiral, a costume which no skill can elevate to dignity, or transform to the graceful—will have received, probably, a mingled impression. Unless they remembered they were looking at an object intended to be seen only at a great elevation, they may have been surprised at a sort of coarseness in the workmanship. Yet it has all the finish that can be required, and it has the great merit of likeness and character—one perhaps inseparable from the other in the countenance of such a man as Nelson. It has the sharp, angular features, the expression of great activity of mind, but of little mental grandeur; of quickness of perception and decision; and withal, that sad air, so perceptible in the best portraits of the warrior, of long-continued physical pain and suffering, the consequence of his many wounds, which accompanied him throughout his brightest triumphs, though it never abated his ardour or weakened his energies. The expression is a peculiar one; it is more afflicting to the eye than the expression of deep thought, and though as mournful, it is less abstracted than that of meditation.

If ever man earned his greatness, both by action and suffering, it was the hero of Trafalgar. While we feel a satisfaction that a public memorial to him is now completed, we cannot help regretting that more than thirty years should have elapsed before so obvious a duty to his renown was accomplished. His monument can hardly be considered as a national tribute to his fame: it is a funeral record, it is raised in a sacred spot, and is consecrated by religion; the interest it possesses is of a higher and more sacred kind. This statue is the public and secular memorial—the tribute of the citizen to the warrior—and till now, in the metropolis of the nation he fought and died for, that tribute has remained unpaid! However, this colossal statue is now completely finished, and the separate pieces of stone, of which it is composed, put together. The figure of the great naval commander measures seventeen feet from the base or plinth on which it stands, to the top of the hat. The whole is cut of stone brought from Scotland, from the Granton quarry of the Duke of Buccleuch. It weighs nearly eighteen tons, and will be taken to pieces in order to be put up. The statue was thrown open to the public last Friday and Saturday, October 27 and 28 [1843], and was visited by a hundred thousand persons.

The Queen's arrival at the Chateau d'Eu

In the middle of August intelligence reached Louis Philippe, King of the French, that Her Majesty Queen Victoria was about to close the session of Parliament, and afterwards to repair on board her royal yacht, in order to seek a change of air and scene. Louis Philippe had recourse to some delicate means of ascertaining the probability of Her Majesty's being graciously disposed to accept an invitation to pass a few days at the royal chateau of Eu; and the result of this preliminary precaution having proved satisfactory, he made preparations for receiving with due distinction the honoured and honouring sovereign. They involved a complete revolution within the Chateau d'Eu; for it was necessary, that the apartments appropriated to the use of the King's own family should be resigned by them for the occasion.

The most extensive dispositions were likewise made for the entertainment and comfort of the Queenly guest and her consort: services of gold, rich porcelain vases, and other beautifully-painted ornaments from the manufactory of Sevres; noble tapestry hangings; and carpets of a texture so delicate that the admiring guest hesitated to put her foot upon them, lest she should mar so much beauty, or crush the lovely and tempting objects represented.

The guns of the battery at Treport announced about three o'clock on the afternoon of Saturday September 2nd that the flotilla conveying and escorting the Queen of England was in sight, the repeated discharge of ordnance, which multiplied and became more deafening as the steamers neared the port, excited the most lively feelings of impatience and curiosity in the minds of the expectant attendants, and of the spectators stationed on the quays and jetties of the port.

Louis Philippe himself proceeded to the Queen's yacht to greet her in person, and whilst the royal recognition was taking place, the batteries ashore and all the vessels in the road, opened their fires and continued to salute the Queen all the time Her Majesty was being rowed ashore. Queen Victoria looked in exceedingly high spirits, and appeared greatly gratified with her meeting. As soon as the commotion had a little subsided, the King of France handed his royal visitors into the state chariot. The shouts of the multitude arose, and the warmth of the cries seemed to please the royal party. At seven o'clock the royal carriage entered *la grille d'honneur* and drove up to the grand entrance, where, amidst the shouts of the soldiery, the sound of the cannon, and the strains of the regimental bands playing "God Save the Queen", Her Majesty alighted and she, led by the King of the French to the front of the balcony, bowed in the most condescending and graceful manner to the brilliant and mixed assemblage before retiring from view.

The second day of Her Majesty's visit being a Sunday, she spent the morning at divine service in one of the noble saloons of the palace, after which she was conducted over the principal apartments of the royal residence. In the evening the Queen attended a dinner of a very grand description, partaking somewhat of a state festival, covers for between seventy and eighty people being laid. On Monday, the preparations for a splendid fête champêtre, which the King had determined upon offering to Her Majesty, were commenced, not withstanding the aspect of the sky was black and threatening. The spot selected for the banquet was the Mont d'Orleans, a spot situated in the interior of the forest of Eu. At a quarter to four o'clock the royal cortège appeared amidst great cheering. The Queen of England sat on his Majesty's right, and immediately behind her, the Queen of the French; whilst the Queen of the Belgians sat behind her royal father. The carriages were six in number, four being drawn by six horses, and two by four. The people were admitted close to the royal table during the collation, and every opportunity was afforded to allow them to observe narrowly the illustrious guests.

That same night, Her Majesty attended a concert in the Galeries des Guises, and the following day, September 5, Prince Albert reviewed a squadron of about 600 men of the 1st Regiment of Carabiniers à Cheval, the afternoon being dedicated to a visit of inspection to the fine old church of Notre Dame d'Eu. The state of the weather on the fol-

The young Belgian princess promenading.

lowing day deterred the royal revellers from making their proposed marine excursion, and a *répas aux bois* was improvised by the King as an agreeable substitute. Tuesday was the day of departure, and was accordingly clouded with regret. At precisely eight o'clock the royal party embarked, amidst a roar of artillery from the batteries at Treport and Mers. The whole of the French royal family went on board the royal yacht to make their adieux, after which they returned to their chateau in the same state and ceremony in which they arrived.

It being generally known that our beloved Queen would return to the shores of her kingdom at Brighton, the authorities of that town made preparations to receive Her Majesty with the honour befitting the occasion; and all their efforts were most cordially seconded by the loyal population of the place, who welcomed her home with boisterous huzzas.

On Wednesday September 13 Her Majesty and Prince Albert landed at Ostend, to be greeted by the King and Queen of the Belgians; the two princes were also there, and the young princess, shown in our engraving, enjoying the sea-breezes on the sands, with her attendants and a royal footman. The royal visitors remained in Ostend until Friday, when they left in a special train to visit Bruges. Every house was decorated; a splendid triumphal arch was erected, and the streets were crowded by the inhabitants, shouting and shrieking with perfect abandon.

The following day the Queen extended her progress to the city of Ghent, visiting the cathedral, attending the theatre, and returning to Ostend in state in the evening. Monday saw the reception of Her Majesty at Brussels, where the preparations were most stately and theatrical; there was a concert of the Grand Harmony in the open air in the park, and a dinner party in the evening. On Tuesday the royal party proceeded to Antwerp, reaching it in the afternoon. On the way there, at the Railway station at Malines, a deputation of several young ladies presented our Queen with a basket of flowers and a scarf of the finest Mechlin lace.

At one o'clock on Wednesday September 20, the Queen and Prince Albert stepped on board the royal yacht, and on Thursday morning at ten minutes to eleven landed at Woolwich Dockyard, where they were received by a guard of honour of the Marines, with their splendid band. Her Majesty appeared in excellent health and spirits, as did also Prince Albert. Her Majesty's progress through Belgium claims this ample record:—it is an event totally unexampled in history, when considered with the friendly nature of her visit, and the manner of her reception everywhere by all classes of people. Not even Queen Elizabeth was received in so welcome, so noble and so national a manner in her progress through England, as Queen Victoria has been in a land to which until now she was a stranger.

Presentation of flowers at Malines.

The royal railway carriage and engine. Illustration below: Interior of the railway carriage.

THE ROYAL RAILWAY CARRIAGE

The carriage constructed for Her Majesty's use is of a very superior description, scarcely parallelled in the records of coach-building. The carriage itself is oblong, about 13 feet by 7 feet, constructed of the finest mahogany; it is double-panelled and stuffed with felt, in order to lessen vibration and increase warmth. The carriage is divided externally into three compartments. The body rests upon a bed of the finest ash, a coating of India rubber being placed between to destroy vibration. At either end of the state saloon, are small compartments, for each a guard, who has a powerful argand lamp, which on passing through tunnels, reflects a strong light through a ground-glass in the panelling. The roof of the carriage projects six inches and rises in the form of a dome, where a ventilating apparatus is fixed. A newly-invented spring has been adopted to render the motion of the carriage perfectly easy. The carriage is painted dark lake relieved with scarlet and gold; the upper quarterings having a broad border of French white round the plate glass windows.

The interior of the carriage is lined throughout with delicate blue satin, wadded and tufted; the hangings of the windows are elegant draperies of blue and white satin. One extremity of the saloon is occupied by an ottoman and two chairs furnished in satin, *en suite* with the curtains. The carpet is Axminster, and by means of a curtain the saloon can be divided into two compartments.

The Dog Smugglers.—The contraband trade carried on by dogs on the Franco-Belgian frontier continues to increase. The number of dogs thus employed is estimated at 80,000. A premium is given for the destruction of each of the quadruped smugglers, and immense numbers have fallen victims to the douaniers, but they are immediately replaced. Their homes are in France, where they are well fed and kindly treated, and their education consists in sending them into Belgium, where they are starved and severely flogged by men dressed as French Customs-house officers; so that they have the uniform in horror, and in the course homeward carefully avoid it, taking a circuitous route as soon as they catch sight of it. When they are let loose to return home, laden with five to six kilogrammes of merchandise, they proceed with rapidity, and they are sure of good treatment on their arrival.

PRINCESS' THEATRE

On Wednesday evening last [February 21, 1844] we imported from the West a biped whose name was *Tom Thumb*, with the military prefix of "General", who strutted about like a miniature Napoleon, and afterwards represented what are called the "Grecian Statues". The production of this little monster affords another melancholy proof of the *low* state the legitimate drama has been reduced to!

This extraordinary minikin man, Charles S. Stratton, known in America as "General Tom Thumb, junior" weighed 9 lb. 2 oz. at his birth, somewhat more than the average weight of a new-born infant. At about five months old he weighed 15 lb., and measured 25 inches in height; since which time he has not increased in stature; and his present weight is but 15 lb. 2 oz. He has light hair and complexion, has a fresh colour and is uniformly cheerful. He is stated to have been born Jan. 11, 1832. He is, however, a *little man* in all save his voice, which is still pitched in "childish treble". He has been exhibited in New York etc. where his miniature palace, furniture, and equipage, excited considerable curiosity. When he embarked for England, he was escorted to the packet by not less than 10,000 persons.

"THE ILLUSTRATED LONDON NEWS" STEAM PRINTING MACHINE

Our readers are doubtless aware of the erection of two new printing-machines, of unusual magnitude and power, for the printing of this paper. There are two separate machines; one for printing one side of the paper, one for the other. These machines are impelled by a six-horse power steam-engine, of the high-pressure variety—that is, the power is that of six horses at a pressure of 25lb per square inch in the boiler; by raising the pressure, the power may be proportionately increased. The engine is considered capable of working four machines, if required.

Each machine consists of a great traversing table and four cylinders, two of mahogany and two of iron; the iron ones being underneath; and a series of endless tapes circulates over each mahogany cylinder and each iron one carrying the paper. The unprinted paper is placed on a table opposite each mahogany cylinder; and the uppermost sheet of the heap being pressed against the cylinder, it is seized and held against it by a small diameter roller, placed at the end of a lever. The mahogany rollers convey the sheets into the toils of the endless tapes, which, circulating round the iron rollers underneath, carry the paper with them. The type is placed upon the traversing table, the iron rollers being so adjusted as to press upon its surface; and the paper thus receives the impress of the type. The printed paper is conveyed by the tapes to a stage above the machines and there deposited.

There are two distinct inking apparatus, one at each end of the table, the types being in the middle; the iron cylinders must rise and fall alternately, so that when one is pressing upon the type the other will not. Without this expedient, the types, after inking the paper on the one cylinder, would, by passing under the other cylinder without an intermediate supply of ink, produce an imperfect impression. To make the paper *register* properly, minute holes are made in each sheet of paper; and when transferred to the other machine these holes are adjusted to corresponding points there, preserving the register with exactness. These points are not stationary on the feeding-board, but are withdrawn the instant the paper is seized by the cylinder.

These machines work at the rate of 2000 perfect impressions an hour.

ACROSTIC APOSTROPHE

ON OUR FIRST ANNIVERSARY.

*T*welve months in frolic round the sun
*H*ave circled since thy task begun,
*E*ncylopede! of all that art has done!

*I*n the May morning of thy birth
*L*oud were the plaudits of thy worth!
*L*earning smil'd as on a flower
*U*nhop'd for in her classic bower—
*S*cience, with friendly hand, was near
*T*o guide thee to her farthest sphere!
*R*eligion frown'd not, but approv'd
*A*nd Poesy gave songs she lov'd!
*T*ime pluck'd the winter from thy wing
*E*ntailing on thee endless spring:—
*D*ecember may salute, but with no sting.

*L*egends tell us nothing great
*O*r good was ever yet create—
*N*othing worthy of the mind,
*D*id not somewhere envy find:—
O'er this thou art triumphant:—Fame
*N*ought but thy "welcomes" doth proclaim!

*N*o! Thou hast reach'd a great and glorious height
E'vn in the onset snatching victory,
*W*ith hands, like infant Hercules, whose might
*S*how'd in his cradle what he yet would be!

HER MAJESTY WITH HER ROYAL GUESTS AT THE OPERA LAST WEEK

One of the most splendid sights that human magnificence could present to the eye was to be seen at Her Majesty's Theatre on this occasion [June 8 1844]. The presence of our gracious Sovereign and Consort Prince alone has often shed a lustre upon this aristocratic and noble *salon*; but, appearing as they did, attended by two such stars, as his Imperial Highness the Emperor of Russia, and His Majesty [? Frederick Augustus, King of Saxony], the spectacle was dazzling in the extreme. No theatre in the world could afford such a *coup d'oeil* of majesty, nobility, beauty, rank—fashion—wealth—power—in short, all that can make a nation great or interesting, as was to be seen and wondered at on last Saturday night at the Opera.

At the end of the first act the National Anthem was sung with admirable effect; for then a beloved sovereign was receiving the heartfelt homage of her people, and the potentates of other lands were congratulating her upon their sincere and ardent affection. Afterwards followed the Russian National Hymn, which was admirably executed by the band. The house was crammed from the floor to the ceiling. The opera "Il Barbiere", and other entertainments, were but heedlessly attended to—his Imperial Majesty's eyes seeming to *basilisk* everybody.

By the way, we pitied many anxious beings in those side boxes which are ingeniously contrived to enable the would-be spectators to look at their *vis-a-vis* neighbours instead of the stage. They stretched and stretched their necks, but they were as far from seeing the "grand sight" as they were from the centre of the earth. When will our theatrical architects gain a *little* knowledge of their business?

THE EPISCOPAL FLOATING CHURCH

The Episcopal Floating Church has been brought so prominently before the public eye that we have prepared a view of the interior for the gratification of our readers. It appears that this marine church was originally a sloop of war in the royal service, where she signalized herself in many desperate encounters. But now her "battered hulk" has been moored in the Pool of London, to serve the peaceful uses of a Christian congregation. She has accommodation for about 500 persons, and is regularly attended by the inmates of the Destitute Sailors' Asylum and Sailors' Home, the Sailors' Orphan Girls' School, and by a changing multitude of sailors from "off shore" and "afloat" in the tiers of ships in the neighbourhood. Boats are provided on Sundays at the Tower Stairs for the free passage of sailors or their connections who may wish to attend the ship service.

Interior of floating church.

PERIODICAL NOVELS.—We must not omit a few lines for the latest periodical novel of Mr. Dickens. The first number of "Martin Chuzzlewit", the new work of the famous Boz, is not of a character decided enough to enable us to speak with much confidence as to its future probable success. The opening passage, intended as a satire on the follies of aristocracy, struck us as exceedingly tame, and wanting in that force and pith which used to distinguish Boz. Cannot he take the friend's advice given by Blackwood in the last number, and be in less of a hurry to multiply the number of his books?

EMIGRATION TO SYDNEY

The St. Vincent, towing out.

It will no doubt be in the recollection of our readers that a Government grant was made to assist families and single men, agricultural labourers, shepherds, carpenters, smiths, wheelwrights, bricklayers and masons, being of good character, to emigrate to Australia, limiting the number to five thousand. Amongst these were to be included a certain portion of single women and girls, between eighteen and thirty years of age, who had been in domestic or farm service. There is, perhaps, something extremely melancholy at the idea of quitting our native land—and true it is that absence only serves to strengthen the links that unite us to HOME; for in whatever part of the world an Englishman may be, he still looks with ardent affection and longing desire to the spot of his nativity. But with all these feelings, dear and precious as they are, on second consideration there is not so much to excite painful sensations in emigration as at first there seems to be. A large field is opened for skill and industry; there is a prospect of gaining a competency which promises a "welcome return"; and unhappily there exists in England so much real distress, that anything in the shape of improving the conditions must be grateful to the feelings. True, the voyage is long, and no one who understands the nature of the fickle elements but must be sensible of the many unpleasantnesses attendant upon a tedious passage in a crowded ship; but where there is health and strength, and a willingness to labour, they are soon forgotten in the quiet of occupation on shore.

On Monday [April 8 1844] one hundred and sixty-five souls, men, women, and children, embarked at Deptford, on board the St. Vincent of 628 tons, preparatory to sailing the following day for Plymouth, where she will receive all who may be assembled there from the western part of England; from thence she will proceed to Cork, and take in emigrants from Ireland, quitting the last-mentioned port on the 16th of April, for Sydney.

The depôt at Deptford is a building fitted up and arranged with bed-places, bedding, etc., in distinct apartments, separating the married from the single, and a large dining-hall, where the emigrants get their meals. Here they continue collecting between the periods of sailing of the respective ships, and all are expected to be present two days before the day of embarkation. On Monday the St. Vincent received her living freight on board from the depôt, and they were immediately counted off into messes of eight or ten each, and victualled for the day. Between one and two o'clock we witnessed the spectacle of taking the first meal, and it certainly was a most interesting scene. The married people were very decently attired, though not so much so as the single, for in several instances, amongst the latter, both male and female, there were indications of gentility in dress and manners that caused surprise.

The apartment of the unmarried females was rather dark, but still there was light enough to show several really handsome countenances and good figures, whose departures from Old England seemed to cast a reflection upon the bachelors they left behind. If there is any gallantry in Sydney, many that we beheld cannot be long after their arrival without husbands. There was not the

The emigrants at dinner amid-ships.

remotest indication of want or pauperism amongst the whole. One married woman, extremely handsome, was rather elegantly arrayed; she was tall and graceful, and her fashionable apparel set off her figure to great advantage; her husband, a quiet, inoffensive-looking man, habited as a mechanic, but very clean and neat, had a cast of reflective thought upon his countenance as he sat near to her, contemplating the surrounding objects, and occasionally glancing at his wife with solicitude and anxiety. What their former history was there was neither time to enquire, nor would it have been delicate to have questioned if there had been opportunity.

We append a statement of weekly allowance, made to each adult during the voyage:—children being victualled at half the scale, and of course the provision is served out in proportions daily:—$4\frac{2}{3}$ lb. of bread, 1 lb. of beef, $1\frac{1}{2}$ lb. of pork, 1 lb. preserved meat, $1\frac{3}{4}$ lb. flour, $\frac{1}{2}$ lb. raisins, 6 oz. suet, 1 pint of peas, $\frac{1}{2}$ lb. of rice, $\frac{1}{2}$ lb. preserved potatoes, 1 oz. tea, $1\frac{1}{2}$ oz. roasted coffee, $\frac{3}{4}$ lb. sugar, 6 oz. butter, 5 gallons and 1 quart of water, 1 gill pickled cabbage, $\frac{1}{2}$ gill vinegar, 2 oz. salt. This, taken singly, is adequate food, but when united in messes (say of ten) where appetites are not equal, is certainly not bad living, and we have not heard any complaints against the respectable agents on account of the quality of the victuals supplied. After the emigrants have arrived in the colony they are allowed ten days free access to the ship, with all its advantages, should they not be hired or obtain employment before the expiration of that time.

The St. Vincent appears to be a fine vessel, well found, and may the Almighty prosper her voyage, which is usually about four months in duration.

THE TELEPHONE OR MARINE ALARM AND SIGNAL TRUMPET

The principle of this Telephone, whose objects are to convey signals to vessels, transmit orders, and prevent collisions, is one of musical accord, composed of four alternate notes, given out separately, played like those of a cornet, and prolonged whilst the finger remains on the note. An Indicator, or Signal Tell-Tale, is placed on the Telephone Drum to denote the signals made, composed of 16 holes in four parallel lines, numbered at the top 1, 2, 3, 4, and coloured red, white, blue and yellow, only one peg being placed in the same horizontal lines of holes. The Telephone gamut notes are arranged for numbers either by the public or private key, the alternate notes of the gamut C, E, G, C, being denoted by 1, 2, 3, 4.

The Telephone will convey signals four or five miles; and as a fleet sailing in three columns will not extend over more than three miles, it will be sufficient for the guidance of the fleet in foggy weather, by day or night.

THE GIRAFFES AT THE SURREY ZOOLOGICAL GARDENS

The above is a faithful and spirited representation of the curiosities whose recent arrival at the Surrey Gardens we noticed last week. They are now regularly domiciled in their new abode, and appear to enjoy the comparative freedom which their commodious dwelling affords. All are in the finest possible health and condition, capering about in the wildest glee, and indulging in the most amusing antics in their rough play with their keepers and with each other. The antelopes are of those extremely rare and beautiful species the *Addax* (Lichtenstein) and *Leucoryx* (Pallas). The two native attendants who accompany the animals seem to divide the attention of the visitors with their quadruped companions, and although perhaps not so extraordinary in their appearance, are more rarely seen here, as they belong to tribes that hardly ever wander away from their own homes on the shores of the White Nile.

On Monday evening [October 7 1844] his Majesty King Louis Philippe reached the picturesque town of Treport. All the houses were illuminated, while the wives and daughters of the fishermen lined the way from the quay to the border strand, where lay the royal gig, each holding a flaming torch; the effect was most striking from its cheerful and primitive simplicity. During the King's embarkation, the marine band played away merrily; and the sound over the waters, coming with the effect of the light upon the waves, the rockets in the air, the cheering of the sailors, and the shouts of "Vive le Roi" from the shore, formed a most beautiful and affecting scene.

On Tuesday morning, the guns of the Queen, 110 gun-ship, at Spithead, began to boom in the distance, announcing the coming in sight of the squadron of the eagerly expected Sovereign, which event occurred at a quarter to eight. The French squadron came on slowly and majestically, each ship of war saluting as it advanced, and each battery in turn taking up the salute. From the moment she anchored at Portsmouth, the Gomer, which bore his Majesty, was an object of riveted and eager attention, nor was this steam-frigate unworthy of such curiosity. She presented an aspect at the same time imposing and interesting. Her form is admirable; the wide expanse of her spotless deck, her masts, yards, and rigging show she has been the pet handiwork of the French shipwrights, and that she is the favourite of her captain and crew, who manoeuvred her in silence, and with a most seamen-like celerity and ease. Below she has all the character of a floating palace—the drawing-rooms are as convenient as they are magnificent; that in which the King received his visitors has its sides lined with crimson velvet, whilst in every direction you behold tables of the rarest woods and luxurious *causeuses* and sofas lined with yellow satin.

By the time the Gomer had reached the Victoria-pier, it was crowded with ladies and gentlemen, and with the Corporation Officers in their robes, so that the place formed a pleasing object when seen from the river. At 25 minutes past 10, Prince Albert entered the yard, accompanied by the Duke of Wellington and walked briskly down the stairs whence he was to embark. A barge with Prince Albert's flag was waiting alongside, into which the Prince stepped, loudly cheered by the spectators, who thronged in the boats that covered the harbour. The Duke having followed the Prince into the boat, they went off rapidly to the Gomer, amidst the cheers of the multitude that surrounded them on all sides.

The harbour at this time was a scene of animation not often witnessed. The shores were lined with people. The fortifications in

Arrival of Louis Philippe at Portsmouth.

the distance, and the roads where they were elevated, showed dense masses of human beings; the surface of the water was one mass of floating life, every boat crammed with people; the craft were dressed in the gayest and most brilliant colours, the larger vessels having the yards manned. Upon stepping on deck the Prince was received by His Majesty in the most affectionate manner, the King embracing and shaking hands very cordially with his Royal Highness. His Majesty also shook hands with the Duke of Wellington, and in a few moments, together with the Prince and the Duke, entered the royal barge, which returned to the stairs with the French national flag flying from the stem, in the place of the royal standard of England. From the time the barge left the Gomer till she came alongside the stairs, excitement continued among the spectators. The King of the French repeatedly acknowledged the cheers, taking off his hat, and bowing. Arrived at the stairs, and when he reached the top, he turned round and bowed repeatedly on all sides, laying his hand on his heart. The King and Prince Albert then entered a carriage, which immediately drove off to the railway station; and the royal train started from Gosport at eleven o'clock, arriving at Farnborough at half-past twelve o'clock, where carriages were waiting in which they immediately went off at a rapid pace towards Windsor.

At a quarter past two o'clock, the escort swept rapidly round the quadrangle of Windsor Castle and formed in front, whilst the first carriage, containing the King, Prince Albert, the Duke de Montpensier and M. Guizot, drove under the portico. At this moment Queen Victoria advanced to the threshold, and in the most cordial manner extended her arms, whilst Louis Philippe and the Prince descended from the carriage. Their Majesties embraced most affectionately at the moment of meeting, and then advanced into the vestibule; whence the royal guest proceeded to his suite of apartments.

The wish of her Majesty, as well as that of Louis Philippe, has been to treat this visit purely as one of a private nature, and consequently a quiet manner of receiving her guests was adopted. The range of rooms set apart for Louis Philippe are situated in the north wing of the castle, looking upon the manoeuvring ground of the Home-park, below the slopes. The suite is that which was recently occupied by his Imperial Majesty of Russia, and is only very slightly altered from the disposition which it received for the Czar's reception. Our engraving shows the crimson or principal drawing-room, which is only used on state occasions. The furniture of this apartment is extremely costly; the screens, chairs, etc., being of carved oak, gilt, and the draperies of satin embossed velvet.

On October 9th the *char-a-banc*, the magnificent gift presented to her Majesty by the King of France, was used for the first time. The royal party proceeded therein to Sunbury Common, and thence to Twickenham, Hampton and Claremont, returning home through Chertsey. On the next day Louis Philippe was elected a Knight of the Most Noble Order of the Garter, and in honour of this auspicious occasion covers were laid that evening in St. George's Hall for 130. The banqueting table was ornamented in a gorgeous and magnificent manner, with gold plate, épergnes, candelabra, vases, wine-coolers, etc. Our illustration shows the central portion of the table, with the Queen, the King, the Duchess of Kent, the Duc de Montpensier etc., in their several positions, at the banquet. The plate seen, are portions of the Prince of Wales's Plateau, a service entirely of solid gold. In the centre is the famous St. George's Candelabrum; on each side are smaller ones of the Hesperides and other classical subjects, the whole resting on massive slabs of plate-glass, bound with gold.

On Saturday the King of France received a deputation in the morning, and in the afternoon the royal and august party honoured Eton College with a visit. The King and the Queen were vociferously cheered by the boys, their reception presenting a right loyal scene of enthusiasm. Throughout Sunday Windsor was thronged with visitors, several of whom proceeded on the Clewer road, to meet the King, on his return from chapel. The demand for accommodation was very pressing; and we suspect that many an unlucky wight returned home to town *impransus*. The rush to the omnibuses, in the evening (more especially on account of the heavy rain), was very great. The view of the Castle, from the Eton road, was truly exciting: the principal windows in the northern front presenting a flood of light. We rarely remember seeing the stately pile to such advantage; it was, even from without, a

Introduction of Louis Philippe to the infant royal family in the Crimson Drawing-room.

The Garter Banquet in St. George's Hall, Windsor.

scene of right regal hospitality, carrying the mind's eye back to the chivalric glories of the feudal age, and assuring us that in the laps of ages—the long vista of seven centuries—Windsor has lost not a ray of splendour and magnificence.

On Monday Louis Philippe, her Majesty and Prince Albert left Windsor for Gosport. His Majesty before leaving the Castle presented six magnificent gold snuff-boxes, with his portrait set in brilliants, to the principal officers of the household who had been appointed to attend him. He also presented a number of brillant rings and brooches to the ladies and other attendants of her Majesty, and a sum of £1000 to be distributed among the domestics generally.

At Gosport, the rain, which had all along fallen heavily, soon increased to a perfect torrent; the wind blew a hurricane, and the rumbling of thunder in the distance succeeded faint flashes of lightning, which gave promise of a stormy night. The crossing from Spithead to Treport would be attended with immense loss of time in the then state of the weather, and it was determined to secure the necessary accommodation for his Majesty's departure via Dover. He and his suite arrived at Dover on Tuesday at half past two o'clock in the morning, by special train from New Cross; he retired to rest at five o'clock in the morning. At half past ten the King received the Mayor with a congratulatory address, and then proceeded to the steamer Le Nord, acknowledging the farewell greetings of the vast crowds who were assembled at the pier head to take a parting glance at the monarch who was leaving our shores.

The King of the French landed at Calais on Tuesday afternoon [October 15] from the Le Nord steamer, in excellent health and spirits, having made a rapid passage from Dover, during which his Majesty felt no material inconvenience, although the swell was considerable.

Her Majesty's departure from Weedon Station.

Her Majesty's visit to Burghley House [November 12–15 1844] has again called forth the loyalty of the inhabitants of the line of country crossed by the Royal party, in various kinds of demonstrations of respect. The weather has been most unfavourable the whole time. But, fortunate as her Majesty is in general, sunshine in this—the gloomiest of English months—could not be anticipated. The old mansion of Burghley would have looked more smiling in the leafy time of June. The flags and banners, and arches, would have been more gay, and the fireworks more easy of ignition and explosion; all these outward manifestations would have been more brilliant and pleasing to the eye had the skies been more propitious. But it is cheering to remark that the loyalty and enthusiasm with which her Majesty is always received suffer no diminution from outward circumstances. The leaf may be in the "sere and yellow", and the breezes cold and cheerless, but the affection of the people for their Sovereign remains as cordial and as bright as ever.

On Friday morning her Majesty, Prince Albert, and the suite left Burghley at half-past nine o'clock on their return to London. All along the route the same demonstrations of loyalty and affection were made by the people as on her Majesty's journey down. The triumphal arches had all remained up, and the houses were very gaily decorated with flags, evergreens, etc.

At the town and station of Weedon great numbers of people had collected. The military (47th Foot) lined the road, and there was a guard of honour (of the 47th) under the Command of Captain Gordon. The train started, amidst the cheers of the people, at five minutes to three o'clock. The regular train had not long preceded it, so that great precaution was required.

Triumphal arch at Broughton.

THE DISTIN FAMILY. Mr. Distin, sen., for more than nine years, was principal trumpet in the private band of King George IV, and the Distin Family has given upwards of seven hundred concerts. In December [1843], they proceeded to the continent to make a trial of some newly-invented instruments, manufactured by M. Adolphe Sax. Upon the introduction of the Distin's improved Sax Horns in Paris, they at once ensured success.

Invariably receiving the most enthusiastic applause, Mr. Distin was requested by the Director of the "Conservatoire Royale de Musique" to perform some of Sebastian Bach's compositions, and also the obligato to Handel's "Let the Bright Seraphim", which had not been heard in Paris for many years, as no French trumpet-player would attempt it.

The Distins are at present the only performers on the Sax Horn, which unites the powers of the French horn and those of the cornet-à-piston, but is infinitely superior to both, for it combines the mellowness and sweetness of the former with all the brilliancy and power of the latter.

Mr. Distin and his four sons.

THE MUSEUM OF THE ROYAL COLLEGE OF SURGEONS

This magnificent Museum in Lincoln's-Inn-fields—the first of its kind in the world—owes its foundation to the untiring industry and talents of John Hunter, the great anatomist and physiologist, who devoted his life to collecting the most important specimens in those great branches of knowledge—Natural History, Comparative Anatomy, Physiology, and Pathology. At present the total number of specimens nearly amounts to twenty-three thousand!

Our view is that which first strikes the sight of the spectator, on entering the chief door from the hall of the College. The first large object seen, on the right, is the fossil shell of a gigantic extinct Armadillo, from Buenos Ayres. A shell of the common Armadillo is placed on this enormous specimen, to show by comparison its vast size. On the left is the fossil skeleton of the Mylodon, a large extinct quadruped of the Sloth family, also found at Buenos Ayres. Beyond this, to the left, is the skeleton of the Hippopotamus, the head of which is just seen in the engraving; and on the extreme right, over the shell of the Armadillo, are the bones of the pelvis, tail, and left hind leg of the mighty Megatherium. The large skeleton to the right of the centre, is that of Charles O'Brian, the Irish giant, and is eight feet in height. Two ordinary skeletons, male and female, are placed on his left side, and on his right, under a glass case, is that of the Sicilian dwarf, which is only twenty inches in height.

Proceeding along the Museum on the left are casts in plaster of the bones of a huge and extint bird, the *Dinoris giganteus*, placed, by way of comparison, by the side of a full-sized Ostrich. Still further, is the skeleton of the American Elk, and under it that of the Great Penguin. Behind this, is a skeleton of the Giraffe; and, on the right, that of the gigantic Irish Elk. The large skeleton in the centre is that of the elephant *Chunee*, who, after being exhibited on the stage, was purchased for Exeter 'Change, where it was shot in 1826.

ST. PANCRAS' BATHS AND WASHHOUSES

Superior bath.

Inferior bath.

This establishment owes its origin to the formation of a society for the providing of the labouring classes of the parish of St. Pancras with Baths and Washhouses. The St. Pancras Society believe that the objections that were at first raised against such projects are fast yielding to the facts and arguments which have been brought to bear upon the subject. Reports show that it is conferring direct and immediate benefit upon those for whom it is intended; and that they are desirous of enjoying it. Indeed, it is hard to understand upon what ground the use of the bath, which is so much lauded amongst the rich, can longer be denied to the poor, whose constant toil not only renders it to them a source of greater luxury, but also more absolutely essential to their very health.

The buildings of the St. Pancras Establishment consists of a range of building forming nearly three sides of a square, the entrance being in the centre. To the left of the receiving-room, at the end of a passage containing 5 vapour baths, are 22 small compartments for men's baths (cold, warm or shower), 6 of which will be at a cost of one penny, 6 at twopence, and 10 (superiorly fitted up, for a higher class of person and reached by a separate door), at sixpence; double these prices being charged when hot water is made use of. At the end of these will be two large plunge, or swimming baths, 60 feet by 21, at twopence and sixpence, with separate approaches. This completes the left wing of the premises. To the right of the receiving-room, and arranged on the same plan, will be 16 baths for women, 8 of them being fitted up in a superior style. Beyond these, with a distinct entrance, is the washing department, containing 64 double tubs for washing linen, the smaller portion answering the purpose of a copper, by a jet of steam which will keep the water in a boiling state. The completed work may be put into a patent drying machine, and with much less injury to them than is done by 'wringing'. In the next room is a hot-air machine for rendering the clothes fit for the iron or mangle, both of which will be provided in additional rooms. For all this accommodation each person is only to be charged 1d., if she does not stay more than two hours at the tubs, and one hour more in the drying and ironing rooms.

THE ETHIOPIAN SERANADERS

A party of five American minstrels, under the above designation, commenced on Wednesday night, at the Hanover-square Rooms, a series of concerts, for the avowed purpose of affording an accurate notion of Negro character and melody. They are painted jet black, with ruddy lips, and large mouths; and being capital actors, the deception created is so great that wagers have been offered that they are really "darkies". They dress in dandy costume, white waistcoated and wristbanded, turned up in the most approved D'Orsay fashion. One plays the tambourine, Mr. Germon, who is the leader; another, the bone castanet; the third, the *accordion*; and the two others, the banjo, or African guitar. The castanet player does not sing; but his four colleagues have good voices, and in glees harmonize charmingly. It is, perhaps, the *buffo* exhibition which will create the greatest sensation, and in this quality they are inimitable. The tambourine performer affects a ludicrous air of pompous sentiment, whilst the castanet sable hero indulges in all kinds of buffoonery and antics. He is a wonderful player—no Spaniard can rival him in the rapidity, delicacy, and precision. A scene called a "Railroad Overture", causes an explosion of laughter; they seem to be endowed with perpetual motion; and the scream of the whistle, at the same time with those of the engine, beggars all description.

DESTRUCTION OF THE "TRIBUNE" OFFICE, NEW YORK

Destruction of the "Tribune" office, New York.

During the terrific storm at New York, on the 5th ult., [February, 1845], a fire broke out at about 4 a.m. in the office of the *Tribune* newspaper, opposite the City Hall. Mr. Graham, the proprietor of the *Tribune*, and a clerk, were sleeping in the second story, until awakened by the roar of flames, and the door and stairway being on fire, they jumped from a window and escaped. The compositors in the fifth story, and the pressmen in the basement, had barely time to save themselves. A few books were saved and nothing else.

No man could have imagined that such an establishment, in which men were constantly at work night and day, could be wholly consumed by fire. There has not been another night, since the building was put up, when it could have been burnt down, even if deliberately fired. But when this fire broke out, under a strong gale and snow-storm of twenty-four hours continuance, which had rendered the streets impassable, it was well nigh impossible to drag an engine at all; and those which reached the fire found the nearest hydrant frozen up, and only to be opened with an axe. Meantime, the whole building was in a blaze.

All that is stated as to the origin of the fire is, that a boy lighted a fire in a stove at four o'clock and half an hour afterwards the apartment was in flames. On the morning after the fire, in searching the ruins for property, a watch and chain, and purse of money, which had been left under a pillow of one of the beds, was discovered. The watch was much injured, but the purse and money were not damaged.

Pic-nic Party, at Ascot Races.

ASCOT-HEATH RACES

This year of 1843—(what part of the year we know not how to call it, for just now it is certainly not summer, and there is a drizzling, Novemberish atmosphere about us which makes us doubt if it be June)—this year of

Chifney. Robinson. Wheatley. W. Scott.

JOCKEYS

1843, we repeat, has been most unpropitious to the turf. In a double sense the Derby received a damper, partly in showers first, and partly in defaulters afterwards, and the winners have been haunting Tattersall's, like so many Canadian emigrants, in search of a *settlement.* The debtors, on the other hand, may be considered as having arrived in America already, upon the banks of the "*Oh, I owe.*" Since then we have had Ascot water parties—the crowds beat by the weather—the worst drivers and the most delicate ladies obliged, in their crisis of difficulty, to take the *rains*—the sun, like the King of the French, confining himself to *St. Cloud*; and the light wine-bibbers, the moselle-mongers and champagne-quaffers obliged to swallow or take in the largest imaginable quantity of *heavy wet.* Drenching, drenching has been the order of the race days and race journies—drenching in the skies—drenching in the stables—drenching in the gutters—drenching by rail and road! The rains accompanied the trains—the horsemen *ran* faster than their horses—dresses became draggle-tails in drags, and many a man, whose *forte* was in his tilbury, would have given his riding-whip for a shelter in Tilbury Fort. Many people, in fact, were inconsistent enough to say of the race what the tippler at Offley's said of his short measure of brandy—that it was *no go*, and abstained accordingly.

But to our theme—Ascot.

Who when the weather is fair, the sky smiling, and heart exultation at the full does not love Ascot race of the nobility—race of the aristocracy—race of the Queen? What a beautiful course it does present! What a glorious assemblage of dashing equipages unfreighting their divine beauty—the patrician loveliness of England—at the Grand Stand! Look up—there is a gush of sunshine from that galaxy of smiles—there is a fair hearty excitement beaming forth happy radiance upon all around, and harmonizing with the variegated picture. See that aristocratic promenade peopled with beautiful women during the intervals between the races. There are as many hearts as wagers won there. Then listen. The time for the Cup race is approaching, and a bevy of royal carriages comes rolling upon the course. A dim indistinct murmur ushers them on from the distance—it gathers into a loud whirring agitating sound—it grows like the gathering of a passion—it has swollen into a mighty

THE DERBY, FROM THE GRAN

STAND.—BY M. S. MORGAN

EPSOM.
DERBY DAY
18 44

shout—"The Queen! the Queen!" There is a short silence—a brief interval of expectation—a rush of multitudes under the royal stand—a beautiful sovereign gallantly escorted by a young and honest husband, presents herself to her people, and in a moment the air rings with joy. That hearty burst of gladness would dissipate a year of pain.

Thus it used to be, and thus it will be again, although our gracious Sovereign has made this year an exception to the condescending presence at Ascot which her subjects have been wont so fondly to enjoy. Those, however, who have seen her go of yore will find pleasure in catching even the reflex of her former journey upon our page. Her royal retinue, too has ever added animation to the dazzling *tableaux* of the Ascot course. The Master of the Buckhounds, the high official patrons of the turf—the huntsmen, the yeomen, all bedight in high costume or bright livery, have made a sprightly episode of the peopled landscape; and the mounted nobles—young bloods on fiery horses galloping from stand to carriage, from post to ring—have thrown striking elements of grace and beauty into the scene. At Ascot, too, the regulations are better than at Epsom—there is a wiser organization of police, a selectness about the visitors, an absence of riff-raff, and a less determined intrusion of the swell mob. In fact there is much more brilliancy about the Ascot-heath races than any other hippodromic exhibition we wot of, and we rejoice in the *comme il faut* ease and elegance by which they are universally pervaded.

So much for our general *prestige* in favour of Ascot. For the special doings of the present year we refer to the details accompanying our cuts, and we commend the reader to take interest in our group of jockeys, the stable or unstable portraiture which it displays, and the flight of pigeons.

As is customary at the present day, the prize is no longer a real *cup*, but its value remains though its form is changed. In this instance we have a splendid *tazza* or salver, containing in high relief an illustration of Schiller's poem "Pegasus im Yoche" (Pegasus in the yoke), moulded in silver after the designs of Mr. Edmund Cotterill. His Pegasus is a noble creature, full of fire and motion, and worthy of the great German poet's eulogium, and the figure of Apollo is graceful and full of life. The vigour and animation which mark the celestial courser are well contrasted with the Boeotian peasant and the dullard ox. The workmanship, in bright and frosted silver, is, as usual, very well executed; but comparing Mr. Cotterill's model with the cast, we find that the latter falls short of the original in several respects; a fact which is, no doubt, to be ascribed to the work being slightly hurried to be ready for the prescribed day. It is, however, a noble prize, and the winner has cause for congratulation. The manufacturers are Messrs. Garrard, of Panton-street, Haymarket.

Pass we now to

THE ASCOT CUPS FOR 1843

Ascot is this year graced, in addition to the prize which we have described above, with

The Aerial Couriers

works of unusual splendour, the Royal Hunt Cup and Ascot Cup, which have been executed by Messrs. Mortimer and Hunt, the eminent silversmiths, of New Bond-street. The Royal Hunt Cup is composed of a beautifully-finished group of a stag and dogs in silver. The Ascot Cup is Herne's oak as now seen in Windsor Forest, surrounded with beautifully-modelled deer in various attitudes, by the same artist. The oak, which is well known, is quite dismantled by age; and the top is made to remove and be replaced by a rich foliage (adapted for lights), adorning it in primitive beauty.

Ascot Grand Stand.—The Race.

The Race—Tattenham Corner.

EPSOM RACES

Every foreigner who has written his experience of a pilgrimage to Epsom on the Derby Day, describes it as one of the most marvellous displays of popular wealth and condition to be witnessed in the world. None have spoken of it as that which it is besides—a true type of the national idiosyncrasy.

John Bull is by no means the mere mass of living lead that gentlemen with no more brains than bladders have thought fit to pronounce him. He is, indeed, in the habit of exercising those properties which distinguish his species from that of the brute, but he can be merry, as well as wise. Of the account he has turned the latter quality to, "the great globe itself" is the monument: you cannot contemplate him making the most of the former more favourably than by accompanying him to Epsom Races. Thither he has gone annually for more than half a century, and thither ye found him going—if ye were in luck, on Wednesday last, with as keen a relish as ever.

Epsom has begun to add to her character of a mighty sporting rendezvous much of the pageant style of Ascot. When both are perfectly blended together she will be peerless as a holyday festival. The Grand Stand is now certainly the grandest edifice of its kind in the country. The entrance is from the rear, where carriages drive into a spacious enclosure, and set down at a noble flight of double steps, surmounted by an awning. The interior arrangements are complete; uniting elegance and comfort in a remarkable degree. In front, slopes a turf-covered lawn down to the course, from which a light iron railing separates it.

Far off, in front, ye see the classic "hill," studded with equipages—where more champagne is drunk in four hours than in any other spot of the globe in as many years—where unheard-of feats of gastronomy are achieved.

The Weighing-Room.

We provide a series of illustrations of the interior economy of H.M.S. "Collingwood", which will be specially interesting at this present moment [November 1845] when points of nautical skill are so extensively discussed. For convenience, we arrange our descriptive details in order to correspond with the succession of the Engravings.

Sick Bay or Hospital.

SICK BAY—Or hospital, is generally on the starboard side of the ship, forward. This part is solely under the charge of the surgeon and his assistants. It is not interfered with in any way, save for the purpose of cleaning in the morning, which is superintended by the mate of the main-deck; he makes his report to the executive officer who reports to his captain, who then inspects.

Lashing the Hammocks.

LASHING THE HAMMOCKS—Lashing is a term used among nautical men. To lash or secure the booms, spars, or boats, is to wind rope round them to the "skids", or other fastenings, so as to secure them from moving about, unless unlashed, which means to untie. Our engraving gives an excellent idea of the busy scene on the "gun-deck", when the sailors are making their beds for the night.

Sailors' Mess Table.

MESS TABLE—Between each gun and the lower-deck is a table, about 12 feet long and 3 feet or more wide, known as the Mess Table. It is generally fixed by a moveable pin in a hinge to the side of the ship, and suspended from the deck overhead by slings or ropes at the outer end, so as to be capable of being removed in an instant, which is done when the ship is cleared for action. The Mess Tables are then conveyed to the orpol-deck, and, being without legs or frame, are placed over the cable, and form a platform or bed for the wounded men when dressed by the surgeon.

Ward or Dining Room.

WARD-ROOM—This is the dining-room and drawing-room of a certain class of officers, and is in the after-part of the main-deck. Here are located the commodore, lieutenants, master, marine officers, surgeon, purser and chaplain. It is fitted with dormitories, or cabins, on each side, and these are furnished by their occupants generally in a style of exquisite neatness and taste.

Six-Water Grog.

SIX-WATER GROG—A seaman used to be allowed half-a-pint of rum or brandy, or, in lieu thereof, one pint of wine, *per diem*; but, when spirits were issued, it was done twice a day. As for instance: a gill of spirits was issued at dinner-time, to which was added three gills of water, making in all one pint of grog. To this liquid, when the ship had been six weeks at sea, a proportion of lime-juice and sugar were added, making a pint and more of excellent punch. But, when the men have abused the use of this beverage by frequent acts of inebriety, it is the custom to give six-water grog, instead of three, thus inflicting a sad punishment on poor Jack.

Weighing anchor

WEIGHING AND WORKING—In well-regulated men-of-war the crew are so disposed of, or stationed, that one watch, or half the crew, are employed weighing the anchor, while the other half are employed in looming and making sail.

Working a Gun.

WORKING A GUN—It will be well if in the course of battle, ships are not blown up by placing live shells amidst the active artillery; for, however careful the gunners may be, it will be next to an impossibility to avoid accidents of this nature with so combustible a material. The thirty-two pounders are generally worked or manoeuvred by thirteen men, and a boy, as follows:—Two forecastle-men, or prime seamen; four topmen, or able seamen; two afterguard, or ordinary seamen; two waisters, or landsmen; two marines, one mizen-top [sic] man, and a boy to fetch powder ("a powder monkey"); they are selected of equal number from each watch, so that when a ship has to fight from both sides, the starboard watch remains with the guns on the starboard side, and the larboard, or past watch, on the port side, and are thus designated:—Two captains—first and second; two firemen, two sail trimmers, two pumpers, two boarders or small-arm men, two spongers, and one powder boy. On any other exigency each gun contributes its quota of two men, who are headed by an officer selected for that purpose. As, for instance, a roll of the drum summons the boarder, and each gun supplies two men who are commanded by the senior lieutenant, assisted by the lieutenants of the small-arm men, and by that division of marines always prepared for that purpose.

Stowing of Stock.

STOWING OF STOCK—There is in all ships, between the fore and main hatchways, on the main-deck, a regular fixed sheep pen of two piers, each about four feet high, and capable of holding 18 to 20 sheep each. One part is appropriated to the admiral or captain, and the other to the officers of the ward-room, the sheep being under the charge of the sheep butcher, who attends them three times a day. When more stock is taken on board, for which there is not room in these pens, the executive officer generally has it placed between such guns on the main-deck as are not likely to be disturbed until the ship goes to sea, and the long-boat, or launch, is hoisted in. The inside of this boat, usually, is then allotted to receive live stock.

OPENING OF PARLIAMENT BY HER MAJESTY

The purpose of the Speech delivered from the Throne at the opening of the Session of Parliament is to shadow forth, in general terms, the direction and tendency of the leading Legislative measures to be brought forward by the Ministers of the Crown. It is not intended that the Sovereign should enter into details, or allude to specific points of those measures; any expression of opinion on the part of the Crown, in anticipation of the discussions on the several portions of a great plan or scheme of policy, would appear like dictation, and be, in fact, an infringement of that perfect liberty of debate which is one of the highest privileges of the Commons of England. The general style in which Royal Speeches are drawn up is often made the subject of censure; but there is a Constitutional reason for it, and, though that generality has sometimes been allowed to fall into vagueness or obscurity, yet, of late years, this fault has been avoided, and the people have derived from the Royal Address a pretty clear intimation of the course of policy to be pursued on public affairs. The Address of her Majesty to the assembled Lords and Commons on Thursday last [January 22, 1846] was a very fair specimen of these State documents: details we cannot gather from it, but the direction of the "Movement" is pretty clearly perceptible.

The first striking paragraph is that containing the reference to our Oregon dispute with the United States. We gather from it a determination fully to assert the "national honour" in the question; and it may be taken as an assurance that from the just claims of this country there will not be the slightest departure.

We next gather that measures of stringency are in preparation for those districts in Ireland where the assassin seems to murder with impunity. Let us hope the Legislature will go deeper than this; the dreadful effects of discontentment must be repressed, but there should be also an attempt to remedy the causes of such social disorder.

It is the remaining portions of the Royal Speech that possesses the greatest importance. The "satisfaction" expressed at the result of the past relaxations of the prohibitive and protective system, results described as a "prosperous state of the Revenue, the increased demand for labour, and the general improvement which has taken place in the internal condition of the country", is the prelude and introduction to that intimation of a further progress in the same direction, which the public has been led to expect would be made. Parliament is recommended to take into its "early consideration" a yet more extensive application of the same principles.

We gather from the Speech that it will not be by any means limited to the Corn Laws; it will embrace "many articles, the produce or manufacture of foreign countries"; it is more than probable that the proposition will be bolder and more comprehensive than the Tariff of 1842. But so near the time of certainty speculation is needless. We may remark, however, that it appears singular the great topic, the Corn Law, should not be expressly mentioned, or alluded to.

Whatever may be the differences hereafter excited, sure we are that every man will heartily respond to the prayer with which her Majesty concludes her gracious Address, that the Councils of our Legislators may "promote friendly feelings between different classes of my subjects, provide additional security for the continuance of peace, and to maintain contentment and happiness at home, by increasing the comforts and bettering the conditions of the great body of my people".

"RAGGED SCHOOLS"

Mr. Charles Dickens, in an eloquent Letter addressed to the Editors of the *Daily News*, describes the places which bear the above name, as an effort "to introduce among the most miserable and neglected outcasts in London, some knowledge of the commonest principles of morality and religion; to commence their recognition as immortal human creatures, before the Gaol Chaplain becomes their only schoolmaster . . . This attempt is being made in certain of the most obscure and squalid parts of the Metropolis; where rooms are opened at night, for the gratuitous instruction of all comers, children or adults, under the title of 'RAGGED SCHOOLS'. The name implies the purpose. They who are too ragged, wretched, filthy, and forlorn, to enter any other place: who could gain admission into no charity school, and who would be driven from any churchdoor: are invited to come in here, and find some people not depraved, willing to teach them something, and show them some sympathy. . . ."

We have selected the School in Jurston-street, Oakley-street, Lambeth. The School is opened on Sunday evenings, at six o'clock; and the year's average attendance has been 250 children and 25 teachers. We gather from a lecture recently delivered by the Rev. Mr. Ainslie, that at Windsor a school on "the Ragged" principle, has been established by a poor chimney-sweep, "who had himself been a bad and abandoned man, but who was reclaimed, and who now sat there, with his dirty face, teaching and doing more good than thousands of others of ten times his capacity."

The Lambeth "Ragged School"—(Girls).

The Lambeth "Ragged School"—(Boys).

THE ROYAL YACHT, "VICTORIA AND ALBERT"

Our artist has engraved the Royal Yacht *Victoria and Albert* passing through the Needles for Plymouth, on the morning of Tuesday week [August 18, 1846]. There was a heavy sea; though the Queen remained on deck the whole of the passage.

We subjoin the details of the interior of the Royal Yacht, with the recent alterations. The Royal Apartments occupy the after-part of the yacht, and comprise the Dining-room, the Drawing-room, and the Bed and Dressing-rooms. The Dining-room occupies the entire stern from side to side, and is lighted from the stern windows, from side windows, and a

Top of the page: The Royal Yacht in heavy seas off the Needles. Above: The Dining-room.

skylight in the centre. It is 20 feet in length, by 22 feet breadth, and 7 feet 7 inches in height. The pannel [sic] work is of a dark colour, with gilt mouldings. Sofas (the under part of which is used for lockers) are attached to the circular stern. The chairs are plain mahogany and green morocco; one of them, with brass knobs, and spikes on the feet for security, always stands on the starboard side, and is appropriated for the Queen. A circular table, but which may be extended to dine 18 persons, stands in the centre. At the sides are ivory hand-holders to catch hold of when removing from place to place when the vessel is in motion.

The Drawing-room is 24 ft. long, 12 ft. 6 in. broad, and 7 ft. 7 in. high. The paint work is lilac in colour bordered with gold beading. It has three windows in the side and is also lighted by strong prismatic glass work in the deck. The chairs are curiously formed to double up, said to be invented by George IV. There is a circular table in the centre, and a square table at each end, as well as a side table, the whole having raised brass work round the edges to prevent anything from rolling off. Two handsome and commodious easy chairs stand abaft and a sofa on either hand. Against the vessel's side is a pianoforte, a Brussels carpet covers the deck, and the whole is extremely simple. On the starboard side of the passage, opposite to the Drawing-room, is the Royal Bed Cabin and Dressing-rooms.

The City has been startled by a robbery on a large scale, a kind of "monster" depredation, planned and executed with an amount of skill truly alarming. It is the last of a series of felonies by which during the space of a year the monied world has been perplexed. The age of the highwayman has departed; Captain Macheath himself could not "stop" a first class train; the attempts of daring villany, then, are not now so much directed against the moving, personal property of society, as against the masses of it that are banked, and they are made either by fraud or force, or a combination of both. But the skill of those who commit such crimes, now bears no proportion to the facilities which society possesses for their detection; but a few hours elapse and every particular is known all over the country; and a few days, at farthest, carries every particular to the capitals of Europe. In either case, the attempts of the thieves to make use of their booty are paralysed; nor does the Continent or America afford an asylum, as of old, to the fugitive criminals. Detection seems almost certain; we scarcely remember one great forgery, fraud, or robbery, within the last few years, that has not been followed by the prompt punishment of the guilty persons.

What is the lesson to be derived from all these skilful and daring acts of dishonesty? That not one of them baffled the pursuit of justice, and that those who "made haste to be rich", by plunging into crime, are now poor, miserable, justly despised; and from good, even exalted, positions, have fallen to a state of the most ignominious slavery. And yet, undeterred by these examples, men still engage in the perilous game against society and the laws, in which so many have failed before them!

Exterior of Cab, with Index.

THE PATENT MILE-INDEX

A simple and ingenious contrivance for measuring and indicating the distance travelled by wheel carriages, has been invented and patented by Mr. H. Von Uster, of the College for Civil Engineers, Putney.

The invention is equally applicable to private carriages as to cabs and other public vehicles, one of its advantages being that there is nothing unsightly in the apparatus which, indeed, can hardly be seen at all when the carriage is in motion. The wheels of the vehicle are coupled to a dial-plate provided with two faces, one inside for the use of the passenger, and the other outside, in which the driver and his fare together can note the position of the hands before the latter steps into the cab. Both dials have exactly the face of a clock, being furnished with an hour and minute hand, and hours and minutes are indicated on the dial precisely as in an ordinary time-piece. The divisions of hours correspond exactly with the miles actually traversed by the vehicle; thus, if the dial indicated 20 minutes past 12 when the passenger entered the cab, he will know that he has travelled exactly a mile when the dial points to 20 past 1. The passenger is thus supplied with a perfect check against overcharge, while the proprietor has the means of knowing the amount of mileage actually performed. The convenience and simplicity of adopting, as the index of distance, a method of calculation so familiar as the face of a clock supplies, need hardly be pointed out.

The possibility of tampering with the apparatus has been effectually prevented.

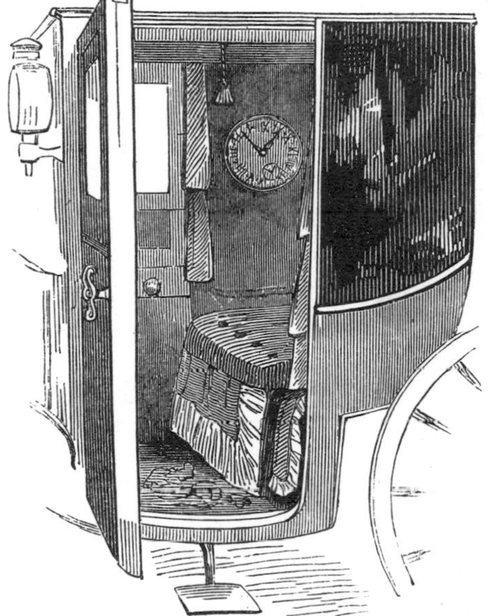

Interior of Cab, showing Index.

The dials are protected by a thick glass, which must be broken before the hands can be reached; and even then they cannot be put backwards or forwards, but must be broken if moved at all.

There can be no doubt that the application of the Mile-Index to public carriages—particularly to cabs—would be very satisfactory to the public; and that a very large increase of passengers would be the result, were they protected from the chance of overcharge, which they may be by this invention.

Lumley's Monster Mortar.

THE BATTLE OF THE OPERAS

The "Battle of Life" between Bow-street and the Haymarket is progressing fiercely, and each party is confident of success. The Haymarket depends upon its *basso monstre*, the threat of which had the power of throwing off notes which usually burst on a house with terrific effect. At either place, the intelligent assistant, who gives the tone to the audience, by directing is in constant practice, and he can now aim with unerring precision.

Mr. Wyatt's Atelier, or Model-room.

This stupendous work was designed and executed by Mr. Matthew Cotes Wyatt and his son James Wyatt. The Model was commenced in May, 1840, and occupied the Artists upwards of three years, the scene of their labours being the Atelier, represented in our first Engraving. The plaister [sic] of Paris used considerably exceeded 100 tons; it was formed upon a revolving platform, upwards of 20 feet across, travelling upon 40 rollers, and weighing in itself several tons. To give strength to the body of the horse, a beam passes through it longitudinally, like a backbone, from which spring transverse timbers, like the ribs of a ship. In the Illustration, the modelled group is incomplete; the head and tail of the horse; the feet, and uppart [sic] of the figure of the illustrious rider; being wanting. The line of projections from the body of the horse are iron bolts, beneath which, in the early stage of the modelling, were placed props for security in shifting the figure by means of the platform, so as to obtain the most desirable position for light, &c.

The entire group represents the Duke of Wellington, as he appeared on the Field at Waterloo, upon his favourite horse, "Copenhagen", in a standing position. The Duke sat to the sculptor for the portrait: the head is remarkably fine, and the likeness good: the warrior wears his customary short cloak, which the artist has skilfully draped, so as to give it something of the grace of a classic costume. The material is bronze, for melting which Mr. Wyatt erected two great furnaces; the first capable of melting only twelve tons at a time; the second capable of melting twenty tons at a time. In order that the legs of the horse should be capable of carrying the great weight they would have to sustain, it was found necessary to cast them solid. The height of the group approaches 30 feet; and such is the bulk of the horse that eight persons have dined within one half of it. The following are some of the other dimensions:—

	ft.	in.
Girth round the horse	22	8
Ditto, arm of	5	4
From the horse's hocks to the ground	6	0
From the horse's nose to the tail	26	0

The group being cast in pieces, they have been joined, partly by screw-bolts, two inches in thickness, and partly fused together by a new process, twelve inches at a time.

The roof of the Foundry was removed and the colossal group lifted out of the pit with shears, and placed upon a carriage, designed and constructed to convey the great work to its final destination—the triumphal arch at Hyde Park Corner. The stupendous labour of raising the Wellington Statue to the summit of the Green Park Arch was commenced at an early hour on Wednesday morning [September 30, 1846]. A body of riggers from Woolwich Dockyard, assisted by a number of labourers, were first occupied in changing the position of the Statue, as deposited the day before, from south to east: and in order to accomplish this end, the whole mass of figure and carriage, weighing altogether sixty tons, was lifted by the tackle, and then shifted to the desired spot. This feat fully proved the competency of the mechanical appliances provided: accordingly the preparations were carried on until three o'clock, when the signal was given to "hoist away". The figure was raised by means of strong six-inch cables fastened round each arm, or thigh of the horse, which were then hooked on to the blocks used in the ascent. Through these blocks, four in number, triple sheaved, and specially made for this occasion, ran six ropes, also quite new, and made of the strongest yarn, each rope being calculated equal to ten tons. Upon the traversing platform above, were four powerful windlasses, worked by eight men each.

The removal of the various fastenings and bolts by which the Statue was secured to the Car, occupied no less than six hours. At a quarter past three, the Statue, having been properly secured in the slings, began slowly to move, and at six o'clock was raised to the height of about forty feet, having gone up at the rate of three inches every minute during the two hours and three quarters that were consumed in the process. Before nine o'clock, the platform, Statue, and all, had been backed westward and fairly landed on the proposed site, and raised to an elevation which would admit the Statue being placed in its position in a very short time, when the crown of the arch on which it was to rest was prepared for its reception. The masons and other labourers resumed their labours on Thursday morning, and just after one o'clock Mr. Wyatt had the gratification of seeing the Statue move steadily into its destined position. Immediately after, the work of securing it was proceeded with, and in a very short time the figure was fixed.

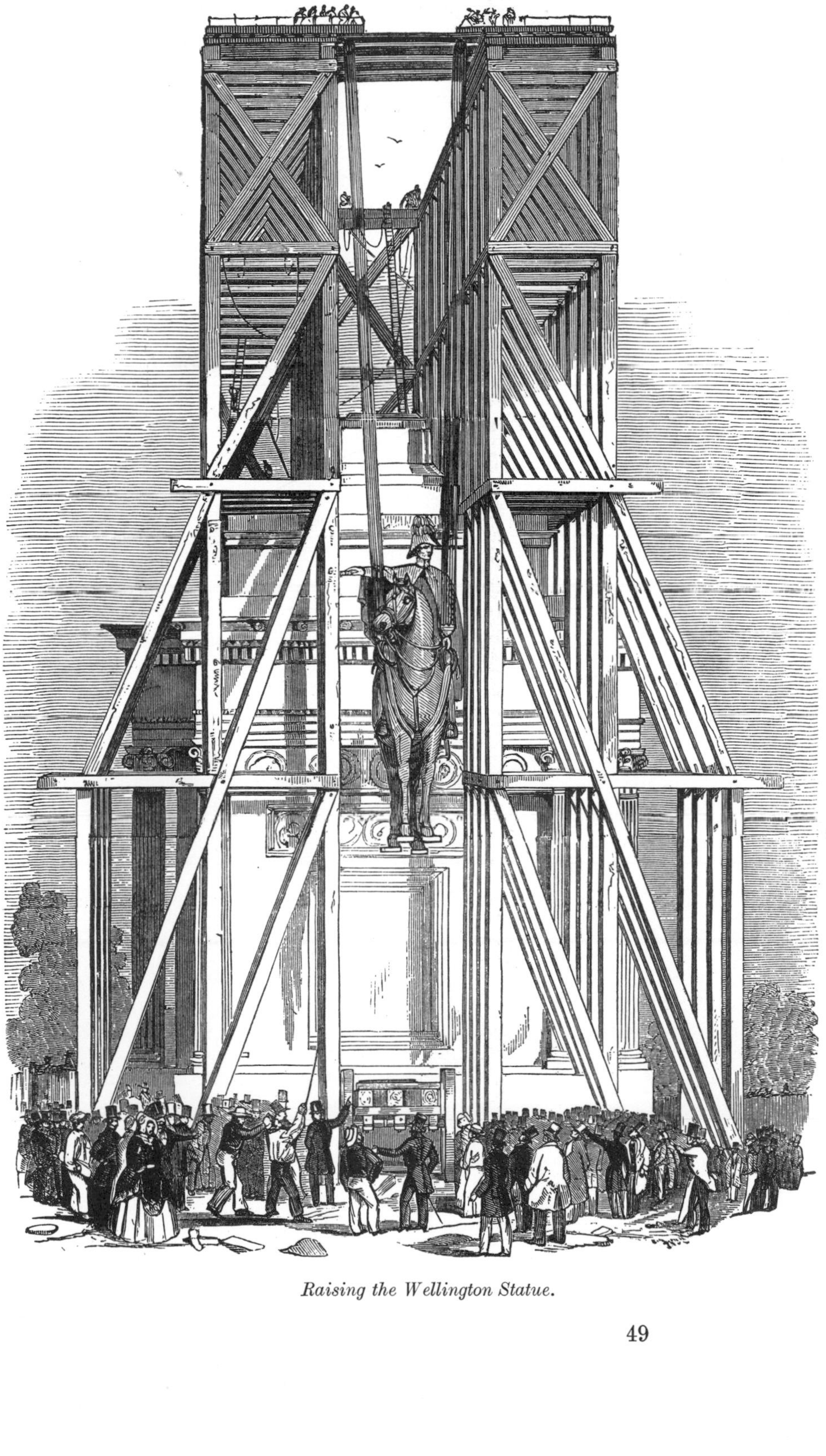

Raising the Wellington Statue.

NEW CACTUS, FROM REAL DEL MONTE, MEXICO

(CEREUS SENILIS)

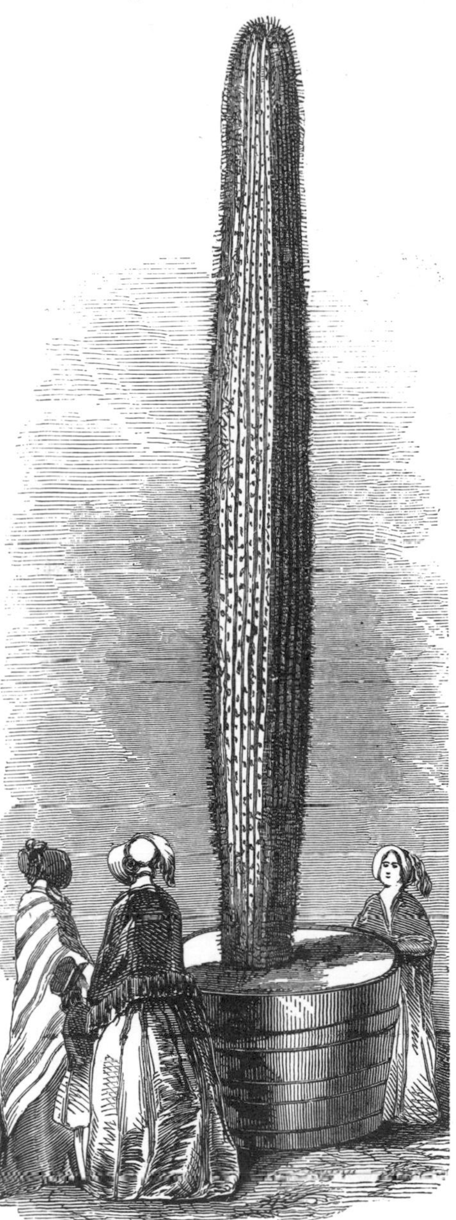

There are three specimens of this lofty Cactus in the Royal Gardens at Kew, $12\frac{1}{2}$ feet, 16 feet, and $18\frac{1}{2}$ feet high; two of the three, however, we regret to add, are now showing evident signs of decay. This species is called *Senilis*, vulgo "Old Man's Head", from the quantity of long, wiry, grey hair which crowns the summit. Unlike the human kind, the old plants are less conspicuous by their long grey hair than the younger ones. For the means of procuring them we are indebted to John Taylor Esq., and the gentlemen of the Real del Monte Company. *Small* plants of this species we know to be twenty and twenty-five years old: from their slowness of growth, as well as from the reports of the inhabitants of Mexico, there is reason to believe that these gigantic individuals are some hundreds (probably a thousand) years old.

The Letter-Carriers' Office.

The great interest excited by the cases of "espionage" at the General Post-office, which have just been brought under the attention of both Houses of Parliament, suggest our continuation of the details of the economy of the great Postal Establishment, commenced in No. 54 of our journal. We propose, in pursuing the subject, to present to our readers the details of the duties of the department, and to give a full description of the internal working of the several branches of this extraordinary machine.

The Newspaper Bin.

THE LETTER-CARRIERS' OFFICE

In the morning, the letter-carriers (to each of whom one partition is appropriated by number) assemble, and assort the letters into their respective walks. The gallery will hold 100 men; and the body, with auxiliaries, 270 more. A portion of the floor is parted off in the middle, where two clerks sit to rectify any mistake which may arise in charging the letters to the carriers. In the evening this room is used for sorting newspapers, to be next described as

THE NEWSPAPER OFFICE

The newspapers from the several vendors and publishers average from 15,000 to 20,000 per night. These are conveyed into the newspaper-office by the northern or letter-carriers' entrance. Those brought by the mail-carts from the branch offices and from the various receiving houses in the metropolis, as well as by the bags of the letter-carriers, are taken in at the lobby, or eastern entrance, into the Inland-office. The newspapers are sorted in the Inland-office; and, for this purpose, the

The Office Letter Railroad.

square partition for the clerks is removed, and a platform placed in its stead; and on this platform is a large bin. The newspapers are brought in in large sacks, baskets, and hampers, and thrown promiscuously into this bin, above which is suspended a crane, used for the purpose of emptying the sacks. A man mounts the heap of papers, attaches the crane to the bottom of the sack, which by means of ropes and pulleys is raised by other men, and thus disgorges its contents.

THE RAILWAY ROOM

The duty of this important department consists in a separation of the letters after the first sorting has taken place into towns, bags for which are conveyed per rail. There is a curious mode of communication opened between the Inland and Twopenny-post departments, by the medium of a tunnel passing underneath the floor of the vestibule or great hall. A kind of tram-way is laid, upon which waggons are drawn by means of a jointed chain worked by a simple crank in the London District Office.

THE SECRET OFFICE, AT THE GENERAL POST-OFFICE

Secret-Office, at the General Post-Office.

The sensation produced by the recent cases of letters being opened at the General Post-office, by the authority of the Secretary of State for the Home Department, has induced us to engrave, for the gratification of our readers, the identical apartment in which this extraordinary power is exercised. It is also used as the Money-Order Office, and is situated on the right of the principal entrance, facing into the great area. A portion of the room is partitioned off, along with the windows, for the payment and granting of Post-office orders. The ordinary business transacted in the room, is the keeping of the accounts connected with the order department, and the franking, &c., of official communications. From one corner of the room is an elegant spiral staircase, which leads to the other offices connected with this division; and beneath the staircase, is a door which communicates by a flight of steps, with the vaults beneath. A door at the side of the room opens into the private office of the principal, Mr. Barth, whose name is signed to all the documents passing through the office.

Few persons are aware how letters are opened and re-sealed by the Post-office. Wafers are opened by the application of moisture, and sealed letters are opened thus:—The letter is laid on an anvil with the seal up, upon the seal is laid a square piece of pure lead, and upon this lead descends a hammer with considerable velocity. The sudden impact converts the lead into a seal as faithful as an electrotype, and accordingly is used to re-seal the letter, which is now opened by destroying the wax bit by bit. For all letters similarly sealed the lead seal will do. A blunderer in the management must have recently led to suspicion. In small country towns, curious postmistresses keep by them an assortment of seals, for the purpose of enabling them to get at little secrets.

Packing the Indian Mail.

FOREIGN AND SHIP LETTER DEPARTMENT

Adjoining the Inland-office is the Foreign and Ship Letter Department, where all letters and papers for foreign and colonial ports are assorted, packed, and dispatched. The India and other mails are made up in this room. The papers are packed in large strong white leather sacks, about as tall as a man, and of proportionate width, the name, as "Smyrna," "Sydney," "Hong Kong," "Demerara," &c., painted upon them.

Our engraving shows the interior of this office during the business of packing the Indian Mail. In this department, too, is a "hoist," for raising bags of letters into the Ship Letter-office.

Folkestone: Arrival of the Indian Mail–Express Omnibus proceeding to Receive it.

CONCLUSION

The number of letters passing through the Post-offices of the United Kingdom is upwards of 219 millions per annum; the gross revenue is about £1,600,000; the cost of management nearly a million, and the net revenue of 1843 was given at no less a sum than £600,000, the cost of the packet service being, as it ought to be, placed to the account of the Admiralty.

THE OVERLAND INDIAN MAIL

We have described in former numbers the course of the Indian Mail from Bombay to Marseilles, together with views of some of the more remarkable localities in the passage of a newspaper express from Paris to the *Times* office in London. Since that period, the subject has grown to be one of greater importance; the states of Hindostan have become more essential to the welfare of the home country; China has been added to our commercial empire; and the course of trading adventure on the coasts of Burmah, Japan, and many wondrous places of the Orient seas, have combined to give all Post-office arrangements with these immense territories a degree of surpassing interest. The flight of the Indian Mail is, in truth, a wonder of the day: thousands follow its course for pleasure or instruction; and even the Governor-General, has at last ventured to take the post passage to Calcutta.

The India Mail—comprehending all the mails from the departments of the East—is made up at Bombay. It consists of bundles of letters, so packed, in strong iron boxes of about two feet by one and a half in depth, securely bound and sealed in *solder*, as wax would be melted by the heat of the climate; these boxes are stamped with a crown, and the words, "GENERAL POST OFFICE—INDIA MAIL." The number of these boxes varies from thirty to forty, or more; together, they constitute the Mail. The boxes, sealed and numbered, are put on board a powerful steamer, and sent direct to Suez, at the head of the Red Sea; then they are transmitted across the Desert in light carts, to Cairo, where they are shipped on the canal, and towed, or steamed, according to circumstances, to Alexandria, where the race against time and tide in reality commences. They are mostly shipped by one of the magnificent steamers in the service of the Oriental Steam Navigation Company, and carried, *via* Malta, direct to Marseilles. At this port, the papers for France are delivered, and an abstract of the Indian news drawn up for the instant information of the French and English Governments. This abstract is sent by telegraph to Paris and thence to Boulogne by a one-horse "*Malle-poste*." On reaching Boulogne, the "abstract" India Mail express, bearing on its envelope the significant words, "*Tres Pressé*," is placed on board a steamer and forwarded, with all possible speed, to Folkestone. In approaching this port the vessel hoists a signal of the "Mail," called a "whiff," or pennon tied at the end in a knot, to give notice to the harbour master and the railroad authorities, to have all things in readiness to speed it on its flight to the metropolis. The answer to these signals, from the pier-head, is made by a double white light, as shown in our engraving. Immediately on the Mail signal being observed, the railway harbour-master, the indefatigable Mr. Faulkner, makes the necessary arrangements for its reception. On landing, the express is committed to Mr. Faulkner, who carries it to the train.

The Abstract Mail having thus reached the Folkestone station in safety, is placed in the carriage of a special train, which is usually in waiting a period—more or less—of three days, for its arrival, and, despatched in less than two hours to the metropolis.

Telegraphing the Abstract of the Indian Mail from Marseilles to Paris.

THE BRITISH MUSEUM

We are happy to state that the noble ediface for the conservation of our "National Museum" is nearly completed; little remains of the grand central portico for construction; and all the rooms at present contemplated, save one or two, are in course of finishing.

Our Illustration shows one of the new rooms in the upper floor of the western wing—the Egyptian Room, the first apartment to the right of the Great Staircase leading to the Ethnographical Room. It has cases ranged on either side, filled with Egyptian deities, sacred animals, statues, household furniture, and other large objects.

But here, as everywhere else, last of all comes death; and the floor of the room is mostly occupied with plate-glass cases of mummies, and various emblems of the painted pageantry to which mortals have fondly clung in all ages of the world. Here are coffins, sepulchral cones, and other ornaments, scaraboei, amulets, &c. Above the cases are bronzes; casts of sculptures from temples, models of obelisks, &c. The casts illustrate the heroic life of Egypt, just as the contents of the cases illustrate the social life. This room has usually crowds of visitors; and, when we remember that Egypt was the cradle of civilisation, we shall not be surprised at its relics being so popular.

PASSAGE OF THE THIRD REGIMENT (BUFFS) THROUGH THE CITY

On Monday afternoon [October 12, 1846] the 3rd Regiment of Foot (Buffs) marched from Vauxhall in the direction of Euston Station, *en route* for Ireland; and, having arrived on the City side of Blackfriars-bridge, the colours were flying, and the band had struck up a lively air, when an ox, which was being driven along Bridge-street in a contrary direction to the military, became alarmed by the music, and dashed suddenly towards the footpath by Chatham-place, where the soldiers were marching. Several of the men met the ox with their bayonets, and the beast became so enraged that he again charged the military, broke their ranks, knocked down some of the men, and threw the arms of others to the ground. Passing the pavement, he threw down a young girl with great violence. She was promptly taken to a surgeon, where she shortly expired from a fracture of the skull, and injuries to the chest.

SURREY ZOOLOGICAL GARDENS

The evening spectacle of the *Siege of Gibraltar*, at this popular resort, is very good, if we take into consideration the terrific realities sought to be represented. The *action* commences about dusk, when the French and Spanish ships begin to take their positions before the town, upon which they commence a brisk fire; this is as sharply returned by the besieged. That represented in the centre of the Engraving is blowing up, and discharging into the air an immense quantity of crackers and other fireworks, which, although they have nothing to do with the Siege, afford great delight to the spectators.

The Improved Omnibus. (*See next page.*)

IMPROVED OMNIBUS

This new omnibus involves two points of importance to the public—improved construction, and consequent reduction of fare.

Several of the new carriages are now building for the Economic Conveyance Company, by Messrs, Adams and Co., who have patented this vehicle. Its prominent differences from the omnibuses in general use, are—its easiness of access, the roof of the carriage being raised, so as to admit the free entrance, without stooping, of a tall person; whilst a safe method of holding on is afforded till the passenger is seated.

The interior of the roof of the carriage is to be appropriated to advertisements, whilst its exterior will form a seat for the outside passengers. Thirteen passengers may be carried within, and about fourteen without. For the interior conveyance, twopence per passenger, and for the outside one penny, for an average distance of a mile will be charged. It is not, however, intended to convey passengers strictly by the mile, but from one part of the metropolis to another, averaging the distance of a mile; and other Omnibuses will be in attendance to convey the traveller to, or towards his destination.

Instead of the ordinary iron-pointed pole, which protrudes through the panel of another carriage, when any accidental collision takes place, the pole of the newly-invented Omnibus has an elastic buffer at the end, similar to that used in railway carriages; so that a motion forward only, and no damage, is occasioned by any contact. To prevent the delay, which usually occurs in pulling up the horses, and stopping the vehicle, when a passenger makes a call to be taken up, a strong break [sic], with a long lever, is under the control of the conductor, which brings up the Carriage instanter, and is sufficiently powerful to supersede the necessity of stopping to put on a drag on descending a hill. The ventilation of the new Carriage is arranged above the heads of the passengers, so that they are subject to no draught, and a mode of communication is thereby made as well with the coachman as with the conductor.

LONDON STREET MUSIC

Of all the itinerant musicians who perambulate the great metropolis, the organ-grinder holds the most conspicuous position. How many suicides have been committed under his melancholy influence has not yet been clearly ascertained; but the effects of the *orgue de Barbarie* on the nervous system have been well known since Hogarth gave to the world his "Enraged Musician". As if the ordinary organ were not enough for anyone's ears, here comes a Monster Street Organ to add to our daily torture. Our artist has resolved that our eyes shall be saluted with its aspect as well as our ears. Look at it and tremble, amateurs and artists! It is from the prolific manufactory of Gavioli, of Modena; and it cost upwards of £150. Here is the march of Street Music; a locomotive Brummagem organ, drawn by a real horse, and exacting two men to develop its orchestral resources. And how hard do the automatons labour in their vocation! How well does the Italian maker comprehend public taste; he gives us plenty of parchment and brass. Ask the "Conductor"—we mean the real one—to display the organic riches of the interior, and how will you revel in reversing cylinders—beating Little's new double-action printing-machines hollow; the difference being, that in the latter there is a myriad of tapes, and in the Monster Organ a shoal of needles. The Great Organ is a street "swell" of the first magnitude—a wholesale dispenser of Rossinian and Bellinian melodies, the hearing of which will cause our modern composers to borrow the strains involuntarily in their forthcoming operas.

PARKHURST PRISON

Dresses of the Officers and Prisoners.

One of the earliest measures contemplated by the Government, in consequence of the discontinuance of the System of Transportation, will be certain alterations on Millbank, Pentonville, and Parkhurst Prisons. The paramount effect will be to substitute for Transportation, imprisonment in the three national prisons above named, or in the county prisons already constructed, which, it is asserted, will meet the exigencies of the case. Pending the consideration of this important change in the Convict System, it may be interesting to introduce to our readers the present discipline at Parkhurst—the Reformatory, or Juvenile Prison, as it has been termed.

The Establishment at Parkhurst was commenced in the year 1838: it is situated nearly in the centre of the Isle of Wight, and presents altogether an imposing appearance; a portion of the buildings placed upon a rising ground, it is visible for several miles around. The original building formed the Hospital to the adjacent Barracks, and was altered for occupation as a prison in 1838. In 1843 were commenced some extensive additions, viz., a ward in the rear, a Chapel, a Probationary Ward, Schools &c.: together with the entire Junior Ward. There were also built at this time residences for the Surgeon, Assistant-Chaplain, Steward, Schoolmasters &c.; houses for Warders; besides two Lodges, and an Infirmary: and there were then completed roads and other works connected therewith. These additions were executed at a cost of about £30,000.

The several buildings are of brick, with cement dressings; and the portions appropriated to the Prisoners are surrounded with walls fifteen feet high. The principle entrance is through a rusticated archway, of Isle of Wight stone; flanking which are two lodges, that on the left for the Porter; and on the right are the office of the Clerk of Works, the Surgery, and the Receiving-room; in the latter are slipper-baths, supply of hot water, and fumigating apparatus. Here each Prisoner, previous to his admission, is examined by the Surgeon; is next washed, and clothed in a Probationary Ward dress, entirely new. The Officers of the Prison wear military undress—blue frock-coats, cloth caps, and leather belt and strap holding keys. Each Prisoner wears a leather cap (made in the Shoemaker's shop) and bearing on its front the Boy's No. in brass figures; the trousers and jacket are of grey cloth; on the left breast of the latter are sewn P.P. and the No.; and P.P. on the left thigh. The rest of the clothing is striped shirt, leather stock, waistcoat for winter wear, worsted stockings and boots, all of which are made in the Prison. On the right breast is worn a brass medal, with No. The Penal Class is denoted by yellow collars and cuffs, and letters of the same colour.

THE PROBATIONARY WARD is a great improvement upon the original system for the reception of Boys on their first arrival. This division of the building consists of THE CORRIDOR, with three tiers of cells, 137 in all; each being 11 feet by 7 feet, and 8 feet 6 inches high, brick-arched, and provided with a hammock, of cocoa-nut fibre, shown in the Engraving of THE CELL, rolled up and laid on a shelf in the corner, to the right of the door; at night it is stretched with straps from wall to wall and fastened with cleats, 15 inches from the floor. Each Cell is furnished with a small table, stool, and writing-desk; a Bible, Prayer-book and Hymn-book, for Chapel use; school books, slate and pencil; and upon the wall of the Cell are placed the Morning and Evening Hymn cards with prayers, and copies for writing; by the side of which is an iron holdfast candlestick, to receive a "Palmer's candle". Immediately over the door-way, is an iron plate for the admission of fresh air, from the Corridor; and in each door is an inspection-plate, of glass and iron wire-gauze, 4 inches by 3. There is, also, a spring-bell, which the Prisoner is to sound when he requires the attendance of an officer; there being affixed to each bell an iron plate inscribed with the number of the

The Corridor.

Cell, indicated, as the bell rings, to the officer in the Corridor.

The Prisoners in this Ward take their meals in their separate Cells, from which they are only allowed to be absent each day, $1\frac{1}{2}$ hours for exercise; $2\frac{1}{2}$ hours in school; half an hour cleaning; and half an hour in the morning, in chapel for prayers.

THE CORRIDOR as shown in the Engraving, is surrounded with galleries and flights of steps leading to the upper tiers. In the

The Probationary Ward School Room.

A Prisoner's Cell.

basement are two Dark Cells for punishment, and two Baths for the Ward. There are Washing-rooms to each gallery, with separate compartments, so that the Prisoners cannot communicate with each other. There are, also, two water-closets on each floor, for night use.

Instruction is given in each Cell according to the knowledge possessed by the Prisoner on entering; when not otherwise employed, he is set to work at tailoring, shoemaking, or other occupations; so that he is not allowed to be for a moment idle.

In the PROBATIONARY WARD, the course of instruction is two hours and a half, on alternate days, of elementary instruction, chiefly religious and moral. By good conduct, the Boys are admitted to the senior division of the School, and instructed at open desks, of which the School Room is provided with 8, as well as fitted with 50 compartments: each of the latter holds but one Prisoner, and is so planned, that the Schoolmaster can inspect and instruct without possibility of the Boys communicating with or seeing each other.

When a School Class is occupied in Cells, the Boys are regularly visited several times a day by the Schoolmaster of the Class for scholastic instruction; as well as by the Chaplain and Principal Schoolmaster, for the purpose of religious and moral admonition. To afford to each Prisoner an occasional opportunity of quiet consideration of his condition and prospects, as well as reflection on the admonition and instruction which he has received, the several School classes are placed for one day in the week in separate cells, and there furnished with light employment, which, while it has afforded manual occupation, has yet allowed time and opportunity for thought.

A visit to Parkhurst Prison—there to witness the exertions of philanthropic enlightenment to reclaim the juvenile offender from the ways of error to the paths of virtue and peace—is one of the most gratifying scenes of philanthropy to be enjoyed in this great Christian country. In the summer of 1845, the Queen visited the Prison, with her suite; and her Majesty was graciously pleased to pardon, in person, two of the Prisoners, one from each Division of the Establishment.

EASTER MONDAY ON THE RIVER THAMES

This is a picture of holiday life, illustrative of the amusements of Easter Monday, when the indwellers of London flock by thousands to Greenwich by steam-boats. Dipping into Mr. Albert Smith's *Christopher Tadpole*, for the present month, we quote the passage:—

"The holiday was Greenwich Fair, whither he was to accompany Mr. and Mrs. Chirpey, and Bessy Payne; and when the little party had assembled in the little shop, it would have been difficult to have found four happier faces, and certainly one prettier, in all London. For the jolly man was still the same—a trifle stouter, perhaps, but that was of little consequence—and his partner had forgotten all her first affections; and, finding that hearts were not daily crushed and blighted as she had once imagined, was as cheerful as her husband; indeed, in the lively, good-humoured Mrs. Chirpey, you would have scarcely recognised the romantic, soul-wearied Miss Twits. She had given up reading the penny romances; for two small publications of her own—one four years old, and the other but a few months—took up all her attention. And the youngest of these accompanied the party,

Mrs. Chirpey insisting upon carrying it herself. And Bessy looked so cruelly pretty—had grown such a trim, plump little woman, and was so elegantly dressed, that Sprouts quite misgave his power over her affections, almost thinking that she was too good for him. . . . And so they set forth, the envy and admiration of the entire court; and proceeded towards the river.

"They had to wait a little while at Hungerford Pier, for there was scarcely standing-room on the packet that was to start first. Tom bought some periwinkles on the sly, 'to amuse himself going down,' he said, which made Bessy pout, and regret that he felt so dull, at which Tom wanted to be affectionate, but was very properly reproved. In a few minutes a boat came up, and the dangerous process of embarking Mrs. Chirpey and the baby having been accomplished, the others followed, and the vessel moved off, rolling under its heavy freight until the water almost washed in at the cabin windows. The folks were so wedged together, that Sprouts could not produce the effect he had intended, with a bottle of stout and a biscuit; and the harp and cornet had as much as they could do to get room to move their arms. But this, said Tom, was an advantage, because it was perfectly impossible for them to come round for money when they had finished playing. At last, after stopping everywhere to take in more people, until the passengers swarmed like bees on every available part of the boat, they got to Greenwich, and made their way towards the Park."

GOING TO THE EPSOM RACE BY TRAIN

First Class

Second Class

Third Class

FATAL EXPLOSION ON BOARD THE "CRICKET" STEAMER

We give an account of the frightful accident which took place about half-past nine o'clock on the morning of yesterday week [August 27, 1847] on board the *Cricket* steamer, one of the boats running between the City and the West-end at the fare of one halfpenny. It appears that the vessel was about to leave the Adelphi pier for London-bridge, having on board about 150 passengers, all quietly seated, when a sudden report was heard, followed by an instantaneous explosion. Immediately the vessel was nearly cleared—some of the passengers being blown up into the air, falling into the water—others had jumped over the sides, and were struggling in the mud.

One part of the boiler was hurled 100 feet

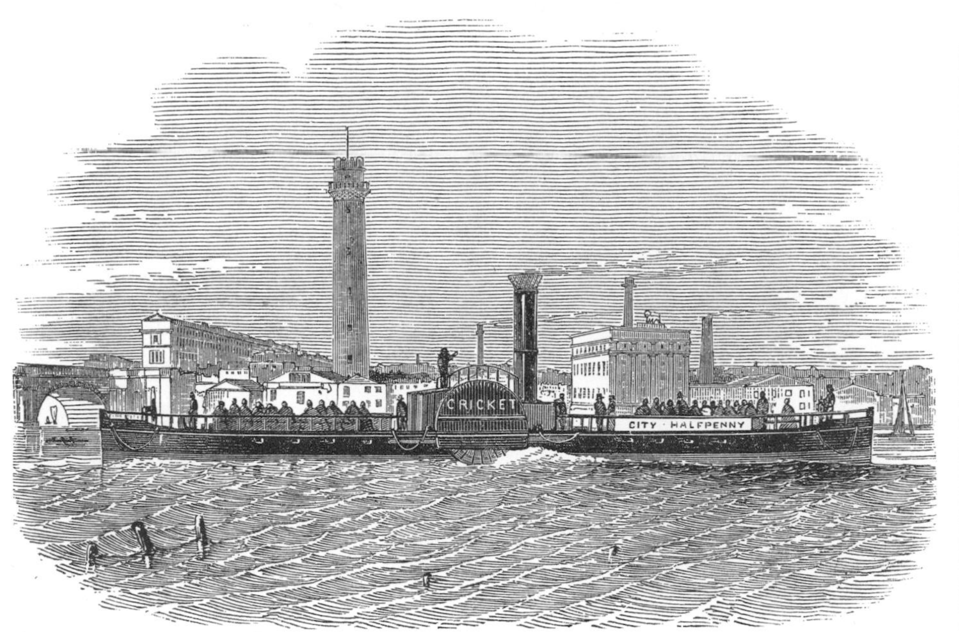

towards the Watermen's Adelphi pier, at the bottom of George-street, and another portion of it in a contrary direction towards Waterloo-bridge.

It is not a little singular that the *Cricket* was condemned, together with the *Ant* and *Bee*, more than six months since, by Mr. Portwine, in his work on the "Steam Engine", &c., in the following plain language:—"There are three vessels on the Thames, called the *Ant*, *Bee* and *Cricket*—boats which profess to work with low-pressure condensing engines. The public is not aware that they are working at 36 lb. on the square inch. These are the boats plying from Hungerford to London-bridge, and working at high pressure; they may when out of order blow up their decks and the myriads of passengers they are burthened with". This extract was published by an engineer six months since, and time has too fatally proved Mr. Portwine's prediction.

Exaggerated reports were spread of the number of persons killed. It amounts to five; but a great many were hurt.

SKETCHES FROM LONDON THOROUGHFARES

Through the London of the present day the rapid current of human life is ever rolling in living eddies, from east to west, and jostling, in its mighty strength, every idle object it meets with on its way; and, in this ever-moving ocean, each human wave has its allotted mission, each tiny ripple "its destined end and aim." So rolls on this mighty river, bearing onwards those who pass and re-pass on each side of its shore-like pavement, and the rapid vehicles which glide swift as full-sailed vessels through its mid-channel!

All at once there is a stoppage! Some heavily-laden waggon has broken down, and the long line of carriages of every description are suddenly brought to a stand-still—all are motionless. You see the old thoroughbred London cabman, who has promised to take his fare either east or west, as the matter may be, in a given number of minutes—dodge in and out for a few seconds, through such narrow openings as no one excepting a real Jehu born on the stand, would ever venture to move in, until he comes to the entrance of some narrow street, the ins and outs of which are known only to a few like himself, when, crack, bang, and he has vanished, giving one of his own peculiar leers at parting, at the long line he has left stationary. Now there is a slow movement, and the procession proceeds at a funeral pace. The donkey-cart, laden with firewoods, heralds the way, and is followed by the beautiful carriage with its armorial bearings. Behind comes the heavy dray, with its load of beer-barrels; the snail-paced omnibus follows; the high-piled waggon, that rocks and reels beneath its heavy load, next succeeds, and you marvel that it does not toppel [sic] over, extinguish some dozen or so of foot passengers, and smash in the gorgeous shop front. The wreck, which left the street so silent for a few minutes, is at length drawn aside, and all is again noise and motion; the police van rolls on with its freight of crime, and is followed by the magistrate's cabriolet, as he hurries off to a west-end dinner.

And all goes merry as a marriage bell.

Burning the Royal Carriages at the Château d'Eu.

FRENCH REVOLUTION, FEBRUARY, 1848

The spectacle of a great and enlightened nation, for the second time within the space of eighteen years, unanimously flying to arms in the assertion and vindication of its political rights, is one which cannot be contemplated with too careful a scrutiny. Its minutest details must be fraught with the most solemn and significant lessons to the people, as well as to the rulers of every contemporary nation. Wherever the light of popular Government has begun to dawn, it behoves all men to watch attentively, in the cause of humanity, the calamitous episodes which may attend its progress, tracing to their origin the results of fraud or impolicy on the one hand, or of overheated zeal on the other. It has been the deplorable destiny of France to furnish more than one such lesson to the world, written in characters of blood, and read by the torchlight of rebellion.

Interior of a Chamber—A Family of Insurgents protecting a Barricade in the Rue du Faubourg St. Antoine.

London, Saturday, February 26, 1848—The events of the week in Paris have proved to Louis Philippe, that, spite of his enormous army, the forts, the limited franchise and unlimited power of buying the electors, spite of his strong majority in the Chambers, there is still something that can check "the system." He is nearly absolute as a King can be, who exists by a charter, and professes to govern by a Constitution, though both are mockeries. A revolt in Paris must always make him feel that as he was raised to the Royal power so he may be hurled from it. And through eighteen years he has crushed the populace as a mass, and escaped the vengeance that worked by the hand of the assassin, yet he is now in extreme old age, with a child for his successor, sitting on a throne that trembles on the wave of popular convulsion! One would think that the sagacity and wisdom which have brought him only to this, cannot be of the highest order.

Constituted as the French Chambers are, filled with men employed by the Government, or hoping to be employed, the opinion of the public is not reflected there. Hence the necessity of a revolt; barricades and bloodshed, even to secure so small, and, as far as the nation is concerned, unimportant result, as the change of M. Guizot for M. Molé. We call it unimportant, for that it will be followed by any real change in the system that crushes the people of France we do not believe. Louis Philippe merely plays an old game over again.

Barricade at the Corner of the Boulevard, Rue Mazagran, near the Porte St. Denis.

We have just received another telegraphic express, to the following effect:—

BY ELECTRIC TELEGRAPH

DOVER, FRIDAY, 9.30 P.M.—A Queen's messenger arrived, bringing news that Louis Philippe has formally abdicated the throne. He proceeded to the Chamber of Deputies yesterday at half-past one, and announced his intention, in favour of the young Count de Paris; the Duchess of Orleans to be Regent. Previous to the abdication, the City of Paris was in possession of the people, who sacked and fired the Tuileries. Louis Philippe, with his family, has departed for Neuilly.

RED REPUBLICANISM

[Saturday, July 1, 1848.] The "Red Republicans" have justified their name. They have filled the streets of Paris with blood. They have enacted scenes unparalleled in the annals of civilisation. The history of the sad calamity which will render memorable in all time the month of June, 1848, is by no means intricate. On the 24th of February the populace of Paris were victorious, not merely by their own efforts, but by the very apathy of the middle classes. The latter could not take up arms for a system of corruption like that of Louis Philippe. But, on that very day, when the old system was overthrown, and a new one was installed in its place, a difference sprang up between the active and the passive agents of the Revolution. The working classes, or "Red Republicans," were imbued with the doctrines of Communism. The middle classes, however, did not share these ideas. They wanted no red flag, which was to them an emblem of terror alone. They were content with the old tri-colour, and with the ideas with which it was so intimately associated. These were ideas of political, not social change.

These two flags and two principles were brought, if not into physical, at least into moral collision, in the hour of their combined triumph over the monarchy. They met face to face upon the steps of the Hôtel de Ville. M. de Lamartine represented the one—the whole populace the other. M. de Lamartine became the chief of the Provisional Government in the interest of the middle classes. Men of his own principles were installed along with him. But by their side were found the men of the new ideas—men who looked for social, more than for political change.

Although trade was at a stand, and although the middle classes were impoverished, and daily lost some portion of the hardly-earned rewards of their industry, enterprise, and economy, the "people" were not allowed to suffer. They were fed with large wages, and supported at the public expense. The breach continued to widen. The Red Republicans determined to found a Republic of their own, upon the overthrow of that previously existing. They commenced operations on Thursday week in the name of the "Red Republic—democratic and social." They fought obstinately. They were obstinately resisted. After a struggle of four days, unparalleled for its savage ferocity, they have been vanquished, but at a cost which it is fearful to contemplate.

CIVIL WAR IN FRANCE

[July 1, 1848.]—Paris has again become the theatre of one of the most sanguinary struggles that even its blood-stained streets have ever witnessed. Nothing approaching the carnage of the last four days has, it is said, occurred in that capital since the massacre of St. Bartholomew. The *ouvriers*—the workmen of the national workshops—have constituted the plague-spot on the Republic, which has developed itself into this frightful disaster. We mentioned in our last Number that the Government had determined on sending out of Paris to the provinces such of the workmen of the *ateliers nationaux* as had come up to the capital since the revolution of February,

Carrying the Wounded.

attracted thither by the wages offered by the Government. This circumstance led to the outbreak which took place on Friday (last week).

THE ILLUSTRATIONS

We append the substance of the notes taken by our Artist, of the appearance of the localities which he visited in sketching the accompanying Illustrations. That such was accomplished at great personal risk will be inferred by each reader; to whom also it will doubtless be satisfactory to learn that in his faithful and devotional discharge of duty, our Artist experienced no personal injury.

Women on the Barricade of St. Denis.—Although this scene appears too melodramatic to be true, still it is the very drama of reality. To the left waves, in grim terror, the flag inscribed "Du Pain ou la Mort" (Bread or Death), and mounted on the barricade are two women heroically calling upon the insurgents to follow their example of self-devotedness. The foremost was well known in the Quartier St. Denis; she was a fine woman, with black hair, and wore a light blue silk dress; her head and arms bare. She and her companion were shot whilst in the attitudes indicated in the Illustration. The scene reminds one of heroines of 1793.

Women on the Barricade, near the Porte St. Denis.

The Great Barricade at the entrance of the Rue du Faubourg St. Antoine.—Our Artist having taken a good view of the scene from inside the barricade on the Place de la Bastile, proceeded to the entrance of the Rue du Faubourg St. Antoine. "Here," he writes, "I inspected the famous barricade: it was as high as the first floor, and more than ten feet deep; the top was covered with double rows of well-armed men. A small passage near the corners was left, through which I passed. When inside this barricade, I was compelled to work like everybody else at removing the pavement, only to show that I sympathised with the insurgents. After this display of *bon volonté*, I was at liberty, and went up the faubourg to the fifth barricade, showing my dirty palms and muddy coat every time when called upon to assist, to prove that I had contributed my share. The aspect of the faubourg was formidable: one universal feeling pervading all the population; women, old men, children, and entire families were in the street,

The Great Barricade at the Entrance of the Rue du Faubourg St. Antoine, from the Place de la Bastile.

whole of the streets which open into Covent-Garden are thronged with vehicles, and buyers and sellers—for either the green-grocer or his man must be here early if our dinner-table is to be supplied with first-rate vegetables; and from the most remote street of the suburbs the greengrocers are compelled to come either to the Borough, to Farringdon, or Covent-Garden markets for their stocks—for these, with the exception of Spitalfields, which is celebrated for potatoes, are the only garden markets. From one or other of these places have all those tempting shows of flowers, fruit, and vegetables, which give such a country-look to the greengrocers' shops been brought at an early hour.

THE QUEEN'S STATE BALL-ROOM

SKETCHED BY PERMISSION OF HER MAJESTY

The State Ball-Room at Buckingham Palace is a very handsome apartment; though too small for its purpose. It is divided into two portions, one, the chief part of the room, and the other a lesser portion, where the orchestra gallery is erected. The apartment is divided into three compartments, by coupled three-quarter columns of the Corinthian order, carrying a highly-enriched entablature; and from that springs a very deep coving, and thence the ceiling, which is flat. The columns are scagliola in imitation of porphry, and the capitals are gilded, as are all the decorations and enrichments of the entablature.

On the western side of the room are three lofty windows, the curtains to which are of yellow satin, with draperies pendent from richly-gilded cornices. By an ingenious adaptation of the curtains of the central window, the effect of a canopy to a throne is produced. A small stage is erected in the bay of the window, filled with the choicest of flowers in blossom, and covered with crimson velvet: and on it are placed chairs for her Majesty and the Royal Family, and long seats for distinguished visitors.

The Sea-Serpent passing under the stern of the "Daedalus."

THE GREAT SEA-SERPENT

A new attestation of the existence of the Great Sea Serpent appeared in the *Times* of the 10th inst. [October, 1848] in a communication from Plymouth dated October 7, as follows:—

"When the *Daedalus* frigate, Captain M'Quhae, which arrived here on the 4th inst. was on her passage home from the East Indies, between the Cape of Good Hope and St. Helena, her captain, and most of her officers and crew, at four o'clock one afternoon, saw a Sea-Serpent. The creature was twenty minutes in sight of the frigate, and passed under her quarter. Its head appeared to be about four feet out of the water, and there was about sixty feet of its body in a straight line on the surface. It is calculated that there must have been under water a length of thirty or forty feet more, by which it propelled itself at the rate of fifteen miles an hour. The diameter of the exposed part of the body was about sixteen inches—its colour a dark brown, with yellowish-white about the throat. It had no fins, but something like the mane of a horse, or rather a bunch of seaweed washed about its back. When it extended its jaws, which were full of large jagged teeth, they seemed sufficiently capacious to admit of a tall man standing upright between them. The ship was sailing north at the rate of eight miles an hour, and the beast was seen by the quartermaster, the boatswain's mate, the man at the wheel, the Captain and officers of the watch. The *Daedalus* left the Cape of Good Hope on the 30th of July and reached St. Helena on the 16th of August."

A gentleman long resident in Norway writes:

"There are, I believe, several varieties of the reptile known as the Sea-Serpent. In several of the fossil reptiles somewhat approaching the Sea-Serpent in size and other characteristics, the orbit is very large, and in this respect, as well as in having short paws or flappers, the descriptions of the Northern Sea-Serpents agree with the supposed appearance of some of the antediluvian species. A great part of the disbelief on the existence of the Sea-Serpent has arisen from its being supposed to be the same animal as the Kraken, or rather from the names having been used indiscriminately."

The State Ball-Room—The Polka. (*See preceding page.*)

THE ELECTRIC LIGHT

On Tuesday night [December 5, 1848] there was a second public experimental exhibition of the Electric Light upon the raised steps forming the entrance to the National Gallery and the Royal Academy. There was a large attendance of scientific gentlemen and noblemen. Upon the summit of the steps a kind of easel was raised, beneath which were placed the battery and a small lamp. About a foot above the battery was the light produced burning upon two pieces of charcoal, backed by a single thin reflector, and the light enclosed within a glass case. The light produced was of a most powerful character, but is, in our opinion, still but a costly experimental toy, whose practicability forms a whole subject for conjecture.

The illustration shows an Experimental Exhibition of the Electric Light in Trafalgar Square.

HER MAJESTY'S VISIT TO IRELAND

The announcement that her Majesty intended to visit Ireland immediately after the prorogation of Parliament [August, 1849] created on the very first day that it was known across St. George's Channel the greatest satisfaction and delight in the minds of all classes of people. A few, perhaps, ventured to throw doubts upon the reception that would be given the Queen and her illustrious Consort; but the large majority of the citizens of Dublin, Cork, and Belfast, and the people of Ireland generally, gave expression to opinions which must speedily have convinced this little party that they had utterly miscalculated the temper of the public. Day by day after that time the popular enthusiasm continued to increase; and it soon became evident that Irish loyalty, exuberant as it was when George IV visited Ireland, had suffered no diminution; but that, on the contrary, it had grown in fervour and extent. In every part of her dominions her Majesty is admired, respected and beloved, both as a Sovereign and as a woman. Not only is public homage cheerfully and spontaneously rendered to her as the model of a Queen, but a warmer and more tender homage is no less spontaneously and universally offered to her as an example to the daughters, wives, mothers, and gentlewomen of her nation, of the conduct they should pursue, to merit the esteem of the wise and the admiration of the virtuous. Ireland participates in these feelings, and the very humblest of the people give expression to them. Even in cases where political rancour might be supposed to rage, the Irish, with exceptions too insignificant to require notice, separate the person and character of Queen Victoria from the occasions of public strife and difference of opinion that are, unhappily, too frequent, and yield to her, individually, the homage of their unaffected loyalty. Many persons now living witnessed and shared in the ceremonies and rejoicings that took place when George IV visited Dublin. Those persons are unanimous in asserting that the enthusiasm of that day, great as it was, was a mere shadow of the loyalty and devotion expressed throughout society during the visit of a more deservedly popular Sovereign—QUEEN VICTORIA.

For at least ten days or a fortnight before her Majesty's arrival at Cove, the citizens of Cork, Dublin, and Belfast were up and stirring to do her honour. Public buildings and private dwellings put on a new face of cleanliness: shops were newly painted and decorated: never was such scrubbing, and rubbing, and beautifying—such running to and fro of busy men.

The whole population felt the impetus. The shopkeepers put forth their richest display of goods. The Killarney arbutus, the tabinets, or poplins, and all the few articles that may in Ireland be considered as of native manufacture were displayed to the best advantage in the windows to captivate the attention of strangers, especially of those who were expected to pour into Ireland from rich England laden with golden sovereigns, and having nothing to do but spend them. The price of lodgings went up at an enormous rate; and seats at the windows of those housekeepers who were fortunate enough to be located in the exact line of procession, were offered for sums, which, if obtained, would have gone

The Statue of Queen Victoria, Royal College, Cork.

The Queen at the Female Infant School, Dublin.

The arrival of the Royal Visitors at Belfast Harbour.

far towards paying the whole annual rental of the speculators. If all the gold of California had been expected, prices could not have risen much higher.

The price of labour went up. Carpenters (and gas-fitters more especially) were at a high premium. For once in the history of Ireland, the supply of labour was not equal to the demand. The streets swarmed with a population almost unanimous in the desire to make her Majesty's welcome in Ireland superior in its cordiality to any that she had ever received in any portion of her dominions.

Our first Engraving shows the statue of her Majesty, which has been presented to the Royal College at Cork by Sir Thomas Deane, and which was elevated at the very moment of the Queen's carriage passing to its proper site on the nearest gable of the structure. Next we show the visit by the Royal party to the infant school of the National Board of Education at Dublin, where a pleasing scene presented itself. The children were arranged in rows one above the other, the front being occupied by the very youngest, some of whom were not above three years of age. They all rose at her Majesty's approach, and sang a hymn in a very creditable manner. Her Majesty looked on with very evident gratification, and seemed especially pleased, if not amused, with the antics of the youngest babies.

Interior of the Royal Railway Carriage.

The next Engraving shows the scene of her Majesty's landing at Belfast, as the gilded sides and rakish yellow chimney of the steam-yacht *Fairy*, bearing the Royal party, were first descried. And finally, we present the Royal railway carriage, which elicited the admiration of all who beheld it. The exterior was painted blue and white, and the French style of decoration furnished a very elegant model for the ornamental work. The windows are of plate glass, and command such an extensive view, that her Majesty was enabled to see all around her. At either side of the roof was a beautifully gilt *fac simile* of the Royal arms, and at each of the four corners was a crown placed upon a cushion. The interior of the carriage where the Royal party sat was eleven feet five inches in length; the draperies consisted of white damask, richly ornamented with gilt devices; the mirrors were of various shapes and sizes; a sofa of blue tabinet, four chairs, and five footstools, constituted what may be termed the essential furniture of the compartment; the ceiling was highly ornamented; and altogether this and every other part of the carriage presented an appearance of beauty and elegance seldom surpassed.

THE NEW SILVER COINAGE

A new silver piece called a 'florin' of the value of 2s. has recently been coined. It has for the obverse the Queen's effigy, crowned, with the inscription 'Victoria Regina', and the date of the year; and for the reverse the ensigns armorial of the United Kingdom, contained in four shields crosswise, each shield surmounted by the Royal crown, with the rose in the centre, and in the compartments between the shield the national emblems of the rose, thistle, and shamrock, surrounded by the words 'One florin, one tenth of a pound'; and with a milled edge.

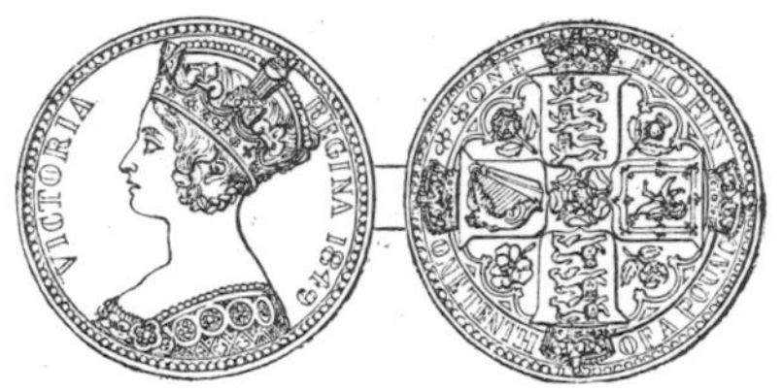

VAUXHALL GARDENS

The season at this still popular place of amusement has proved, on the whole, successful to the new *entrepreneurs*. The result has been fairly earned; for the proprietors have provided for their visitors a succession of novel attractions of a superior class.

On Wednesday the great attraction was the Night Ascent of Mr. Green in his superb Victoria Balloon, which was seen by aid of the Electric Light, at the back of the spectators' gallery, as shown in our Illustration.

The Balloon ascent did not take place till eleven o'clock. The occupants of the car were but two—Mr. Green and a friend. When set at liberty, the Balloon rose slowly, and, after poising itself, soared easily into the air, and was soon lost in the shadow of the starless sky. The display of fireworks made from the car, however, soon rendered its course observable for a considerable time.

The illuminations on Wednesday were on an extended scale of magnificence and effect; and it must be acknowledged that a great improvement has been made in the character of the scenic contrivances. We remember when the tinkling tin waterfall and the hermit in the dark walks were the best ingenuities of Vauxhall. In their place, we have indications of more artistic taste: such as the Italian Walk, with its sculpture and fountain, illumined by the electric rays. It is, certainly, one of the most elegant localities of the Gardens.

The Medical Inspector's Office.

emigration from Scotland or Ireland. In the year 1849, out of the total number of 299,498 emigrants, more than one half left from the port of Liverpool. We learn from a statement in a Liverpool newspaper, that in the months of January, February, March, and April of the present year, the total emigration was 50,683 persons; and as these four months include two of the least busy months of the year, it is probably that the numbers during the months of May, June, July, and August, the full emigrational season, will be much more considerable, and that the emigration for the year will exceed that for 1849.

It would appear that very few out of the vast army of Irish and other emigrants that proceed to the United States, or the British Colonies, go out as mere adventurers, without some knowledge of the country, or their chances of doing well, when they get there. The sums received by them before they leave this country are sufficient proofs that they have prosperous friends upon the other side; and it is to be presumed that the friends who send them the money, do not avoid sending them advice, and giving them full information, to the best of the means, as to their movements upon arrival.

No passenger-ship is allowed to proceed until a medical practitioner appointed by the emigration office of the port shall have inspected the medicine-chest and passengers, as shown in our first Engraving, and certified that the medicines etc. are sufficient, and the passengers are free from contagious disease.

There are usually a large number of spectators at the dock-gates to witness the final departure of the noble ship, with its large freight of human beings. It is an interesting and impressive sight, as may be seen in our second Engraving: and the most callous and indifferent can scarcely fail, at such a moment, to form cordial wishes for the pleasant voyage and safe arrival of the emigrants, and for their future prosperity in their new home. As the ship is towed, hats are raised, handkerchiefs are waved, and a loud and long-continued shout of farewell is raised from the shore, and cordially responded to from the ship. May all prosperity attend her living freight!

The Departure of the Emigrants' Ship.

This Exposition usually takes place annually in the Louvre; but, owing to the repairs at that place not being completed, the locality has been changed; and this year [1851] the novelties of French art have been exhibited in a temporary building provided for the purpose in the court-yard of that scene of so many vicissitudes—the Palais Cardinal, Royal, and at present National.

The collection contains specimens of the best works of the French modern school: and we are informed that during the present season we shall have the opportunity of seeing the more remarkable of these pictures in London; a Committee being now in course of formation in the metropolis with the object of giving to French and other Continental artists the same hospitable reception which has been so liberally accorded to the industrial world in the Crystal Palace in Hyde Park.

The accompanying Illustration shows one of the ground-floor saloons of the Paris Exhibition; in which, for the first time, is presented the happy combination of pictures and statues, reciprocally setting off their merits.

This portion of the Exhibition is admirably arranged, and may serve as a model for that neglected class of building, our galleries of art. The temporary barrack-like house was built in two months. The room contains but a small portion of the contributions of the French artists; for we find the catalogue to contain no fewer than 1664 names, whose productions amount to 3952, and fill 34 rooms and galleries. The contributors are—painters, 1306; sculptors, 204; architects, 44; engravers, 78; lithographers, 32.

THE MANUFACTURE OF STEEL PENS IN BIRMINGHAM

A brief account of a visit to the largest manufactory of steel pens, in Birmingham, or the world, will enable the reader to understand the magnitude of the operations through which a piece of steel passes before it becomes that flexible instrument which has superseded the quill as the recorder of our wants, our business, and our affections.

The manufactory is that of Messrs. Hinks, Wells, and Co., an immense establishment giving employment to 564 hands, consuming $2\frac{1}{2}$ tons of steel per week, turning out 35,000 gross of pens weekly, or 1,820,000 gross in a year.

The metal in its crude state, best quality cast steel, is clipped from the original sheets into lengths from $1\frac{3}{4}$ to $4\frac{1}{2}$ inches wide, placed in a "muffle", heated to a white heat, and annealed. The strips are then put into the rolling mill and rolled until they are quite flexible. Next, in the "cutting-out room", the pen first begins to assume a form. Along this room a number of woman are seated at benches, cutting out, by the aid of hand-presses, the future pen from the ribbons of steel. The "blanks" are then taken to be pierced, and after a second annealing they are each stamped with a distinctive mark. The

Ground-floor Saloon of the Paris Exhibition Building.

The Pen Grinding Room.—(*See preceding page.*)

distinctive marks in this manufactory number about 3000.

By being placed in a groove, and having a convex tool dropped upon it, the pen is bent into a tube of the required shape. To remove roughness, the pens are scoured, and then taken to the "grinding-room" which employs one-fourth of the entire number of hands engaged in the manufactory. The quality of the pen very much depends on the grinding, which serves the same purpose as the scraping the back of the quill did. The pens are then taken to the "slitting-room", and then varnished and boxed.

The younger girls earn from 5s. to 7s. a week; the elder, 12s. and 14s. Even at work they are generally well dressed.

THE FIRST PUBLIC EXECUTION AT SAN FRANCISCO

Lynch law was never carried into execution with greater deliberation and more solemnity than at San Francisco on last June 10th and 11th [1851]. About 9 o'clock on Tuesday night, a man carrying a bag containing something apparently very heavy, attracted the attention of the Whitehall boatmen, at their station on Central Wharf. He jumped into a boat with his bag, and pulled away. But few moments had elapsed before a gentleman who keeps a shipping office on the wharf came down to the boat-stand in pursuit of a person who had just robbed his office of a small iron safe, containing a considerable sum of money.

A number of the boatmen succeeded in capturing him, while the bag proved to contain the stolen safe. He was at once taken possession of by the Vigilant Committee, who conducted him promptly to their headquarters, where he was tried in presence of about eighty members of the conclave in secret trial, by them convicted, and sentenced to be hanged in the Portsmouth-square that very night.

The citizens had accumulated in large numbers, the bell on the engine-house having rung a signal to apprise them of the proceedings. The populace were very much excited as the bell commenced to ring the prisoner's funeral knell. About two o'clock the doors of the committee room opened, and the condemned was for the first time presented to the populace. A number of the police made several attempts to obtain possession of the prisoner, but they were roughly handled and prevented—had they persisted, they would have been riddled with balls. Several citizens denounced the execution and sought to aid the police.

The prisoner by this time was nearly dead with fear and rough handling, when a rush was made towards him, a noose thrown over his head, the rope manned by twenty ready hands, and the heavy form of the convicted felon swept through the air and dangled from the block. A few fearful struggles, a quiver of the hempen cord, a few nervous twitches—and the crowd gazed upon the lifeless corpse of him upon whom such speedy and terrible vengeance had been executed by an outraged populace. At six o'clock the Marshal repaired to the spot, cut down the body and consigned it to the dead-house. Of the guilt of the prisoner Jenkins there was no doubt. He had been known to the police for some months as a desperate character from the penal colonies, where he had passed many years as a transported convict.

Lynch-Law in California.

REPORT FROM THE INTERIOR OF CALIFORNIA

Certain travellers who have visited California have reported the country to be strangely deficient in natural beauty, a statement which the accompanying View goes far to refute.

This scene has been sketched by our Correspondent near Russian River, 100 miles north-west of San Francisco. Within thirty miles, the country changes from the "oak plains" of Santa Rosa to the alpine scenery of this sketch. The land is equally rich; the game equally abundant; the climate, if possible, more beautiful. The red-wood pine predominates, but oak of a hardy description is not sparse; the wild grape and raspberry are very luxuriant; salmon and trout are plentiful; and the grizzly bears a little *too* numerous, if anything. This district, the "further back" (from the centre of civilisation), is fast populating. The rocks in the foreground of the Sketch contain 25 and 30 per cent. of gold; but, at present, the expense of working by machinery would not repay labour and cost. The scene of the Sketch is now the residence of an English gentleman, who intends cultivating as much of the surrounding soil as is practicable. The accompanying figures are portraits from the native population of this district.

Mr. M'Collum's equestrian feat on two horses.—(*See next page.*)

DRURY LANE—EQUESTRIAN TROUPE

The star riders continue attractive, and the public crowd the theatre to award the prize of their plaudits to the French and American competitors. But by far the most astonishing miracle-worker of the number is an American equestrian, Thomas M'Collum by name, whose feats with two horses are the most remarkable examples of pirouetting and somerseting [sic] that we ever witnessed. While the horses are proceeding with the utmost rapidity, he describes several curves in the air repeatedly, and comes down safely on their backs, having meanwhile compassed a leap over a flag.

We present our readers with an Illustration. [*See previous page.*] Others might have been given of still greater beauty and daring, exciting wonder at the rider's agility, and the training of the noble animals that so implicitly obey the master's volition. The excitement of these exhibitions is exceedingly great; and they have, indeed, in them a certain poetry of their own, calculated to affect the *stable* mind with a sense of beauty. If the highest dramatic poetry be necessarily banished from the Drury-Lane stage, owing to the fault of the proprietary, in omitting to fit the machinery for scenic purposes, we see no reason why the equestrian spectacular poetry may not be substituted, until the requisite duty behind the scenes be performed by those who have this Temple of the Muses in trust.

''*Swan-Upping*'' *from Brentford Ait.*

SWAN UPPING ON THE THAMES

Yesterday [July 19, 1844] the Lord Mayor and his civic friends proceeded in state to spend a festive day in the haunts of the regal and privileged swans of the Thames. On this occasion, the state barge, followed by a gaily dressed shallop, conveying the company, were towed to Brentford Ait, a little above Kew-bridge, where the celebrated barge, the Maria Wood, was moored to receive them: his lordship disembarked and continued his ''voyage'' to Twickenham on board the barge Maria. A splendid banquet was served on board, and dancing kept up with much spirit on the ample deck.

The swan is, perhaps, the most beautiful living ornament of our rivers and lakes. Poets of all ages and countries have made this bird the theme of their praise, and by none with more characteristic truth of expression than by our own Milton who, in his ''Paradise Lost'', says:—

'The swan with arched neck
Between her white wings mantling, proudly rows.'

In the Thames, at present, the greatest number of swans belong to the Queen, and the Companies of Vintners and Dyers own the next largest proportion; but the birds are far less numerous than they used to be. They are marked upon the upper mandible with a knife or other sharp instrument. The ''Swan-upping,'' or ''Swan-hopping'', as it is vulgarly termed, is the catching and taking up the swans to mark the cygnets, and renew that on the old birds, if obliterated, in the presence of the royal swan herdsman, which is still continued by the companies above mentioned. This was ostensibly the business of the civic excursion yesterday, but the birds are actually marked in the month of August.

The Dyers' and Vintners' Companies of the City of London have long enjoyed the privilege of keeping swans upon the Thames, from London to a considerable distance above Windsor; and they continue the ancient custom of proceeding with their friends and visitors, with the royal swan herdsman, and their own swanherds and assistants, on the first Monday in August in every year, from Lambeth, on their ''swan voyage'', for the purpose of catching and marking the birds. The struggles of the swans, when caught by their pursuers, and the duckings which the latter receive in the contest, make this a diversion of no ordinary interest.

At one period the Vintners' Company alone possessed 500 birds. In the language of the swanherds, the male swan is called a *Cob*, the female a *Pen*.

The Great Exhibition Building.—View showing the Ribs of the Transept.

THE GREAT INTERNATIONAL EXHIBITION

The design by Mr. Paxton, F.L.S. of a building for the Exhibition of the Industry of All Nations in 1851, has been considered and planned with a view to its fitness for the objects intended, as well as to its permanent occupation or removal to another site for a winter garden or a vast horticultural structure; and which might, if required, be used for a similar exhibition to that intended in 1851.

The building is a vast structure, covering a space of upwards of twenty-one acres; and, by the addition of longitudinal and cross-galleries, twenty-five per cent. more space may be obtained. The whole is supported by cast-iron columns, resting on patent screw piles: externally, it shows a base of six feet in height. At each end there is a large portico, or entrance veranda; and at each side there are three similar entrances, covered in for the purpose of setting down and taking up company. The longitudinal galleries running the whole length of the building, together with the transverse galleries, will afford ample means for the display of lighter articles of manufacture, and will also give a complete view of the whole of the articles exhibited. The whole being covered in with glass, renders the building light, airy, and suitable.

One great feature in its erection is that not a vestige of stone, brick or mortar is necessary. All the roofing and upright sashes would be made by machinery, and fitted together and glazed with great rapidity, most of them being finished previous to being brought to the place, so that little else would be required on the spot than to fit the finished materials together. The whole of the structure is supported on cast-iron columns, and the extensive roof is sustained without the necessity of interior walls.

Only a few years ago, the erection of such a building as the one contemplated would have involved a fearful amount of expense; but the rapid advance made in this country during the last forty years, both in the scientific construction of such buildings and the cheap manufacture of glass, iron &c., together with the amazing facilities in the preparation of sash-bars and other wood-work, render an erection of this description, in point of expense, quite on a level with those constructed of much more substantial materials.

The progress of the Crystal Palace for the Great Exhibition, next year, is sufficiently advanced to enable us to commence a series of Illustrations by which we hope to inform our readers of the general character and details of the structure, and also of the various ingenious modes and contrivances adopted by the contractors for executing the works with the greatest certainty and rapidity.

The central avenue will present a corridor, uninterrupted, 1848 feet in length, extending from the east to the west end of the building. The most difficult and complicated part of the work is that which is to cover in the old elm trees, more than 90 feet high; and the contractors have wisely determined to execute this part in the first instance. Semicircular ribs, which will cover the trees, will rest upon columns placed in three tiers, one above the other. The first series of these tiers, connected together by light cast-iron girders, will make squares of 24 feet, or an area of 576 superficial feet. These girders will also support a gallery extending down the whole length of the building, on both sides of the central passage. Underneath this gallery, the squares will form excellent spaces for the exhibition of decorated ceilings of all kinds; and we understand that the Executive Committee are about to announce that these spaces will be placed at the disposal of decorators.

Every one of these girders is tested by an ingenious hydraulic press as soon as it reaches the ground, and the enormous ribs, 72 feet in span will be completed and ready for fitting this week. There will be sixteen of them, and the last was being finished when we visited the ground. The foundations of the columns are made of concrete, formed of Dorking lime, and the gravel which is obtained in digging them. Upon the concrete is laid the base of the column, and forming part of it; the lower portion is a hollow pipe, purposed to carry off the rainwater, which will flow down through the columns themselves. Nearly the whole of these foundation bases, to the number of about 1500, will be fixed in their places this week; and thus one of the most important operations will have been safely and conveniently performed in fine and dry weather. Upwards of 500 men may be seen busily at work; and, as more castings are supplied, the numbers will be considerably increased. [October 12, 1850.]

[November 30, 1850.] There is no flagging on the part of the contractors, for the steady progress of the building is manifest even to the spectators outside the hoarding. The promise held out, as the Duke of Wellington remarked at his visit last week, by what has been done in seven weeks, shows what may be accomplished in the remaining month. The western extremity has been reached, both the lower and second tiers of columns have been fixed. Some thousand feet of the joists and framework for the flooring have been fitted, and the glazing of the roofs has proceeded uninterruptedly, though attempts to delay the work have arisen with some of the men. An attempt at an intimidation, for a higher rate of wages, by the glaziers, has been promptly suppressed. The progress in their work was deemed insufficient, and it was determined that they should be paid by piece-work. Urged on by some disaffected individuals, a party of the glaziers struck; but, as men to replace them were readily found, several relented, and asked for re-employment, and were informed that their application would be considered when any additional hands were required.

Elm Tree in the South-West Portion of the Building.

Glazing Waggon.

GLAZING WAGGON

Taking advantage of the continuous lines of longitudinal gutters, covered waggons have been constructed for the use of the glaziers in bad weather, each mounted on four wooden wheels, which run on the bottom of the gutters as the wheels of the old coal-waggons in the North of England ran on the wooden or iron trams before the introduction of the edge-rail; on either side of the platform is a box for the glass—being *eight* feet wide, there is sufficient space on the platform for two or three men. In the View, the tarpaulin covering is not shown.

THE ELM TREE

[January 4, 1851.] The elm-tree which is here presented, is commemorated as the rallying post for the objectors to the selection of the site in Hyde-Park for the Great Exhibition. It may be remembered that last session, after Lord Brougham's philippics against closing "the lungs of London," came Colonel Sibthorp's appeal for certain dispossessed Hamadryads of Rotten-row. Of a clump of ten small trees, which would have especially obstructed the south-west portion of the Building, nine were quietly cut down and removed, without being missed by the most observant frequenters of the Park; it was then that the gallant Colonel stepped forth, and claimed immunity and a reprieve of the doom of the tenth. Lord Seymour, the Chief Commissioner of the Woods and Forests, moved in Parliament, by the protector of arboreal privileges, accordingly suspended the sentence, and the spared elm has ever since been allowed to stand in the way of the completion of the Crystal Palace itself.

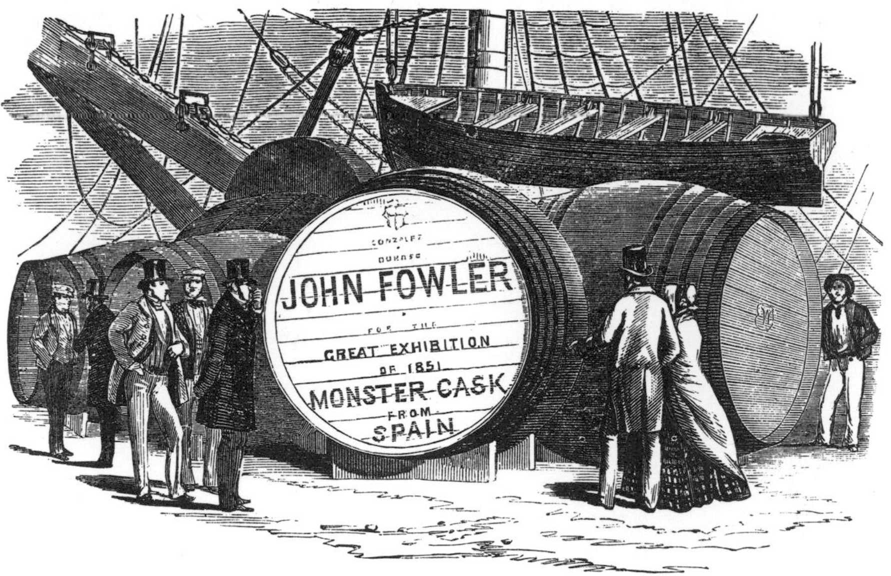

Monster Casks of Sherry in the London Docks.

[January 11, 1851.] Such a stream of visitors of all grades as flowed through Hyde-Park last Sunday had never been remembered by "the oldest" park-keeper: led by the beauty of the day, and the attractions of the palace itself, the unbroken throng wound itself round the precincts of the building so thickly that the ordinary pathway was obstructed to any pedestrian who did not sympathise with the gazing propensities of the thousands present. From the north bank of the Serpentine, the view of the noble building destined to be the shrine of industry of the present year, is extremely imposing, and the lofty trees add to its character and eminence in a picturesque sense. The contest respecting the decoration of the interior is by no means quieted: the advocates for employing a bronze colour are warmer than ever, relying for their strong point on the *metallic* character of the material; all confidence in the strength of the columns, say they, is lost, if you paint them in colours used for wooden poles. Employ iron grey, with a relief of gold, exclaims another party. We ourselves heard a third counsellor suggest a *bamboo cane* hue, to preserve the *lightness of the structure*. Mr. Owen Jones himself originally asked the opinion of more than twenty of the principal architects, house decorators, &c., and found that no two agreed in their advice, before he made his own experiments.

TESTING THE GALLERIES

[March 1, 1851.]—"Are the floors of the Crystal Palace sufficiently strong to sustain the moving masses that will daily pass over them?" That question was satisfactorily answered on the 18th ult., when, in the presence of her most gracious Majesty the Queen, severe tests were applied to a 24-feet square of gallery floor, framed complete, and resting on four of the cast-iron trellis girders, which, during the experiment, were supported on four points, corresponding with the condition in which they are fixed in the Building. The approaches to the square of flooring to be tested were formed by inclined gangways, consisting of planks placed close together. It is to be hoped, that the fears which have hitherto been expressed in so many quarters, as to the stability of the great example of the Victorian style of building, have, by this time, been entirely rejected from the minds of those who have gone so far as to predict that the 1st of May would but prove fatal to the thousands who will enter the great Industrial Palace on that occasion.

ARRIVAL OF GOODS

MONSTER CASKS OF SHERRY

In connexion with the Great Exhibition incidents, we have to notice the importation of four Monster Casks of remarkably fine Sherry, by Mr. John Fowler, wine-merchant, Wells-street, Cripplegate, by the ship *Traveller*. These casks are larger than hitherto known to have been imported from Spain, and their shipment caused some sensation in that country. The larger casks contain 2900 gallons, and the two smaller ones half that quantity. They have been branded, by the express command of the Queen of Spain, with the Royal arms. The casks are of English manufacture, and were shipped to Spain,

Testing the Galleries of the Great Exhibition Building.

Departure of the French Goods by the Great Northern Railway of France, for the Great Exhibition.

where they have been for seasoning since the Great Exhibition of 1851 was first broached, in anticipation that they would have been admitted, and the wines sold for refreshment; but the object of the importer is more particularly, we understand, to shew the connoisseur and the trade, that wines of this high order, and purely free from brandy, cannot be shipped to this country in small quantities without great deterioration in quality. [May 24, 1851.]

Unpacking Goods in the Great Exhibition Building.

THE GOODS IN STORE

The opening-day draws near. But two short months, and the World's Fair will be displayed to its thousands and tens of thousands of visitors. Of this fact there is no question for one moment; and they who dream of any delay, or who presume that the whole of the Exhibition will be deferred one hour, from the incomplete or dilatory arrangements of any part or portion of its foreign or English collection, will wake to the unpleasant reality of finding a punctual observance of the announced intention.

The eastern or foreign half of the interior is now definitely divided into its respective compartments, the hoardings and counters having been completed, and the spaces in the galleries alone being clear and unoccupied, though properly marked out. Most of the goods repose in their wooden cases, or swathings of cloth or matting, giving the various divisions the air of a vast repository of unpacked furniture, camp baggage, &c. Some reluctance, it appears, has been expressed by the foreign representatives, to the immediate inspection of the contributions by the Custom House officers. It is quite certain that any inconvenience is preferable to the delay of this necessary duty; the examination which is inevitably to be performed could not take place amidst the hurry and confusion of carpenters, and cabinet-workmen fitting up shelves, glass cases, decorations, &c., which will soon commence.

Opening of the Great Exhibition.—Entrance of Her Majesty and His Royal Highness Prince Albert.

OPENING OF THE GREAT INTERNATIONAL EXHIBITION

The ceremonial of opening was as auspicious and imposing as the object was novel, and even in a time when people are but little inclined to let their imagination run away with their judgment, or to accept the grand and the indefinite for the small and comprehensible, the fancy of the coldest and most calculating of the spectators was warmed into enthusiasm by the scene. It was not alone the sight of a youthful and beloved Queen, surrounded by her family, lending the aid of an universal and well-won popularity to that solemn consecration of industry; nor the presence at her side of the illustrious Prince, to whose clear and comprehensive intellect and philanthropic heart the Exhibition owes its existence; nor that of the aged warrior—the most notable man in all Christendom, and to whom we are indebted for the repose that has enabled the nations to show that they can work as well as combat; nor that of the chief officers of a state compared with whose power and dominion the empires of old were but as provinces, that made the scene so imposing. It was not alone the presence of myriads of people shouting with "heart and voice" the anthem which speaks both the humble piety and the exulting loyalty of Englishmen; nor the concourse of strangers from every quarter of the globe, and especially from that great nation with whom our rivalry has always, until now, been on the bloody battle-field; nor the magnificent display of every conceivable article of usefulness or luxury invented by the ingenuity of men; nor the gay and brilliant appearance of the exterior of that Crystal Palace, glittering in the rays of a lovely May morning; nor the still more brilliant interior, realizing to the hard matter-of-fact men of Saxon England in the nineteenth century the gorgeous descriptions of fairy palaces born in the luxuriant imaginations of the Oriental story-tellers; nor the reflection that forced itself upon all minds, how truly great and how full of good augury for all humanity such exhibitions might become hereafter; nor the pardonable exultation felt by Englishmen in the fact, that in England alone at the present day such an exhibition was possible: it was not any one of these facts, but a combination of them all, and of a thousand other circumstances equally significant and pleasing, that made the scene within and without the Crystal Palace, the most affecting and cheering, as well as the most remarkable event in the modern history of mankind. [May 10, 1851.]

LONDON DURING THE GREAT EXHIBITION

For the nonce, and until further orders and new arrangements, London is not simply the capital of a great nation, but the metropolis of the world. The Exhibition has deprived it of its local character, and rendered it no longer English merely, but cosmopolitan.

The English are great travellers. Ever since the peace of Waterloo let loose the swarms of our sight-seeing countrymen to visit every nook and corner of Europe—to admire fine scenery—to pry into collections of pictures and curiosities, and to cultivate the national taste for the foreign, the nations of the Continent have been familiar with the long purses, the eccentricities, and the polyglot accomplishments of the restless English of the upper and middle classes. But our Continental friends have not returned our visits. They have seen us abroad, and not at home; and have, for the most part, been slow to understand what inducements we could have to travel. While it has been rare to find an educated Englishman who did not speak French, or perhaps German and Italian, more or less perfectly, and who did not know by personal inspection the main features of the most celebrated of the Continental cities; it has been still more rare, among the same classes in France or Germany, to find a man who personally knew anything about London or who could speak, or even read, the English language. But what with the Crystal Palace and the facilities afforded by the railway system, without which the Exhibition would not have been possible, the people of the Continent have, for the first time, been smitten with the love of seeing strange parts. Already this intercourse has produced a good effect: the columns of the French press bear pleasant testimony to the more kindly feeling consequent upon more intimate knowledge which the Exhibition has been the means of producing; and a whole host of errors, misconceptions, and prejudices bid fair to be driven for ever out of the heads of our nearest neighbours. John Bull is no longer an ogre, but a genial and courteous gentleman. The old joke about the gloom, smoke and dirt of London, and the austerity, inhospitality, and semi-lunacy of the English character, has been dissipated, and our Parisian friends confess that the "sombre" city has produced the gayest, most fairy-like, most beautiful and original building in the world, and that these gloomy English people are positively well dressed, as pleasure-loving, as agreeable, and as polite as the French themselves. They joke us a little about our public statues and buildings, but they forgive much for the sake of the Crystal Palace.

There was at one time a fear that London would suffer in the estimation of strangers, for all time to come, by the extortionate prices demanded for lodgings and food during the period of the Exhibition. But this fear has blown aside. The lodging-house keepers and the *exploiteurs* of furnished houses, though at one time inclined to be exorbitant in their demands, have come to their senses, and foreigners in London may be lodged almost, if not quite, as reasonably as usual. The price of food has remained the same, and the only extortion that has really taken root and flourished, and served to give us a bad character in the eyes of our visitors, is the vile attempt of the omnibus proprietors to raise their fares twenty-five per cent. But we rejoice to see that the omnibus people are likely to be losers by their impudent rapacity, and that the fourpenny fares will not pay.

The cosmopolitan aspect of London is striking. We have not only the ILLUSTRATED LONDON NEWS, in French and German, appealing to the sympathies of our guests in their own language, and telling them all about the Exhibition and other matters, but the daily papers are interlarded with French and German articles. With a kind regard for the stranger, our police and other authorities have become as polyglot as the press. An announcement in the Strand directs the German to the "Eisenbahn", and the Frenchman to the "Chemin de Fer". The Government aids to the good work of fraternization, and throws open the arsenal at Woolwich, and the great national dockyards, to the inspection of strangers; and our great nobles throw open their picture-galleries and parks to the visits of people, whether native or foreign.

Until the present time, the upper and middle classes, both of Great Britain and the Continent, are the only classes who have come to London. The multitudes have not yet made their appearance; but when the price of admission shall be reduced to a shilling, the excursionists will rush in by the cheap trains from every part of the United Kingdom, as well as from the Continent. Paris will land its thousands per day upon our shores; and the workers of Sheffield and Birmingham, of Manchester and the West Riding, of Glasgow and Belfast, and of countless other industrial towns and districts, will pour their teeming myriads into the great cosmopolitan metropolis, to carry away with them, there cannot be a doubt, a remembrance of pleasure and instruction to last them for the remainder of their lives. For six months or more, the intelligent mechanics of our distant towns have been clubbing their weekly shillings and pence for this rational purpose; and among the many interesting spectacles which London will shortly offer to foreigners, none will be more interesting than the visits of these hordes of working-men—the men who made the Exhibition what it is, and who, we fervently hope, will derive the greatest advantage from it.

The Carriage Department.—From a Daguerreotype by Claudet. (*See page 88.*)

Agriculturists at the Exhibition.

But the Great Exhibition has its unpopular as well as its popular side. City merchants and their correspondents say that it has "killed business" for the season, and they grumble accordingly. The caterers for public amusement are still louder in their complaints. The theatres do not fill; panoramas are losing speculations; and people are so busy with the one Great Exhibition, that they cannot encourage any minor ones, or find time for them if they would. But all these things will right themselves. Business cannot be "killed" when so much money is spent and spending; and although it is possible it may have slept for awhile, it is certain that it will awake in due season. As for public amusements, we believe that there is a chance even for the panoramas.

THE GREAT EXHIBITION.—THE

TRANSEPT, LOOKING SOUTH.

THE CARRIAGE DEPARTMENT

The Carriage Department, which is included in Class 5—that of "Machines for Direct Use"—is not without its wonders and its attractions for the whole locomotive community, from those who "ride in chaises" of their own, to those who take their fourpenny-worth in a " 'bus," or make their last journey in a hearse. And all may be here provided. The contributions are abundant, coming from every part of the United Kingdom: Dublin, Edinburgh, Southampton, Birmingham, Bath, Bristol, Worcester, Hastings, Greenwich, have each their display, of some sort or another. Long-acre and Bond-street, of course have the largest, and perhaps the stateliest show; but Dublin and Southampton are not far behind. The supply of cars and dog-carts struck us particularly, for their novelty in structure in many cases, and generally for their extremely dashing appearance. Model omnibuses of gorgeous colourings, and unlimited resources, are sent in in competition by various makers, and we hope some of them will be tried in place of the rusty, uneasy-going rattle-traps which ply upon many of the roads contiguous to the Great Exhibition, to the great astonishment and discomfort of the bones of her Majesty's liege subjects.

Koh-I-Noor, as arranged in the Great Exhibition.—Exhibited by The Queen.

This engraving represents the Koh-i-Noor, or Mountain of Light, once the property of Runjeet Singh, now exhibited by her Majesty, and which, for the purpose of better inspection, is mounted upon pillars, within a gilt iron cage, prepared for the occasion by Messrs. Chubb. The machinery connected with it is so arranged, that, at the close of each day's exhibition, this valuable gem is lowered into an iron case for security during the night. Below the jewels themselves are exhibited the settings in which they originally stood.

Walnut-Tree Couch.—by Jackson.

WALNUT-TREE COUCH

The back, of walnut-wood, is divided into three portions, each richly carved, and upon which the three national emblems, the rose, the thistle, and the shamrock, are represented.

CLOCK-CASE

Mr. Bell has contributed more to ornamental manufacture, in the plastic line than, perhaps, any other artist of the day; and the present is by no means the least happy of his productions. It is styled the "Hours Clock-Case," from the fact of the face being embellished with a bas-relief representing the twelve hours circling round the clock; which itself has an enamelled dial, "representing the sun, its centre a flying phoenix, which fable relates is born anew every 500 years."

FOUNTAIN

This little fountain, studded with dolphins and sea-monsters, and crowned with a figure of old Neptune himself, is cast in bronze, and is supplied with water by a small engine. It is well adapted for the decoration of a summer-house or a cottage verandah.

Clock-case, designed by J. Bell.

FIVE SHILLING DAYS AND ONE SHILLING DAYS

The day of the great folks, and the day of the little folks—the day of the peach-coloured *visites* and the gaudy mousselaines de laine, and the day of the cotton prints and the handkerchiefs at 1s. 11¾d.—the day of the shiny boots, and the day of the ancle jacks [sic] with hob-nails—the day of the newest paletot, and the day of the most primitive smock-frock—the day of vanille, ices, and wafers, and the day of hunches of crust and lumps of meat and liquid refreshments in small bottles—the day of languid lounging and chatting, and the day of resolute examining and frank amazement—the day of the West-End of London, and the day of all the other ends of the earth—the five shilling day in fact, and the one shilling day, come—pass each before us with your votaries: exhibit each your phenomena and your usages; introduce us each to your train of company; tell us, each, your comparative value; read us, each, your separate lesson: for you have and you present, each of you—crown day and twelve-pence day—your distinct train of appendages and characteristics. Sunday in the world is not more unlike Saturday, than Saturday in the Exhibition is unlike Monday. On one day, society—on the other, the world. On the one day, the Nave crowded in such fashion as opera corridors and Belgravian saloons are crowded, and the aisles and galleries empty. On the other day, the aisles and galleries crowded, and the Nave a thoroughfare—a street—swarming, bustling, pushing with loud voices and brusque movements; and people who have sharp elbows, and can use them, and who push along as in Fleet-street or in Cheapside, intent upon going somewhere, determination in their muscles and purpose in their eyes—the energetic business-like march of this energetic business-like nation. On Saturday St. James fairly ousts St. Giles; the latter worthy, but unfashionable saint, taking, however, ample revenge on at least four other days of the week.

Fountain.—By Jabez James.

The Five Shilling Day at the Exhibition.

The Shilling Day.—Exterior of the Exhibition.

PEDESTRIANISM.—MANKS'S 1000 MILE WALK

Some years since, the feat of walking one thousand miles in one thousand hours was considered next to an impossibility; but here we have to record the wonder performed. It has been accomplished on the Surrey Cricket-ground, Kennington Oval, by Richard Manks, whose feats of walking present instances of the capacity and endurance of the human frame altogether unparalleled. On Friday the 10th October [1851] he commenced his great task at four o'clock in the afternoon, finally going, for his 1000th mile at half-past eleven o'clock on October 31.

On Tuesday night, 28th October, there commenced a heavy fall of rain, which continued for nearly six hours. This was very trying for the almost worn-out pedestrian; and, although so near the finish, many persons were apprehensive that he would not be able to complete his task; still onward Manks went, against the most fearful odds and obstacles; although his feet were severely blistered and covered with sores, his limbs in great pain, and he altogether showed the frightful effects of his incessant labour. Manks has been heard to declare that never again will he attempt such a frightful feat.

Richard Manks completing his thousandth mile on Kennington Oval.

Herr Kaufmann and Son's performance at Buckingham Palace.—(*See next page.*)

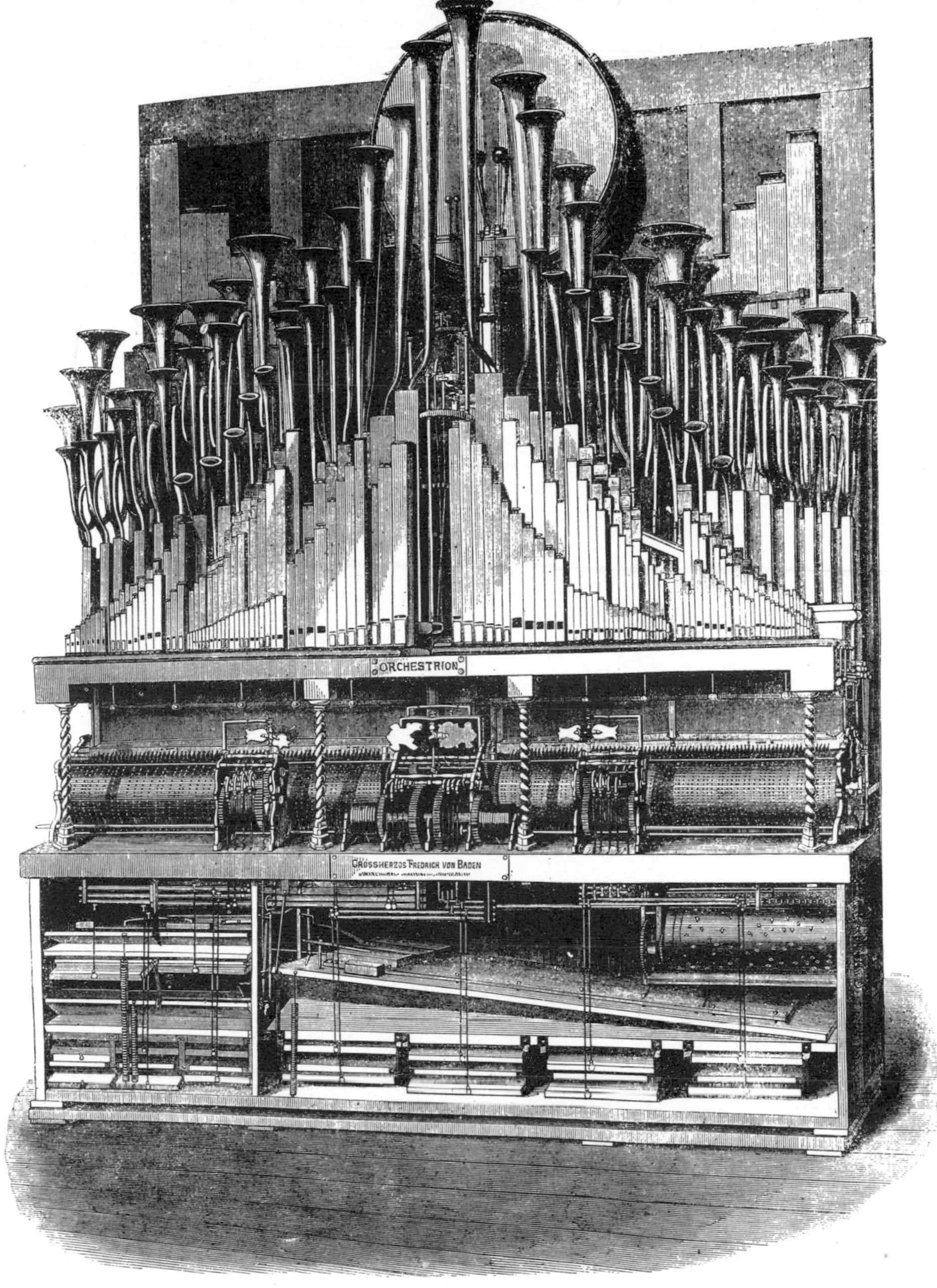

The Orchestrion by M. Welte of Vöhrenbach.

SELF-ACTING MUSICAL INSTRUMENTS

On Saturday the 21st ult., [June 1851] at St. Martin's Hall, there was a private exhibition of new instruments—The "Orchestrion", the "Chordaulodion", "Symphonium", and "Trumpet Automaton", four self-acting instruments. There was also exhibited the "Harmonichord", which is played upon like the organ with manuals and pedals. Herr Kaufmann and his son, the inventors of the above instruments, are from Dresden, and for many years have been unremittingly occupied in perfecting their novel conceptions. The "Orchestrion" is the most picturesque in appearance, and most complete in its actions of the five instruments. It is a combination of the brass and wind instruments; for every one of those metallic and wooden tubes has an eloquent speaking voice. The front of the lower portion of the case being opened, discovers the percussion instruments, the kettle and military drums, and triangle. The Orchestrion was invented by Herr Kaufmann, Jun.; it was five years before he completed this marvellous mechanical contrivance—the tones of flutes, flageolets, clarionets, cornets, bugles, trumpets, bassoons, horns, oboes, trombones, drums, &c., being most successfully imitated. There can be no mistake—all the instruments depicted actually emit sound, and are by no means decorative. It is almost miraculous to hear the light and shade of this invisible instrumentation, to mark the just gradations of crescendo, diminuendo, and sforzando, besides the usual fortes and pianos. We never heard anything so perfectly astounding as the *finale* of the "Don Giovanni": shutting one's eyes, it seemed as if the famed vocal and orchestral forces of Costa were exclaiming at one time, with portentous effect, "Trema" In the dance music, the three different times going on in the *finale* were observed with unerring precision, the mechanical agents doing what the living artists will rarely accomplish—keep together.

The first public performance was on Tuesday, the 24th ult., the instruments having been exhibited on the 11th ult., at Buckingham Palace before her Majesty, Prince Albert, the King of the Belgians and the Royal Family. On their way to this country Herr Kaufmann and son gave concerts, with the greatest success, at Leipzick and Hamburg. The Royal amateurs expressed their high gratification at the quality and ingenuity of the inventions, and complimented Herr Kaufmann and Son on their success.

Another self-acting organ or "orchestrion" has been constructed for his Royal Highness the Grand Duke Frederick of Baden by Mr. Welte. This instrument has 39 barrels, 15 different registers, with 524 pipes—imitating flutes, flageolets, piccolos, oboes, trumpets, horns, trombones, &c. The wind for these instruments is supplied by three pairs of bellows, which again supply four wind-reservoirs, whence it is conducted to the pipes. These bellows are all worked by self-acting machinery. Besides the wind instruments already named, the instrument contains a big-drum, kettle-drum, small military-drum, triangles and cymbals.

The orchestrion performs a number of overtures and pieces of music, among which are the overtures to "Der Freischutz", "Oberon", "William Tell", "Martha", some symphonies of Beethoven, &c., played with considerable precision and correctness, and in excellent time, and the forte passages are given with great effect. When the full number of instruments is played the tone is very powerful, and the effect equal to a small band.

We understand that a great many orchestrions have been sent by the manufacturer to Russia, where they are much patronised by the wealthy. Mr. Welte has had a manufactory for these instruments for many years. The orchestrion illustrated is very expensive, but he makes them of all sizes and prices.

EVIL INFLUENCES OF OUR DAYS

All the voices which have any real influence with an Englishman in easy circumstances combine to stimulate a low form of energy, which stifles every high one. The newspapers extol his wisdom by assuming that the average intelligence which he represents is, under the name of public opinion, the ultimate and irresponsible ruler of the nation. The novels which he and his family devour with insatiable greediness have no tendency to rouse his imagination, to say nothing of his mind.

Even religion is made to suit the level of commonplace Englishmen. There was a time when Christianity meant the embodiment of all truth and holiness in the midst of a world lying in wickedness. It afterwards included law, liberty, and knowledge, as opposed to the energetic ignorance of the northern barbarians. It now too often means philanthropic societies—excellent things as far as they go, but rather small. Any doctrine now is given up if it either seems uncomfortable or likely to make a disturbance. It is almost universally assumed that the truth of an opinion is tested by its consistency with cheerful views of life and nature. Unpleasant doctrines are only preached under incredible forms, and thus serve to spice the enjoyments which they would otherwise destroy.

Submarine Railway between France and England.

SUBMARINE RAILWAY BETWEEN FRANCE AND ENGLAND

The communication between England and France is daily becoming a more and more important object. To consummate the international union, means of conveyance between the opposite shores, so as to avoid the perils and uncertainties of passage by sea, remain to be provided. Bridges have been proposed by some; by others it has been suggested to tunnel the earth beneath the sea. But another projector, M. Horeau, has just appeared in the field, with what he allows to be a bold plan: his project consists in crossing the English Channel, 21 miles in extent, by means of a tube, or tubular tunnel, made of strong plate iron, placed at the bottom of the sea, containing the two lines for the trains.

The slope given to the submarine railway, M. Horeau considers, would admit of a motion sufficiently powerful to enable the carriages to cross the Channel without a steam-engine. The greatest depth of the sea in the middle of the Channel will admit of the construction of inclined planes by means of which the train would be enabled to reach a point where a stationary engine or atmospheric pressure might be employed in propelling the train to the level of the land railways of France and England.

These tunnels beneath the sea would not prevent navigation: lighthouses might be erected to indicate outwardly the position of the submarine railway, so that mariners should not cast anchor near it, as the tube might be damaged.

The day and night lights of the lighthouses should be transmitted through the tube by means of reflecting metal plates. The upper part of the tube should have some strong glass windows placed at equal distances, and gas, which would complete the lighting between the beacons. According to an estimate made, the cost might amount to about £87,400,000.

EXTREME PERIL OF THE "CASTOR'S" LAUNCH

The first attempt to lay down with accuracy the position of the rock on which was wrecked the ill-fated *Birkenhead* was attended with an adventure of a most dangerous character. Toward the end of March [1852] directions were given to Lieutenant O'Reilly, and ten men, of her Majesty's ship *Gladiator*, to hold themselves in readiness for this duty, as well as make a chart of Danger Point. The launch of the *Castor* was selected, and at midnight, 25th March, the party embarked and after knocking about for two days arrived off Danger Point [70 miles south of Cape Town] at midnight. Before morning the south-east wind increased to such a violent degree, that there was nothing left but to run for it to the westward, running all day and being about 140 miles from land, a long way west of Cape Point. The gale continued, and the boat was with difficulty kept afloat. Once a heavy sea struck her, and the waves closed over the heads of the whole party. But by the mercy of God the boat was saved; and made Green Point on the night of the 29th.

Barricade of the Faubourg St. Antoine.

THE REVOLUTION IN PARIS

France is embarked in a new revolution. Louis Napoleon has staked at once his fortune and his country's destinies upon one bold throw of the dice. Whether he will win all or lose all, remains to be seen. With one effort of his will the President has annihilated the Constitution, and in breaking the highest has broken all laws at once. Louis Napoleon has flung away in a moment a character for moderation and steadfast good faith which he was so long in making, and which, had he preserved it, would have stood him well in stead. He was assuming a great moral superiority to the Assembly; he was gaining the confidence of the middle classes, and disarming the hostility of the Monarchical factions. All this he has undone with a breath. Success is the revolutionary touchstone, and the sure guarantee for contemporary popularity; but even if Louis Napoleon gains his utmost ends, he will not the less have marched to power, perhaps to empire, over broken promises and reckless political gambling. [December 6, 1851.]

SUMMARY OF THE EVENTS OF THE LAST WEEK

On Monday the French Constitution of 1848 was in full force. On Tuesday it had ceased to exist by the *sic volo, sic jubeo*, of the President of the Republic, who proposed to the army and people to re-elect him for ten years, and to accept such a Constitution as he would frame. On Wednesday some of the members of the Mountain got up an insurrection, but the mass of the working classes did not rise. The withdrawal of the first decree relative to the voting, and the re-establishment of the vote by ballot, unquestionably did much to prevent the spread of the insurrection on Thursday. In this instance the President was compelled to yield to the force of public opinion. Had he not made this concession, he would not now be at the head of a triumphant military dictatorship. [December 13, 1851.]

THE ILLUSTRATIONS

Barricade of the Faubourg St. Antoine. This barricade was formed at the corner of the Rue St. Marguerite at about noon on Wednesday, the 3rd. Vehicles were upset and stones and other materials raised into a barricade, which was attacked by the Colonel of the 19th Light Infantry, but the troops did not fire until the insurgents discharged their muskets and a soldier fell mortally wounded. The infantry fired a volley in return, and M. Baudin, the Representative, was killed, and Madier de Montjau wounded.

Troops Shooting Insurgents. (From the special correspondent of the *Observer*):—Mr. ———, a wealthy trader, assures me that on Saturday last (Dec. 6), about ten at night, five companies of infantry preceded by 50 of the secret police, appeared in the Rue de Constantine, where they arrested all the men they found in their apartments. The result was that some three hundred workmen left their homes, and darted through the streets like hunted hares. To provide for such an attempt at escape the tranverse streets were well posted with infantry and cavalry, and every one of the wretched men fell into the hands of the various guards. Those who resisted being captured were shot upon the spot, while the remainder were led before the court-martial, and, being deemed dangerous characters, were shot at midnight in the Champ de Mars.

Shooting Insurgents in the Streets of Paris. (From the special correspondent of the *Morning Chronicle*):—On the Thursday night, when all resistance had ceased, information was given to a party of soldiers that some young men who were suspected of being implicated in the events of the day had taken refuge in a *café* in the Passage de Saumon. The officer in command marched thither, and found the information correct. They were ordered to come out from their hiding-place, which they did, and at once surrendered themselves as prisoners. They were dragged out into the passage, and, despite their prayers for mercy, or at least for a trial, were deliberately shot upon the stones there and then.

Troops Shooting Insurgents.—*(See preceding page.)*

The Troops shooting the Insurgents in the Streets of Paris.

Drinking the General's health in the Indian Tent.

GRAND MASONIC BANQUET AT RUGBY

On Monday, the 14th July, a grand entertainment was given by the Freemason of the Lodge of Rectitude, No. 739. Rugby, to General Sir Charles James Napier, G.C.B., late Commander-in-Chief in India.

The Right Worshipful the Provincial Grand Master of Warwickshire (Earl Howe, G.C.K.) having called a Grand Lodge for the occasion, it was attended by a large and influential body of Masons from this and most of the other provinces of the kingdom.

The Lodge was held at the George Hotel, when Earl Howe, after expressing the deep regret he felt at the absence of the principal guest, read a letter from Sir Charles, lamenting his inability to attend owing to a severe relapse of a dangerous illness, and enclosing a note from his physician, which was also read, which cast an unforeseen gloom upon the meeting.

After lodge, the brethren walked in procession to the field belonging to Brother Bingham, of the College of the Deaf and Dumb, W.M. of the Lodge of Rectitude, where the banquet was provided in the celebrated Indian tent belonging to Brother Russell, of Leamington. During the evening Messrs. Carpenter and Ransford, senior and junior, sang several songs, duets, and glees. Altogether the meeting was a happy one, although its main intention was frustrated by the absence of their distinguished guest.

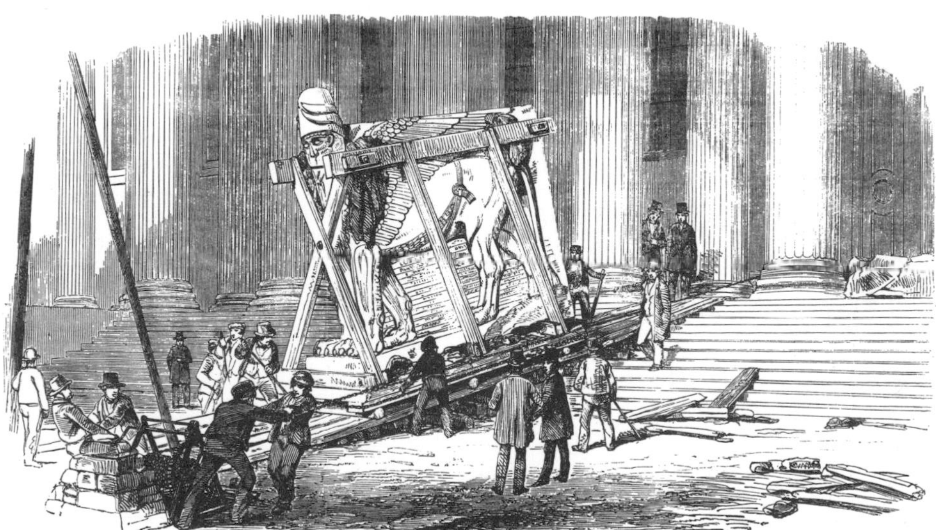

RECEPTION OF THE NINEVEH SCULPTURES AT THE BRITISH MUSEUM

Amongst the recent arrivals from Nimroud, the most striking and important is a colossal Lion, whose weight is upwards of ten tons.

Our Engraving represents the Lion in its transit from the courtyard in front of the Museum into the building. The sculpture was brought from the Docks on a truck drawn by eleven horses, and when in the courtyard was lifted from the carriage and placed securely on a massive framework of wood; being shored up on each side, as shown in the Engraving, to keep it from swaying over whilst it was being dragged to its place, which operation did not occupy more than one hour.

We believe the Lion is the largest monolith which has reached England from the buried city of the East. [February, 1852].

DINNER IN THE IGUANADON MODEL, AT THE CRYSTAL PALACE

The Directors of the Crystal Palace have confided the novel and great undertaking of constructing the gigantic restorations of the Extinct Inhabitants of the Ancient World, which are now, with anatomical severity, being reconstructed, to Mr. B. Waterhouse Hawkins.

On Saturday evening last Mr. Hawkins invited a number of his scientific friends and supporters to dine with him in the body of one of his largest models, called the Iguanadon. In the mould of this colossal work of art, Mr. Hawkins conceived the idea of bringing together those great names whose high position in the science of palaeontology and geology would form the best guarantee for the severe truthfulness of his works.

Invitation cards were issued at the beginning of last week:—"Mr. B. Waterhouse Hawkins solicits the honour of Professor —'s company at dinner, *in the Iguanadon*, on the 31st December, 1853, at four p.m." The incredible request was written on the wing of a Pterodactyle [sic], spread before a most graphic etching of the Iguanadon, with his socially-loaded stomach, so practicably and easily filled, as to tempt all to whom it was possible to accept, at such short notice, this singular invitation. Mr. Hawkins had one-and-twenty guests around him at the dinner, which was luxurious and elegantly served. The repast being ended, Professor Owen took occasion to explain the means and careful study by which Mr. Hawkins had prepared his models, and had attained his present truthful success; adding that it had been a source of great pleasure to him to aid a gentleman who possessed the rarely-united capabilities of an anatomist, a natural artist, and a practical artist, with a docility and eagerness for the truth which ensured Mr. Hawkin's careful restorations the highest point of knowledge which had been attained up to the present period.

Professor Forbes also bore testimony to the truthful care and study with which these great models were produced by Mr. Hawkins, and which would render them trustworthy lessons to the world at large in a branch of science which had hitherto been found too vast and abstruse to call in the aid of art to illustrate its wonderful truths.

After several appropriate toasts, the agreeable party of philosophers returned to London by rail, evidently well pleased with the modern hospitality of the Iguanadon, whose ancient sides there is no reason to suppose had ever before been shaken with philosophic mirth.

The new Post-office Letter-box at the corner of Fleet-street and Farringdon-street. (*See next page.*)

NEW STREET LETTER-BOXES

The accommodation at the Post Receiving Houses in various parts of the metropolis has long been of a very imperfect kind. Formerly a Receiving House was denoted by a richly-emblazoned pane, in which the time-honoured British lion shone in full national emblazonry; and here and there the tutelar animal's mouth was the receptacle of letters; just as the famous Lion's head at Button's coffee-house, received contributions for the *Guardian*. Few shop-fronts, however, bore so distinctive a feature; but the letter-mouth might be seen at various levels—rarely, as an artist would say, "one the line"—so as to render its discovery somewhat perplexing when the mixed topography of shop-windows is considered. Then came the mean-looking iron crown upon the top of the nearest street-lamp, which did not much enlighten the public in their pursuit of a post-office under difficulties. Next, the example was set by the French Post-office authorities of having cast-iron pillars set up in various streets of Paris, for the reception of letters; and this experiment having been found successful, a similar plan has been adopted by the authorities in St. Martin's-le-Grand. At stated points have been erected cast-iron letter-boxes, one of which—that at the corner of Fleet-street and Farringdon-Street—is shown in the accompanying Illustration. It is much less ornamental that the Paris pillar. Our Letter-box is a stove-like design, reminding one of the latest of London conduits. The Town delivery is complete in about 1½ hours, the Suburban takes from 1½ to 3 hours from the time of dispatch, according to distance.

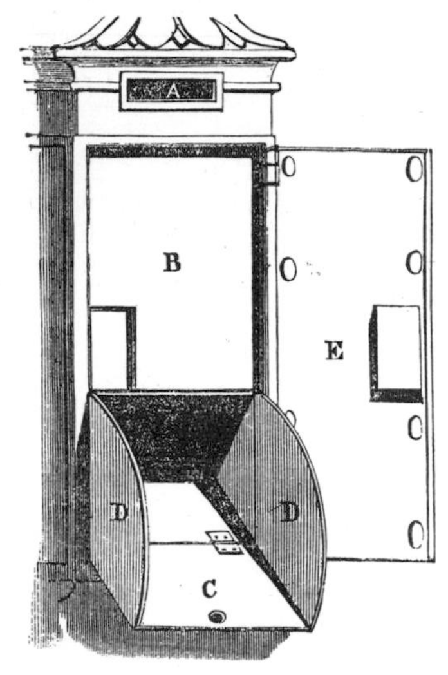

Interior of the new Letter-box.

The front of the Letter-box is shown in the Engraving; and the Diagram shows the interior contrivance for taking out the letters:—A, opening for letters; B, inner wooden front of box; C, flap, which opens and forms an inclined plane with the bottom of the box, by which means the letters are shot into the postman's bag; DD, slides to the flap, to prevent the letters falling over; E, inside of the iron door. The locks are Messrs. Chubb's "patent detector."

Nasmyth's anti-Invasion Floating Mortar.

A NEW IMPLEMENT OF DESTRUCTION

We have been favoured by Mr. James Nasmyth with the following description of the means which he has devised "for destroying, by one masterly blow, the largest ship of an invading enemy.":—

"The principles on which the arrangement and construction of the Floating Mortar is based, consist of a monster self-exploding shell, so arranged as to explode on having its breach end crushed against the breach of the Mortar, the self-exploding cap being situated there. In order to enhance the destructive effect upon the enemy's ship, the shell is so far submerged as to tear its way into the enemy six feet under water-line.

"The shell is inclosed within a perfectly water-tight copper case, which will secure it from the action of the water for years in the chamber of the mortar, submerged six feet under water-line, and ready for service at any time.

"The crush consequent on coming in contact with the side of the enemy is the agent whereby the monster shell is made to explode. A very moderate velocity would prove sufficient for this purpose; so that, in order to obviate the chance of its explosion by accidental contact I have so placed the flange joint of the copper case against the mouth of the Mortar, that the crush against the side of the enemy, resulting from a speed of two or three miles per hour, shall be sufficient to cause it to explode and tear its fearful way through the side of the enemy. No ship that has ever been built, whether of wood or iron, could survive the fearful hole which a monster shell thus exploded would produce.

"The next feature is the intimate union of our mortar with the hull of the screw steam-vessel, which transports it direct to the object which we desire to destroy. Next, the crew who attend to the navigation of the Floating Mortar are protected from the action of shot, whether red-hot or cold, by giving the vessel, in all directions where assailable, such a thickness of timber as that no shot can penetrate to the *interior*.

"The hull will be made at least ten feet thick, of poplar wood, by reason of its lightness, toughness, and incombustibility. Red-hot shot might lodge in it, but would fail to set it on fire.

"This class of vessel is chiefly designed for *defence against invasion*, and would not have to act against an enemy, probably, at greater distances than one or two miles from our shore, so that it could easily return for another shell."

The Cabin on the Grands Mulets, Mont Blanc.

During the long, dreary months of last winter [1852], the guides of Chamouni employed themselves in making the frame-work of a hut, to be erected on one of the rocks on the side of Mont Blanc, known as the *Grands Mulets*, whereby travellers might be sheltered from the cold during the night bivouacs. Hitherto blankets and railway rugs have formed the chief protection against the low temperature, and these, under ordinary circumstances, were found sufficient in the majority of cases; but as the rocks themselves are situated at an elevation of 10,300 feet above the level of the sea, and consequently about 2,000 feet above the Alpine line of perpetual snow, and, moreover, are frequently exposed to fearful and unexpected storms, the want of some sort of refuge, however rudely contrived, has long been felt.

The present hut—by far the highest habitation, if it may be called so, in the old world—is constructed after the manner of the dissected barns sold in the toy shops, and kept together by wooden pegs and braces. Its external walls are formed of flat blocks and splinters of the rock, and these also serve to keep the roof in its position, during high winds, by their weight. It is fitted up with a few rough planks, forming the tables and

shelves. There are two sliding windows, glazed; a door, which closes tolerably well; and an iron fire-place, the chimney of which passes out at one of the windows. Its size is about fourteen feet long by seven broad, and the roof of the lean-to slants towards the west, so that the afternoon sun melts the snow thereon, and the water that drips from the eaves is carefully collected in bottles, as there is no other chance of getting any, except by the stove. As soon as the sun goes down, if there be the least puff of wind, the cold is very sharp and biting, and icicles form, almost immediately, at the edge of the roof.

In consequence of the erection of the hut, the Grands Mulets has become one of the excursions from Chamouni. Whilst it avoids the expense and risk of the actual ascent of Mont Blanc, it is a greater feat for ambitious tourists to attempt than the journey to the Jardin. There is, besides, the excitement of sleeping one night amidst the eternal snows of the mountain, and the wonderful view of sunset and sunrise from so great an elevation; whilst the lover of dangerous enterprise will always find more than a sufficient number of precipices, fissures, and obstacles generally, amidst the wild horrors of the upper part of the Glacier du Tacconay, to satisfy him.

Skating in Regent's Park.

ON THE ICE

The snow has left its card for us this season [January, 1854] without doubt. London has resembled a sheet of white paper in the past week, on which was written the footprints and activity of its myriad population. The metropolis has put on its winter robe, and taken it off with coquettish frequency. There have been fifty pretty little amateur snow-storms from one to a hundred minutes in duration—intermittent in their calls, coming and going with unsatisfactory celerity. The ornamental waters of the Park are ice-bound; and much obliged to the weather are the thousands of pleasure-seekers who extract amusement from ice, and manage to cut out as much pleasure on a pair of skates as less

Collision between the "Duchess of Kent" and the "Ravensbourne" off Northfleet Point.

enterprising folks would languidly enjoy on a day of brilliant summer sunshine.

There is a class of clumsy skaters who do nothing but tumble, and try the ice fearfully; these persons may excel on *terra firma*, but ice is beyond their power; their action might be elegant on a gravel walk, but the frozen carpet of the lake demands more skill than they possess.

The clumsy portions of the visitors are not without their uses. They produce their share of the general fun, for what they lack in grace and management, they abundantly compensate for in cause of merriment. The comic tumbles and droll mishaps—the merry struggles and old mistakes—all of which seem to take place in a good-humoured way, make up a sum of gay mischance that we would be sorry to part with. Ice is a great provocative of amiability, and many a man is good-natured where it has frozen, who is not particular in this respect away from the ice. Looking about the lake, we observe skaters, sliders, pedestrians of either sex and all ages, moving and shifting about like the changes of a kaleidoscope.

LOSS OF THE "DUCHESS OF KENT" STEAMER

A collision of a most frightful character occurred on Thursday afternoon [July 1, 1852] in the river Thames, off Northfleet Point, by which the *Duchess of Kent*, Margate and Ramsgate steamer, was run down by the *Ravensbourne*, bound to Antwerp with nearly 200 passengers and full cargo. The *Duchess of Kent* was coming up the river against tide, and hugging the southern shore—the tide running very strongly. The *Ravensbourne* was about three parts over the river on the Kent shore, and as she neared the *Duchess of Kent*, the latter crossed; in an instant, consequent on the heavy way on the *Ravensbourne*, before the *Duchess of Kent* could cross her, she ran into her about twenty feet from the figure-head, just before the wind-lass, on the starboard bow. The crash was frightful; the *Duchess of Kent* immediately began to fill, and to sink, bows foremost. The scene among the passengers, a large number of whom were ladies with children, was truly frightful. At this moment the Gravesend steam boat *Meteor* arrived alongside, and the passengers and crew were dragged on to her and the *Ravensbourne*. In the meantime the vessel sank, bows first, almost perpendicularly, the keel being lifted as she sank twenty or thirty feet out of the water. From the moment of collision to the time the *Duchess of Kent* sank beneath the surface was little more than eight or nine minutes.

SLAVERY IN THE UNITED STATES

We here engrave the oaken case containing the Address of the Women of Great Britain and Ireland to the Women of the United States, on the subject of slavery. The Address, with its more than half-a-million signatures, is contained in twenty-six folio volumes, inclosed in the case, and, we understand, will be dispatched to the United States this day [April 9, 1853].

It is feared from a letter received in Glasgow on Monday by the agent for the New York steamer, that Mrs. [Harriet Beecher] Stowe will probably not visit England this season, She is very sick and unable to leave her bed.

DEATH OF THE DUKE OF WELLINGTON

The Duke of Wellington is dead. The great soldier, the wise statesman, the able administrator, the profound thinker, is no more. We cannot but call the event, which has deprived the country of the living presence of so illustrious a man, a national calamity. Yet the star of his usefulness had culminated and fallen; and his death, when he was full of years and of honour, is an event that was yearly, if not daily, expected. It will excite no poignant sorrow, because it was natural and timely, but it will call forth that manly and general sympathy which death always demands, especially in the case of individuals so great and so good as he was.

There never arose in this realm a man who conferred so many services on his country as Arthur Duke of Wellington. His fame is entirely pure. There is not a dark spot upon it. As a soldier and a conqueror the annals of no period and of no country can show a reputation more brilliant or deeds so unselfish, as well as so grand and so beneficial, as his were from his youth to his maturity, and from his maturity to his venerable old age.

Yet it was not simply as a soldier, great as he was, that the Duke of Wellington rendered such infinite service to his country. He was a high-minded, disinterested, and honest statesman, and possessed in a remarkable degree a clear, sound, sagacious, and straightforward intellect. As a politician these qualities were of inestimable value to himself and to Great Britain.

Bust of the Duke of Wellington and the Waterloo Flag, in Windsor Castle.

For the last ten or twelve years of his honoured and honourable life, his public appearances were public ovations; and he was as affectionately loved, and as sincerely respected, by the humblest street pedestrians whom he met in his daily walks, as he was by by the more favoured few with whom he associated in public, as well as in private and domestic life.

THE ROOM AT WALMER CASTLE

The room in which the Duke expired is of moderate size and plainly furnished: but everything neatly and methodically arranged, something like an officer's room in a garrison. On the right-hand side stands an ordinary iron camp bedstead, with a single horse-hair mattress, and a horse-hair pillow covered with leather, which the Duke usually carried with him and used in town. Summer or winter the little camp bedstead was without curtains. Here the Duke always slept and wrote, when at Walmer. Over the bedstead is a small collection of books, evidently selected for use. Among them are some of the best English writers of Anne's Augustan age, in poetry and prose. In the centre of the room is a mahogany table, well stained with ink, and covered with papers; and here for some hours every day the Duke sat and wrote. Near this is a more portable one, and contrived so as to be used for reading or writing while in bed. This, with two or three chairs, comprises the whole.

The room at Walmer Castle in which the Duke died.

The Funeral Procession in Pall Mall.

THE DUKE'S FUNERAL

The grave has closed over the mortal remains of the greatest man of our age, and one of the purest-minded men recorded in history. Wellington and Nelson sleep side by side under the dome of St. Paul's, and the national mausoleum of our isles has received the most illustrious of its dead. With a pomp and circumstance, a fervour of popular respect, a solemnity and a grandeur never before seen in our time, and, in all probability, never to be surpassed in the obsequies of any other hero hereafter to be born to become the benefactor of this country, the sacred relics of Arthur Duke of Wellington have been deposited in the place long since set apart for them by the unanimous decision of his countrymen. All that ingenuity could suggest in the funeral trappings, all that imagination and fancy could devise to surround the ceremonial with accessories that most forcibly impress the minds of a multitude, all the grace that Royalty could lend, all the aid that the State could afford in every one of its great departments, all the imposing circumstances derivable from the assemblage of great masses of men arrayed with military splendour and in military mourning, together with the less dramatic but even more affecting grief expressed by the sober trappings of respectful and sympathetic crowds, all the dignity that could be conferred by the presence of the civil and legislative power of a great and ancient kingdom; and, lastly, all the sanctity and awe inspired by the grandest of religious services performed in the grandest Protestant temple on the world, were combined to render the scene inside and outside of St. Paul's Cathedral on Thursday last [November 18, 1852] the most memorable in our annals. Nor in the popular estimation were these, great and imposing as they were, the only circumstances that invested the funeral of the great Duke with extraordinary interest. To the minds of the people, and to the superstition of thousands who would be loth to confess, although they would find it impossible to deny, the hold of such feelings upon their imagination, "the signs and the portents of nature" were added to the commemorative deeds of men, to render the last scene in the history of the hero more awe-inspiring than it might otherwise have been.

Amid the rise, and perhaps the fall, of empires, amid "fear of change perplexing the nations," amid earthquake and flood, a trembling earth and a weeping sky, Wellington was conveyed from his lonely chamber at Walmer to the more splendid halting-place of Chelsea, and from thence to his grave, in the heart of London. The very elements seemed to sympathise with the feelings of living men at the loss of one so mighty as he had been in his day and generation.

But the hero is entombed, and the voice of his contemporaries has spoken his apotheosis. Every incident in his long and honourable life has been sought for and recorded. Every trait in his simple, direct, and manly character has found its chronicler. The stores of his wisdom have been arranged and classified into apophthegms, brilliant as epigrams, and many of them as immortal as his victories.

The Hero sleeps well. May we never miss in a future day the guiding hand and the clear judgement of him who gave nearly forty years' peace to Europe, who was the benefactor of every kingdom in it; who gave France constitutional liberty—since lost, but sure to be regained; and who raised his own country to a height of power, influence, and true glory she had never before reached. No Caesar ever approached such deeds as these; and all Greek and Roman fame are but small and mean compared with the pure fame of the GREAT DUKE OF WELLINGTON!

LAST MOMENTS OF THE DUKE OF WELLINGTON

(ILLUSTRATION ON NEXT PAGE)

On Tuesday morning, September 14, [1852] the Duke of Wellington complained of uneasiness in the chest and stomach. At this time there were no symptoms indicative of danger, but shortly his Grace became much worse, became unconscious and breathed laboriously. Remedial measures which in former attacks had been useful were now of no avail. Soon after one o'clock he became very restless—the eye glassy. Respiration became very difficult, but easier when his Grace was placed in an easy chair; but the pulse sank: and at twenty-five minutes past three o'clock p.m. his Grace expired.

The persons present at this historical moment were Lord and Lady Charles Wellesley, Dr. M'Arthur, Mr. Hulke (the apothecary), and his son; Mr. Kendal, the valet; and the butler.

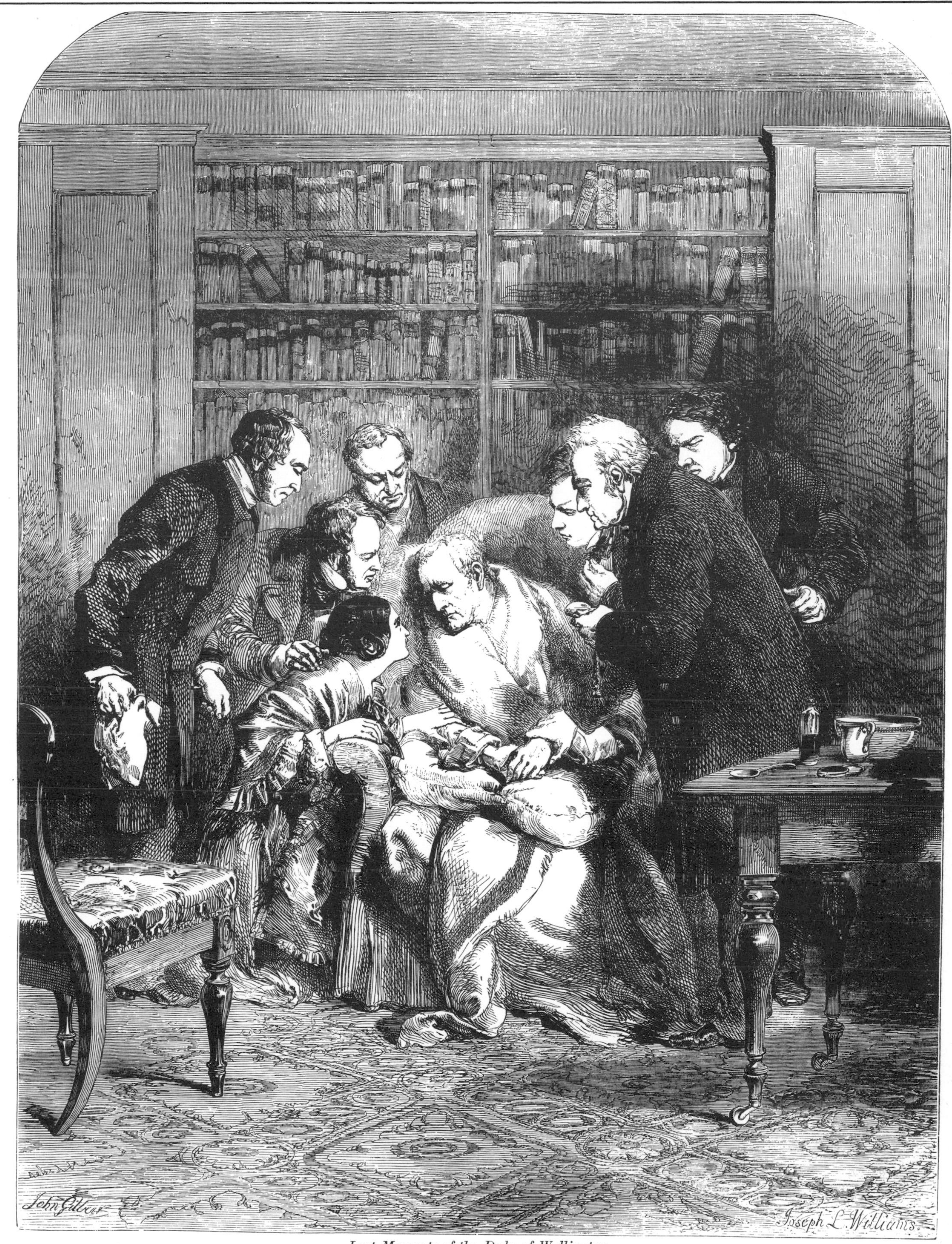

Last Moments of the Duke of Wellington.

Shipment at Trieste of Wooden Houses, Furs, etc., for the Allied Armies in the Crimea.

DECLARATION OF WAR AGAINST RUSSIA

The Emperor of Russia, with a contemptuous insolence, unbecoming his position, though on all hands expected of him, has refused to return any answer to the demand made upon him by Great Britain and France to evacuate the Danubian Principalities. No alternative was therefore left to the Allies but an immediate Declaration of War. On Monday evening a formal Message from her Majesty, announcing the fact, was communicated to both Houses of Parliament. On the same day a similar communication was made by the Emperor Napoleon to the Senate and Legislative Assembly of France. On Tuesday evening a Declaration of War by the British Government against Russia was published. With a unanimity which has characterised all the steps taken by Great Britain and France during the momentous negotiations, of which these acts are the close, the French Government simultaneously proclaimed war against the wicked disturber of the peace of the world. The struggle will immediately commence and the most ardent wish, the most sincere prayer of every honest man in the civilised world will be formed for the speedy downfall of the Imperial Barbarian, whose pretensions are an outrage to Europe, and an insult to the right feeling and common sense of mankind. [April 1, 1854.]

THE ENGLISH AND FRENCH ALLIANCE

The great war which is now raging on the banks of the Danube, and in the Baltic and Euxine, is a war whose present object is the independence of Turkey, but whose ulterior objects may become far wider and more important. When Society punishes a murderer, it is not merely to avenge the victim that its arm is raised, but for the vindication and maintenance of the law upon which Society itself is based. In resisting the felonious designs of the Czar against the dominions of his neighbour, the British and French nations do not simply resist the ambition of an unscrupulous despot, who sets all considerations of justice at defiance, but they take arms in defence of a sacred principle, upon the recognition of which the tranquillity and the civilisation of the world depend.

These things may be truisms to those who look dispassionately around them, but they need to be repeated occasionally to meet the loud and incessant objections of the covert friends of the Czar, who insist that the evident destiny of the Turks is to be driven into Asia, and that they are not worth the powder and shot which Great Britain and France are expending in their cause. We do not admit the likelihood of such predictions, or the justice of the picture which is drawn by the pro-Russians; but—even were the Turks a thousand times more worthless than they would have us believe; were the Mahometan religion infinitely more inimical to the progress of civilisation than it is; were the stability of the Turkish dominion in Europe utterly hopeless—it would be the duty of this country, and of every other in this hemisphere claiming to be Christian and civilised, to resist to the most this nefarious aggression. [April 22, 1854.]

THE CRIMEA EXPEDITION

The startling announcement in the *Times* of last Saturday, that on that very day (August 5) a force, made up of English, French, and Turks, and amounting to between 80,000 and 100,000 men, would invade the Crimea, and attempt to effect a lodgment on the heights commanding the harbour of Sebastopol, has not yet been confirmed in every particular by the news from Constantinople; but the most recent intelligence shows that great preparations were making for the conveyance of a large body of troops, whose destination was understood to be the Crimea. [August 12, 1854.]

This long threatened enterprise—one of the most gigantic military movements ever undertaken—has, at last, been effected, so far as regards the embarkation of troops and artillery, under the most favourable circumstances. [September 23, 1854.]

CHARGE OF THE CHASSEURS D'AFRIQUE

The part which this body of French cavalry took in the action at Balaclava, although every way worthy of the fame which those gallant troops had won by their conduct on former occasions, has not received so much notice as the doings of our own soldiers. It was about 10.50 on the morning of the 25th ult. that the Chasseurs d'Afrique took up their position in advance of the ridges on the left of the British army. About the same time General Canrobert attended, by his staff, rode up to Lord Raglan, and the staffs of the two Generals mingled together in praise of the magnificent charge which had just been made by the Scots Greys and Enniskilling Dragoons.

It was during the charge made by our Light Cavalry Brigade on the Russian army that the Chasseurs d'Afrique took part in the battle. With fearful impetuosity, they dashed down upon a battery on the left of our army, which had been telling most severely upon our men, and cut down the gunners. Unfortunately, however, they could not get the guns off without support; and had to retreat, with the loss of two Captains killed, and 20 men killed and wounded, out of their little force of 200 Chasseurs. Of course there were some very narrow escapes. "One of my friends in this squadron," says our Artist, who has forwarded the Sketch here engraved, "had his horse killed in the very square—in the midst of the enemy; but was fortunate enough to catch an artillery horse, which he mounted, and got off safely, along with his companions." [November 25, 1854.]

The Battle of Inkerman.—Repulse of the Russians.

THE BATTLE-FIELD OF INKERMAN

The scene which our Artist has here depicted is one which he witnessed in crossing the battle-field on the 5th of November, at the time when the Russians were retreating. On horseback or on foot it was impossible to pass along without treading on the wounded or the dead, so thickly was the ground covered with them. A sergeant who had been in the very midst of the deadly struggle thus describes how he felt when he went home to the Camp and found none of his comrades there:—

'The worst I felt was, when I came home and found all my comrades missing, and did not know whether they were dead or wounded; but had to go amongst the dead and wounded in the dark to see whom we could find. I was passing, with some more of my comrades, with as many of the wounded as we could get along, and there was one of our poor fellows, lying on the ground beside some that were dead, with both his thighs shot through, one

Charge of the Chasseurs d'Afrique, October 25.

Our Artist on the Battle-field of Inkerman.

of which was fractured very much. He did not even utter a groan, but simply said, "Sergeant, is there any chance for us to-night?" I said, "We will come back and fetch you;" but the night was so dark that we could not find him, neither did anybody else, so he had to lie all the next day; but the poor fellow has since died of his wounds . . .'

Another soldier gives the following description of the battle-field, a few days afterwards:— 'I have just been over the ground on which the Battle of Inkerman was fought. Many relics of that day still remain—Russian cartridges not yet broken — ramrods—Minié-balls — Russian pouches — belts — old gun-barrels doubled up — fragments of clothing, &c.; but, above all, some hundreds of round shot and shells unburst lay about in all directions. The graves of our brave men who fell on that day are also to be seen, their heads marked by pyramids of the deadly missiles by which so many fell. The graves of the enemy are still more conspicuous. From the number left dead on the field it was found impossible to dig a grave for each; so that their last resting-place is known by the dimensions of the earth thrown up—a piece about eight feet wide and as many yards long, containing, perhaps, some twenty or thirty of these poor fellows. Twice had the ground been fought over; twice have the enemy been repulsed; twice have we toiled to bury their dead. Thus I went musing on, until a shell burst in the air some hundred feet over my head, fired from the mud tower—from the steamer which moves up and down the harbour, and from a three-gun battery on the Inkerman opposite.' [February 3, 1855.]

Mr. Fenton's Photographic Van.—From the Crimean Exhibition.

MR. FENTON'S CRIMEAN PHOTOGRAPHS

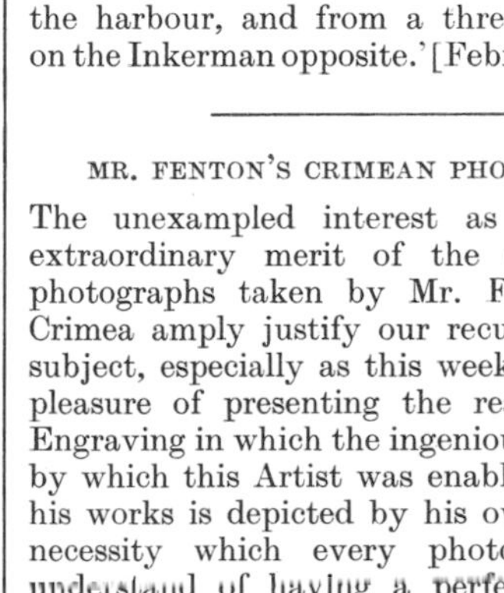

The unexampled interest as well as the extraordinary merit of the exhibition of photographs taken by Mr. Fenton in the Crimea amply justify our recurrence to the subject, especially as this week we have the pleasure of presenting the reader with an Engraving in which the ingenious contrivance by which this Artist was enabled to execute his works is depicted by his own hand. The necessity which every photographer will understand of having a perfectly-darkened room, a locality not likely to be found on the field of battle or before the beleaguered wall of Sebastopol, induced the eminent firm to whose spirited enterprise Mr. Fenton's expedition is due to have such a place constructed in a portable, or rather transportable, form; and here it is. This is the studio of battle, the room whence have emanated the three or four hundred engravings which will be preserved as records of the dreadful Crimean struggle, long after the traces of war's iron hoof have been effaced by time. The historian of the war in future years will be seen bending over these memorials, and comparing them with the *literae scriptae* of the correspondents of the journals, in order that, before setting himself to deck out his epigrammatic paragraph, or to roll his sonorous period, he may be well "up" in the features of the country and the bearing of those who fought on its soil. [November 10, 1855.]

THE FALL OF SEBASTOPOL

There is no mistake this time. Sebastopol has fallen. The town is a mass of ruins. The Russian fleet—whose only achievements were to overawe Turkey, and to inflict the cowardly massacre of Sinope—has been burned by the victorious Allies, or sunk by the orders of Prince Gortschakoff. The dread spectre of Russian aggression no longer fills the world with alarm; and none remain to deplore or regret the result, except the friends of tyranny and wrong. [September 15, 1855.]

RAFT IN THE SEA OF AZOFF

(*From a Correspondent*)

I send you a Sketch which perhaps may serve to acquaint the authorities at home "what is really useful in the Sea of Azoff." During the recent rapid and brilliant operations in that sea it was found that the shallowness of the water prevented the heavy guns of the ships being brought into play. A raft was accordingly constructed on board the *Stromboli*.

It consists of twenty-nine casks placed in six rows, cradled, as it were, in a framework of spars 45 feet long and 15 feet broad; a portion of the upper part is firmly planked over; a spar lashed athwart ships is ingeniously fitted with straps, to which the side tackles, &c., are hooked; the train tackle being hooked to one similarly fitted abaft; while a spar taken to two stout towing bollards abaft serves to keep the raft in any direction required. When this novel gunboat was finished, the *Miranda* hauled alongside the *Stromboli*; purchases from both vessels were applied, and the enormous mass was raised a little above the *Stromboli's* gunwale, by steadily heaving in on their cables, the ships slowly separated, the purchases were lowered, and the wide-famed *Lady Nancy* was added to the British navy.

Seldom has a more lively scene, or a more perfect display of energy been witnessed, than that which presented itself on the quarter-deck of the *Stromboli* during the building of the *Lady Nancy*. The ever-being-swept dazzling white parade ground, was now a building yard; all hands saw not only the importance, but the necessity of the work; and in the incredibly short space of twelve hours the *Stromboli's* zealous crew had provided themselves with a gun-boat, which, when carrying a long 32-pounder gun, weighing forty-two cwt, 100 rounds of ammunition, a seven-inch hawser, and eighteen men, drew only twenty inches of water. I hear it is cheerfully admitted by the squadron, how nobly, and coolly her crew fought her. At Taganrog this flaming *Lady Nancy* fired more than eighty rounds with a precision that elicited hearty cheers from our allies. She has been towed more than 200 miles, in boisterous weather, not a nail or lashing has started, she is still what she was designed to be—perfection.

THE RUSSIAN OVERLAND TRADE

The transport of goods between St. Petersburg and Kowno has, in consequence of the blockade of the Bay of Finland, attained a magnitude that affords employment to some thousands of carriers, waggoners, &c., and it is computed also to 30,000 horses. In addition to this amount of traffic the number of troops marching from the capital westwards often make the roads impassable for private travellers for half a day at a time. The unconscientious conduct of these *kibitka* drivers, as regards the goods committed to their care, has given rise to so many complaints, that the Minister of the Interior has found himself compelled to issue special police instructions with reference to these gentry. It was notorious that they not unfrequently threw away to the road-side goods entrusted to them to convey, or purposely left them at railway stations or in private houses.

The "Lady Nancy" Raft attacking Taganrog, in the Sea of Azoff.

THE RUSSIAN HOSPITAL AT SEBASTOPOL

Our Artist in the Crimea has given a Sketch of one of those "chambers of horrors," to which the *Times* correspondent refers in the following passage:—"Of all the pictures of the horrors of war which have been presented to the world, the hospital of Sebastopol presents the most horrible, heartrending, and revolting. It cannot be described, and the imagination of Fuseli could not conceive anything at all like unto it. How the poor human body can be mutilated and yet hold its soul within, when every limb is shattered, and every vein and artery is pouring out the life stream, one might study here at every step,—and at the same time wonder how little will kill!

"The building used as an hospital is one of the noblest piles inside the Dockyard wall, and is situated in the centre of the row at right angles to the line of the Redan. The whole row was exposed to the action of shot and shell pounding over the Redan, and to the missiles directed at the Barrack Battery, and it bears in sides, roofs, windows, and doors, frequent and destructive proofs of the severity of the cannonade. Entering one of these doors I beheld such a sight as few men, thank God, have ever witnessed! In a long low room, supported by square pillars, arched at the top, and dimly lighted through shattered and unglazed window-frames, lay the wounded Russians, who had been abandoned to our mercies by their General * * *. With the roar of exploding fortresses in their ears, with shells and shot forcing through the roof and sides of the rooms in which they lay, with the crackling and hissing of fire around them, these poor fellows, who had served their loving friend and master, the Czar, but too well, were consigned to their terrible fate. Many might have been saved with ordinary care. What must have the wounded felt who were obliged to endure all this; and who passed away without a hand to give them a cup of water, or a voice to say one kindly word to them? In the midst of one of these 'chambers of horrors'—for there were so many of them—were found some dead and some living English soldiers, and among them poor Captain Vaughan of the 90th, who has since succumbed to his wounds." [October 6, 1855.]

Hospital in Sebastopol.—Dr. Durgan attending the Wounded.—From a Sketch by E. A. Goodall.

MISS NIGHTINGALE

Although the public have been presented with several portrait-sketches of the lady who has so generously left this country to attend to the sufferings of the sick and wounded at Constantinople, we have assurance that these pictures are "singularly and painfully unlike." We have, therefore, taken the most direct means of obtaining a Sketch of this excellent lady, in the dress she now wears, in one of "the corridors of the sick," in the Hospital at Scutari. A recent letter in the *Times* bears the following testimony to the humane services of Miss Nightingale:—

"Wherever there is disease in its most dangerous form, and the hand of the spoiler distressingly nigh, there is that incomparable woman sure to be seen; her benignant presence is an influence for good comfort even amid the struggles of expiring nature. She is a 'ministering angel' without any exaggeration in these hospitals, and, as her slender form glides quietly along each corridor, every poor fellow's face softens with gratitude at the sight of her. When all the medical officers have retired for the night, and silence and darkness have settled down upon those miles of prostrate sick, she may be observed alone, with a little lamp in her hand, making her solitary rounds. The popular instinct was not mistaken which, when she set out from England on her mission of mercy, hailed her as a heroine; I trust that she may not earn her title to a higher though sadder appellation. No one who has observed her fragile figure and delicate health can avoid misgivings lest these should fail. With the heart of a true woman, and the manners of a lady, accomplished and refined beyond most of her sex, she combines a surprising calmness of judgment and promptitude and decision of character. I have hesitated to speak of her hitherto as she deserves, because I well knew that no praise of mine could do justice to her merits, while it might have tended to embarrass the frankness with which she has always accepted the aid furnished her through the Fund. As that source of supply is now nearly exhausted, and my mission approaches its close, I can express myself with more

Miss Nightingale, in the Hospital, at Scutari.

freedom on this subject; and I confidently assert, that but for Miss Nightingale the people of England would scarcely, with all their solicitude, have been spared the additional pang of knowing that their soldiers, even in hospital, had found scanty refuge and relief from the unparalleled miseries with which this war has hitherto been attended." [February 24, 1855.]

Newly-Invented Drying-Closet, for the Hospital at Scutari.

NEWLY-INVENTED DRYING-CLOSET

This Closet has been recently forwarded to Scutari, for the convenience of the sick and wounded in the Hospital. Its cost has been defrayed by the munificence of Miss Burdett Coutts, who has made herself acquainted with its capabilities to the most minute details, and has sent an engineer to Scutari with it, to superintend the working of it for a time. The Closet consists of six "horses" of galvanised iron, inclosed in a double case of corrugated iron; the intervals between the two cases being filled with earth or sand, to prevent the external radiation.

Its capabilities were previously tested before Miss Burdett Coutts, when it was shown that 1000 articles of linen can be thoroughly dried in twenty-five minutes by means of this contrivance. The working temperature is 240 deg. The waste heat from the furnace heats the water in the boiler of 100 gallons capacity. There is also the convenience of a washing-trough and a wringing-machine attached. The whole apparatus is portable, and easily fixed in any situation.

This Closet was made from a suggestion from Lieut. Tracey; the entire management being left to Mr. Jeakes, of Great Russell-street, Bloomsbury, under whose energetic direction it was completed and got ready for trial in sixteen days. [June 2, 1855.]

Jenny Lind singing at Exeter Hall.

JENNY LIND AT EXETER HALL

Madame Goldschmidt—or to call her by that which must ever be her artistic name, Jenny Lind—appeared a second time at Exeter Hall on Monday evening [December 17, 1855], in Mendelssohn's "Elijah." She was again received with enthusiasm by a vast assemblage, and again justified that enthusiasm by a performance of incomparable grandeur and beauty.

At this time of day it is the idlest thing imaginable to expatiate on the merits of a work respecting which the opinions of the world is so completely and decidedly fixed. "Elijah," of all the emanations of genius in the highest branch of the musical art, stands second to the "Messiah" alone, not only in intrinsic excellence, but in the affections of the people of England, for whom, in truth, it was produced. On the present occasion the great novelty was the illustrious *prima donna*, though she was not altogether a novelty, even in the performance of this oratorio. It was in it that she made her last public appearance, before she left the country six years ago, and the impression she then produced is still fresh in the minds of many who heard her. The general characteristics of her style as an oratorio singer were still more strongly marked in the performance of Monday last. There was not as much room for the brilliant displays of voice and execution which are afforded by the "Creation", which she performed last week; but there was a greater scope for her powers of dramatic and impassioned expression; while she was enabled to show the exquisite purity of her style, her faithful adherence to the composer's text, and her matchless gift of enchanting and moving the heart by that divine simplicity which, though seemingly artless, is in truth the consummation of art. Nothing could be more beautiful and pathetic than her performance of the scene in which she represented the Widow of Zarepatha, whose child is restored to life through the prayer of the prophet. Her mournful, imploring cry, "Help me, man of God, my son is sick!"; her agitated phrases, so full of anxious suspense; and her burst of joy and thankfulness when she sees the miracle wrought, were the very language of the heart, and went to the heart of every one present. In the great air, "Hear ye, Israel," she rose to a height of sustained grandeur which had never been reached or even approached by any other performer. It was the very perfection of vocal power and deep dramatic feeling. Among the most beautiful things in this Oratorio are the concerted pieces—trios and quartets—supposed to be the voices of angels, and full of divine purity and beauty. In all of these Jenny Lind took part, and gave them a new charm.

THE DEATH OF a somewhat remarkable personage took place a few days ago [August 1862] in Paris. M. Santini, the "guardian of the tomb" of Napoleon I, in the Church of the Invalids, has just tranquilly expired at a very advanced age. Santini was a Corsican, and one of the band of devoted men who accompanied the ex-Emperor to St. Helena and shared his dreary exile. He occupied a subordinate position in the household of Longwood, and after a couple of years' residence was sent home to Europe under the suspicion of having meditated the assassination of Sir Hudson Lowe. Santini brought, sewn up in the lining of his coat, the famous letter traced on a piece of white silk, the discovery of which led to the expulsion of Count Las Casas from St. Helena. He also wrote, or had written for him, an account of the captivity of Napoleon I, of which performance the illustrious exile himself did not entertain a very exalted opinion, characterising it as so many *coglionerie*. At the establishment of the Second Empire, Santini was made *Gardien du Tombeau*, and in that peculiar and honourable post he quietly ended his days.

THE PATENT ELEVATOR AND OBSERVATORY

During the siege of Sebastopol a good deal of natural anxiety was felt to obtain a view of the enemy's works. Two or three weeks before the town yielded to the Allied armies, Mr. Stocqueler, the military writer, conceived that a machine constructed upon the principle of the "lazy tongs", with a vertical action, might be made available for carrying a person up a considerable height, and at a safe distance, so as to afford a perfect view of the interior of the fortifications.

Our engraving shows a series of tiers of expanding laths, each six feet in length, worked by a wheel acting on a spindle; these rise from the three sides of a triangular base, carrying up an individual, secured by a circular railing, to a height of fifty or even one hundred feet, according to the dimensions of the base.

Its utility in superseding scaffolding to a great degree is obvious. For cleaning the inside of the roofs of churches, chapels, halls, and museums; painting and repairing the fronts of houses; assisting firemen to direct the jets of water on burning houses; facilitating reconnaissances and observations; for gathering fruit and lopping the branches of tall trees; for watering conservatories; painting and caulking the sides of ships; in fact, for all purposes in which a certain elevation is requisite this invention will prove of much value.

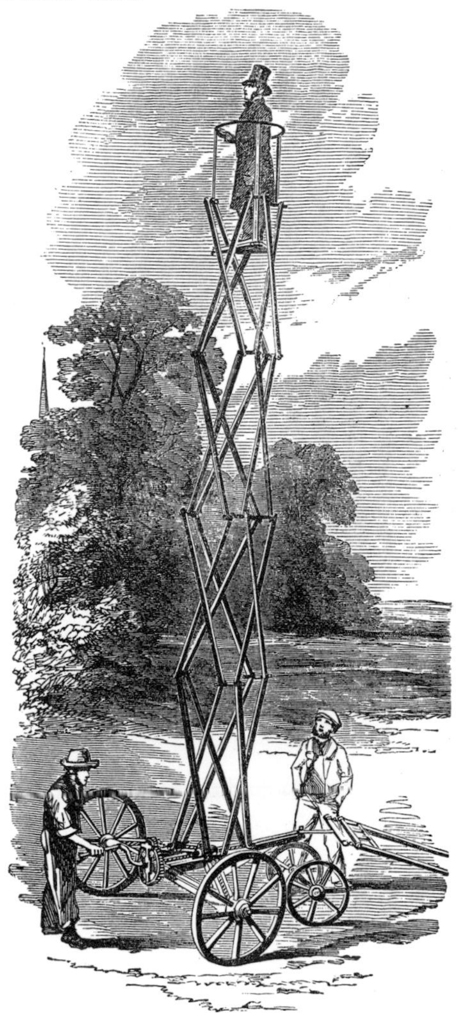

Explosion at Castel Nuovo, Naples.

TERRIFIC EXPLOSION AT NAPLES

The whole of the Quartigie del Mercato in Naples, on the 13th ult. [July, 1855], was alarmed by a fearful accident. Shortly before mid-day a terrible explosion was heard to proceed from the interior of Castel Nuovo, from its architecture and history one of the most interesting buildings in the capital. The alarm was communicated to the whole neighbourhood.

Clouds of smoke were seen rising up from the interior of the Castle, and floating over the adjacent streets, whilst with them were intermixed hats, caps, and clothes, stones and timber. The noise of the explosion was as that of thunder. Some thought that an earthquake had taken place, others that Vesuvius had broken out, and many that it was the first blow of a revolution. The accident took place in the rooms used by the Government for the manufacture of percussion-caps; but how it is impossible to ascertain, as most of those who were spectators are either dead or not expected to live; and those who are aware of any antecedant circumstances which threatened danger dare not speak of them. A considerable number of lives were lost—various statements give the number from fourteen to thirty; whilst very many are in the hospital in a hopeless state.

The King came over the following morning; and, immediately visiting the spot, with his usual activity urged on the excavations for the relief of the sufferers. Some were found without their heads, others without arms or legs. Some were so blackened as to be beyond the power of recognition, and many were fractured and destroyed by the falling of timber, stones, and furniture of the upper apartment. It appears that some time since His Majesty pointed out some defects in the machinery, as he did in the large granary before it fell four or five years ago; in the dry dock also; and more recently in a building called the Maddaloni—in all which cases, through inattention to the Royal commands, accidents took place, involving the loss of considerable amount of life and property.

THE CRIES OF OLD LONDON

Many of the London cries which once resounded through our crowded thoroughfares, and which the old inhabitants still remember, are no longer heard, though we occasionally pick up a few stray notes in the suburbs, that come falling upon the ear like the faint echoes of other days. The cry of "green boughs", to deck the summer parlours, and "green rushes", to strew upon the floors, has long since ceased. The fire-place is no more adorned with branches of the blossoming hawthorn, branches of sweet-briar, and huge pots filled with the fragrant and trailing honeysuckle; art, with its paper ornaments, has driven away these beautiful products of nature, and the less healthy carpet has carried off the meadow-like smell of the rushes. "Cherry-ripe" we occasionally hear, sung out as clear and silvery as when Herrick composed his inimitable little song. "Water-cresses", though no longer borne by a nymph, who paused every now and then to throw aside the long hair which fell over her nut-brown and weather-stained cheeks, is a cry we still hear; but the figure that conjured up Sabrina and the "glassy cool translucent wave", has long since departed. Lemons and oranges are cried by the wandering race, whose dark-haired mothers, in ancient days, poured forth their songs in the land of Israel. The primroses and violets of Spring are still sold in our streets, but the cry of "come buy my pretty bow-pots" is now rarely heard. The apple-stall, with its roasted chestnuts, the oyster-stall (a simple trestle), and the pie-man who is ever ready to try his luck at pitch-and-toss, still haunt the corners of a few of our obscure streets, as they did in by-gone days. The grinder and the tinker, and those who yet follow many a primitive old calling, and who set up their workshops in every open street where they can find a job, have been driven with their quaint cries into the suburbs, and the men themselves are but shadows of the jolly tinkers and merry pedlars who figure in our ancient ballad-lore. The rattle, and roll, and thunder of our modern vehicles have drowned their old-fashioned cries.

Shelling of Boats reconnoitring the Passage to Wyborg.

THE BOATS OF THE "ARROGANT" AND "MAGICIENNE" OFF WYBORG

A few weeks ago [summer 1855], the boats of the *Arrogant* and *Magicienne*, with a gun-boat in company, manned and armed, were sent to reconnoitre in the passage leading to Wyborg. When within some 200 yards of the shore an ambuscade of Russian sharpshooters opened fire upon them, which was sharply returned by our men. Finding that they were too much exposed to the Russian musketry, the boats retreated under cover of the gun-boats. In this encounter we regret to add that four or five men were severely wounded, and, in consequence of the explosion of one of the boat's magazines, a midshipman was thrown overboard and drowned. Owing to the shallowness of the water, the *Arrogant* and *Magicienne* were unable to render any assistance.

The Baltic fleet has for some time been reconnoitring all the channels near Sveaborg, and has found many valuable anchorages, and several points where the coasting trade between Borgo and Helsingfors, which was carried on to a considerable extent, can be entirely stopped; and some surprise is expressed that so little was attempted in this way last year by the vessels stationed in that vicinity. The Admiral had placed the *Dragon* and a French and English gun-boat under Captain Kay's orders, and they met with no resistance whatever, except from shoals, the gun-boats having grounded several times.

All the gun and mortar boats are going over to Helsingfors. The town will probably be shelled; but it is not expected that the fortifications can be destroyed.

PORTABLE SCHOOLS

Portable School—exterior.

Portable School—interior.

While we possess portable buildings for nearly all kinds of purposes, there seems to be no reason why this species of accommodation should not be extended to the business of education. Mr. Robert Ault, a builder, at Stourbridge, has the merit of this new application.

He has erected at Wordsley, in Staffordshire, a school-room of this kind. It is called a portable school-room, because its sides, ends, roof, and floor are framed in compartments screwed together, which can be taken to pieces and removed to any other site. It is 24 feet long, 16 feet wide, and 8 feet high to the springing of the roof. The roof is open to the ridge, which is 16 feet from the floor. The whole is constructed of timber, and capable of holding 100 children. A composition has been applied to the exterior which renders it quite weatherproof. It is well warmed, with one cwt. of coals per week, by a new kind of stove; which, together with the whole building, was designed by Mr. F. Smalman Smith, architect, Stourbridge, and which was made by Mr. Ault for the sum of £60, including a belfry and shutters.

Such a school-room would be very useful where a site or funds are difficult to obtain, or where the ground is undermined, or the population fluctuating. This school-room has been provided to accommodate a mixed school, in a newly-built district, for which a permanent building will be erected as soon as the title of the site can be made clear, when it will be removed to another part of the parish, to serve the purpose of a Ragged School.

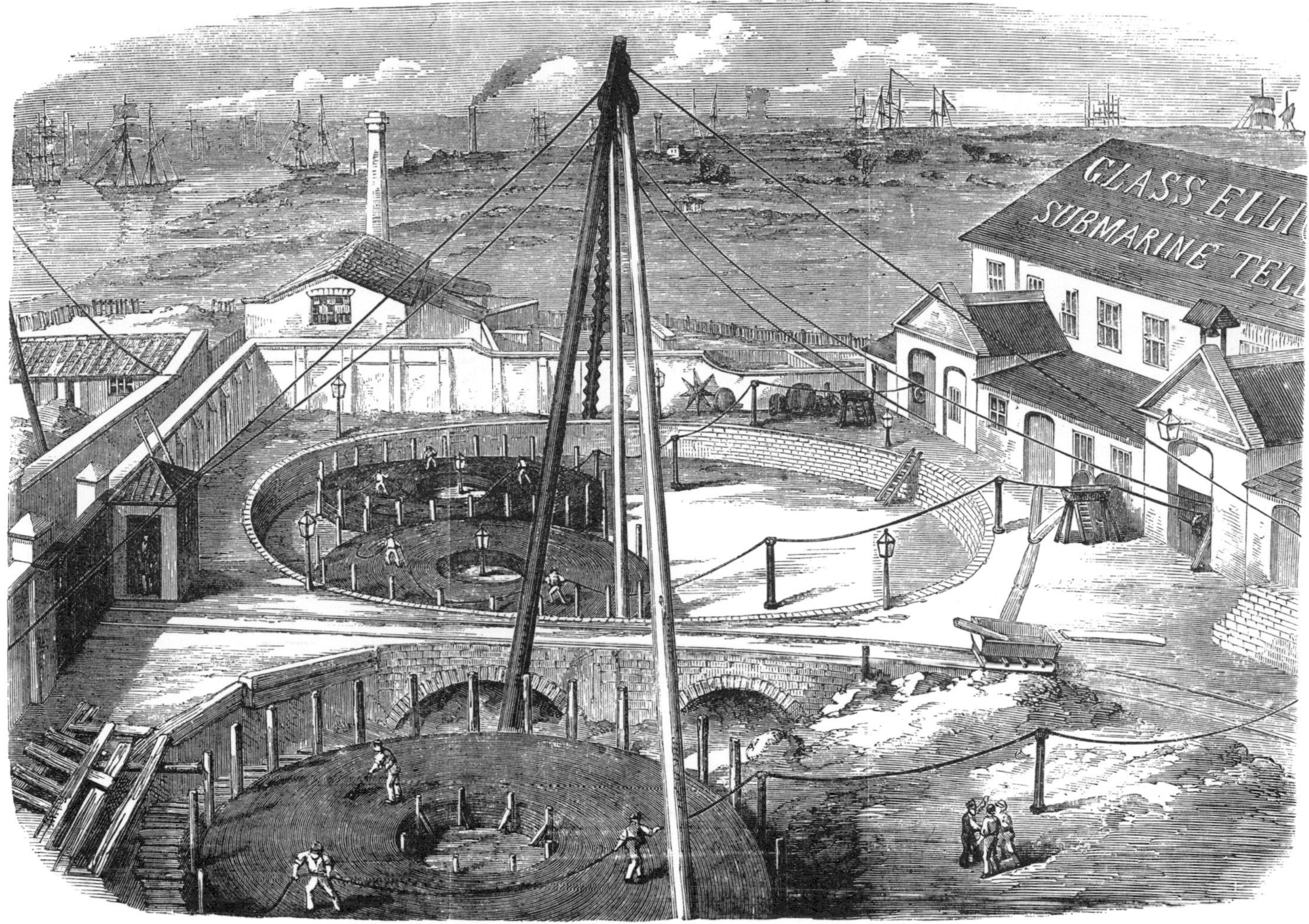

The Atlantic Cable, eady for Shipment, Morden Wharf, East Greenwich.

MANUFACTURE OF THE ATLANTIC TELEGRAPH CABLE

The several extensions of the Electric Telegraph present rare combinations of science and the arts, which are fraught with interest. Of the submarine cable which is to connect the Old and New Worlds the public has already heard much; but comparatively few persons are aware that it differs in structure, weight, and other conditions from most of the ropes hitherto laid, and embraces several valuable improvements suggested by successes or failures with previous lines.

The cable from Dover to Calais, that of the Magnetic Telegraph Company between England and Ireland, and others less generally known, being laid for the greater part of their length in comparatively shallow water, where the consideration of danger from anchors is a very grave point to be met, weigh seven or eight tons to the mile and are of strength sufficient to resist almost any strain to which they are liable, except, perhaps so enormous and exceptional a force as that to which the Ostend rope was subjected in the recent storms, when a large ship held on to the cable for a long time, but finally broke it asunder by the tremendous power of the gale. The injury was repaired on the renewal of fair weather, and the rarity of any interruption happening to lines of such calibre (this being the only instance of accident occurring to any of the stronger kinds of rope, while those of a lighter character laid in similar depths to the Hague and elsewhere ave been frequently repaired, and require a large annual outlay for their maintenance) may be accepted as evidence of the sound judgment exercised in the selection of a heavy class of rope to span frequented and shallow seas.

Near the shores of Newfoundland and Ireland, and until the depth is so increased as to be far beyond any risk of danger from anchorage or the grounding of icebergs, the Atlantic cable will be stronger even than the most massive rope yet laid; but in the chief portion of the route, where the great depth bears with its disadvantages and difficulties the advantage of perfect rest and security for the wire when laid, the weight will not exceed a ton per mile.

The Atlantic cable may be divided into two parts, the core and the armour—the former being the conductor to be actually employed in the transmission of electrical sensations under the ocean between Europe and America, the latter only a protective and strengthening assistant whereby to deposit the insulated wire at the bottom of the sea. The core is composed of seven copper wires of the gauge known as No. 22, wound spirally together so as to form a strand or cord; the object of this arrangement, instead of a single wire of the same sectional area, being to provide against the possibility of any break of continuity taking place in the metal. This strand, which will stretch twenty per cent of its length, is covered with three layers of the purest gutta percha.

The core of this gigantic cable (2500 miles in length) is now in the course of manufacture, under the superintendence of Mr. Samuel Statham, at the extensive works of the Gutta Percha Company, Wharf-road, City-road, London. The outer protection of iron wire has been committed to two eminent firms—viz., Messrs. Newall and Co., of Gateshead; and Messrs. Glass, Elliott, and Co., of East Greenwich. The core is conveyed to East Greenwich upon large reels, each containing rather more than a mile of wire, and there being placed on standards in a lower floor of the factory, the reels being so arranged as to allow of the wire being readily drawn off. Messrs. Glass and Co.'s works were erected in 1854 for the express purpose of manufacturing submarine telegraph cables. They have the advantage of a river frontage of 200 feet, with great facilities for coiling the cables directly on board vessels lying within a distance easily connected by a floating platform. The depth

The Method of Taking the Atlantic Telegraph Cable on Board—sketched from the stern gallery of Her Majesty's ship "Agamemnon."

of the wharf from the river front to the manufactory is 400 feet, and in this area are sunk tanks capable of containing from 2000 to 3000 miles of cable, with ready means of admitting water from the river to submerge the cable from time to time during the progress of manufacture, to prove the perfect insulation, if necessary.

SHIPPING OF THE CABLE

The shipping of the great cable has been a gigantic labour, of which we illustrate that portion which was executed at East Greenwich. Here the *Agamemnon* was moored off the wharf at Glass and Elliott's yard. She had anything but a sightly aspect, the dead weight of the cable and the rather ponderous appliances for paying it out having altered her trim appearance for the worse. In the large Engraving of the vessel in the present Number the wire is being wound over the floating stages from the wharf into the hold of the vessel. The machine by which this is done registered each fathom, furlong, and mile as it passed, while the usual apparatus was employed to test the integrity of the conducting wire. From the small machine on deck it was wound at once to the hold, where it lay in one stupendous solid coil 45 feet in diameter, and nearly 14 feet high.

The *Agamemnon* was to proceed at once to Queenstown, where the other vessels composing the squadron—the *Niagara*, *Susquehanna*, and *Leopard*—will also rendezvous. During the trip from Sheerness to Queenstown experiments were to be made by laying down about 20 miles of cable, in order to ascertain that everything was in good working condition. After taking in coals at Queenstown the four vessels were to start for Valentia Bay. The month of August has been chose for the submersion of the cable, as likely to afford the best conditions for the enterprise in regard to weather.

LAYING THE ATLANTIC CABLE

The construction and shipment of this wonder of the age having already been fully illustrated in our Journal, it remains but to present to our readers, in picture and descriptive detail, the laying of the cable from the extreme point of Ireland to St. John's, Newfoundland. The *Niagara* and *Agamemnon* were the two vessels which actually contained

The "Agamemnon" in a storm.

the telegraphic cable to form the connecting link between the two continents. Shortly after one o'clock (Wednesday, August 5) a boat well manned from the American vessel [the *Niagara*] was let down, and one of the paddle-box boats of the *Leopard*, with a crew, was placed immediately under the stern of the *Niagara*, when the operation of paying out the shore end of the cable commenced. The expedition sailed on Thursday, but had scarcely got four miles when the cable becoming entangled with the machinery, broke, and the ship's boats were engaged until the afternoon of Friday in under-running the cable from the shore to the place where it was broken, and there joining two ends. This operation was successfully performed, and the squadron set sail again on Friday. All went on smoothly to four o'clock on the following Tuesday, up to which period constant signals and messages had been received. At that period the signals suddenly ceased. The return of the squadron confirmed the fears entertained—the cable had broken in deep water. Although this unfortunate accident will postpone the completion of this great undertaking for a short time—possibly for the season—no doubts are entertained of its ultimate and even speedy completion. [August 22, 1857.]

Breaking adrift of the Coal on Board the "Agamemnon."

A NEW ATTEMPT

The *Agamemnon* on the voyage out with the other vessels of the squadron encountered a succession of tremendous gales which scattered all the ships for some days. The *Agamemnon* rolled so heavily and dangerously as to lead to serious fears that she would capsize completely and founder. In these heavy lurches the coals which were stowed in the main and lower decks broke away, and seriously injured several of the crew. Only on the 25th of June was the rendezvous made, and the other vessels sighted. The first splice was made on the 26th and was broken an hour afterwards on board the *Niagara*. After two other splices parted, the *Agamemnon* returned to the rendezvous and cruised for five days. Unfortunately, the *Niagara* did not return to the rendezvous, so that the only fine weather which the expedition had was totally lost, and the *Agamemnon* had to proceed to Queenstown on the 6th of July. There are still 2500 miles of wire on board the two ships. [July 1858.]

Paying out the Land End of the Cable from the Stern of the "Niagara."

Celebration of the Laying of the Atlantic Telegraph Cable at New York.—The Illumination of the City Hall.

FÊTES AT NEW YORK TO COMMEMORATE THE LAYING OF THE ATLANTIC TELEGRAPH CABLE

Of the fête at New York on the 17th ult. we have the following particulars from the gentleman who supplied us with the sketch of the City Hall as it was illuminated on the night of the 17th, and which is engraved here:—

The publication of her Majesty's message to the President of the United States on the morning of August 17, carrying with it, as it did, the assurance that the telegraphic wires were really capable of transmitting despatches, caused an outburst of enthusiasm in the Atlantic States which might almost be characterised by the American qualificative "universal." Wherever the news penetrated there was a public jubilee. In Boston, Portland, Philadelphia, Baltimore, and other places, bells were rung, salutes fired, illuminations spontaneously undertaken; but in New York the most thorough and systematic display of popular joy took place. A little after daybreak on the morning of the 17th the celebration was commenced by the discharge of cannon in the park; and as the sun rose above the heights of Long Island his rays fell upon an assemblage of cities—New York, Brooklyn, Jersey City, Hoboken, Williamsburgh,—decked in flags and resounding with the merry peals of a thousand bells. But the principal feature of the celebration was the illumination of the city at night, together with the display of fireworks provided by the municipality. Not only that unparallelled thoroughfare, Broadway, was illuminated and decorated for two or three miles of its length, but the lesser streets were also brilliant in many-coloured fires. Wall-street—the centre of American commerce and finance—glittered strangely under the quiet sky. Nassau-street, crowded with newspaper-offices, was a thoroughfare of light. Bonfires blazed in every direction. Transparencies were displayed upon every hotel and many private dwellings. Epigrammatic and laudatory mottoes glowed upon the fronts of granite and marble stores. The City Hall, which stretches its white façade half across the narrow, triangular park, was lit up as never before; every pane in its innumerable windows bore a light. The watcher in the illuminated clock-tower looked down (for the last time, as it proved) on a throng such as the park, used as it is to vast assemblages, has never before contained. The heavy foliage of the lime and elm trees with which it is studded was scarcely denser than the crowd assembled in expectation of the pyrotechnic display. The night was moonless, and a cloudy sky favoured the occasion, so that by eight o'clock the signal rockets were sent up, accompanied by fire-balloons. Streams of fiery particles and globules of variegated flame shot up far into the heavens, as if to announce to the lightning its final triumph in submission. Roman candles rose and fell in perpetual ebullition; erratic rockets hissed and surged upwards in contending streams; serpents, cometlike, darted through the air; and at length the great flame-structures erected upon the wings of the City Hall were fired. The illumination paled before their rippling lustre; and cheer after cheer arose from the immense assemblage as the designs became developed in succession. Among the most elaborate pieces was one representing a British and an American vessel, with the union-jack and the stars and stripes at each side, surmounted by the inscription—"All Honour to Cyrus W. Field! Franklin, Morse, and Field." (Mr. Field is a gentleman, a resident of New York, who has been very active in the telegraphic enterprise, and Professor Morse was one of the first to elaborate the idea of electro-telegraphic communication.) Other pyrotechnics presented similar devices and allusions, during the continuance of which the National Anthem of Great Britain, together with "Hail Columbia!" and "St. Patrick's Day," was played by an attendant band. With a further discharge of rockets the display was concluded, and by half-past nine the spectators had dispersed.

It unfortunately happened that some sparks fell upon the woodwork of the clock-tower of the City Hall, and flames burst out there about midnight, which finally consumed the tower, and largely damaged the building itself. As the central fire-alarm was located on this spot, the intelligence could not be communicated instantly, as usual, to the engine-houses, and the delay which ensued proved fatal to the structure. The scene, however, was magnificent. The statue of Justice, a familiar sight to all New Yorkers, stood wrapt for a length of time in the flames of the grand illumination, and serenely endured the fiery glow for more than an hour, until at length she was observed to totter and fall into the flames. Many valuable paintings, and some relics of General Washington, were injured by the water; but the city and judicial records were, fortunately, not endangered. Fifty thousand dollars are required to repair the injury caused by this disaster. [September 25, 1858.]

WHALE STRANDED AT WINTERTON

This fine specimen of the whale tribe was driven ashore at Winterton by the gales which visited the coast of Norfolk on the 5th inst [January 1857]. When the whale found himself upon the land he roared loudly, and he struggled most lustily to regain the deep. His full length is 48 feet; compared with which the proportions of the jaw are very small, measuring only 8 feet; the eye small, the span of ball 5 inches, sight of eye between the lids 1½ inch; and there are two orifices in the middle of the head. The upper jaw is provided with about 400 (on each side) plates of whalebone or baleens, and each is furnished with very soft tufts of white hair sprouting from the inner part to the blowing tubes, which is quite bare, and formed with a pinky horny substance.

SOME FACTS AND FIGURES

Some of our readers may be interested in the following calculations of our last week's numbers:—

The Papers placed separately would reach 678 miles 672 yards, exceeding the distance from the Land's-end to John O'Groats. The Weight of Water absorbed in the process of wetting, 4 tons 9 cwt. 3 lb. The Weight of Printed Paper 30 tons 10 cwt. 51 lbs. The Paper would cover a surface of 367,468 sq. yards. 10 ft. 32 in., or 75 acres 4468 sq. yds.

Cut into slips of one inch, would reach round the Earth, a distance of about 24,000 miles. Excise Duty paid on the Paper £365. Duty for Penny Stamps 1250 [sic].

The whole cost of the Print alone was upwards of £2000.

THE FIFTH OF NOVEMBER

Powder Plot is a general holiday in our calendar, but with many modifications from the olden state. It was first appointed in 1605, as a day of thanksgiving, when all persons were required to go to church. In Spelman's time the judges went to church in state on this day.

The sacred observance of the day has formed a feature of the revivalism which characterises the present age: thus far the solemnity may not have waned. But the secular treatment of the subject has assumed a great variety of complexions, varying almost with the year itself. Last year Guido Fawkes gave way to the Pope and an offending Cardinal, whose notoriety was in full force at the time. On Wednesday last [1851] there was no lack of observance of the anniversary, and the Pope and the Cardinal were not forgotten; but the street humour took another turn, and certain persons—no friends to the legitimate subject of the day—allowed their fancies to riot in effigies of the Emperor of Austria, Marshal Haynau, and the Czar Nicholas; and, to complete the chapter of absurdities, a monster "Bloomer" was added to the grotesque bevy. But, like another pageant we could name, that of Guy Fawkes was, in many instances, too theatrical or stagy; and they appeared to excite a good deal of curiosity among foreigners, not well versed in the calendar of our Church.

By the way, a 5th of November display has of late years been made subservient to the cause of charity as well as mere amusement. Here is a laudable instance. On Wednesday evening a grand display of fireworks took place on the grounds of the Merchant Seamen's Orphan Asylum, Bow-road, in aid of the funds of the institution. The grounds were illuminated somewhat after the fashion adopted at Vauxhall, and a band of music was engaged. In the rear of the premises was a gibbet, to which was suspended an effigy of the Pope; and around it were several barrels of tar, which at the proper time were consumed in a most formidable blaze. The exhibition was attended by a large concourse of people, and the result promised to be of considerable benefit to the funds of the charity.

Release of 300 balloons from the Esplanade des Invalides.

BAPTISM OF THE PRINCE IMPERIAL

Among the entertainments provided for the working classes at the fête on Sunday [June 22, 1856 in Paris], the flight of balloons showering bon-bons afforded most amusement. Three hundred balloons were let off in the Esplanade in the course of the afternoon, and at about five a large balloon was sent up, from which bags of bon-bons were thrown down amongst the crowd. At all the theatres gratuitous performances were given, each house performing its best and newest pieces. Immense audiences attended, and, as is usual with the French public when admitted without payment, the greatest order prevailed. The Boulevards and public promenades were crowded all day. Towards evening the crowd divided into two vast streams—one proceeding to the Place de la Concorde and the other the Barrière du Trône, where two splendid *feux d'artifice* were to be simultaneously displayed. We may here add that the Prefect of the Seine has presented a bag of bon-bons to each of the 50,000 children attending the primary schools of Paris.

The ball given by the city of Paris to the Emperor and Empress, in honour of the baptism of the Prince Imperial [Eugène Louis Jean Joseph, son of Napoleon III: killed in the Zulu War 1879], was of rare magnificence. Their Majesties arrived at about half-past ten from the Tuileries, which they had reached about half an hour before from St. Cloud. From the Palace to the Hôtel de Ville, and in the vicinity of the latter the mass of human beings was so dense that movement was nearly impossible. The splendid illumination of the Palace enabled the spectators to distinguish perfectly the occupants of the several carriages. Buffets were disposed in every convenient part of the building, and on each a profusion of dragées were placed, to show that the fête was a baptismal one. One o'clock struck before the Imperial party thought of retiring. The front of the Hôtel de Ville was lit up at the moment of departure with Bengal lights, and the effect on the illuminated buildings was charming. Dancing continued in the three ballrooms with undiminished spirit, and many of the guests remained until nearly four in the morning.

MR. CHARLES DICKENS

Our illustration presents a portrait of Mr. Charles Dickens when reading at St. Martin's Hall one of his admirable little books to a numerous audience [Summer 1858]. It is a good thing when the author can be thus induced to come forth from his library and mingle with his fellow-men, as a living teacher, uttering his "living reasons", visible and audible to sympathising pupils. The monitor of his kind, speaking in parables, they see and hear him, not through the dead pages of a printed volume, but in his own person, directing the force of the sentences that he had previously written, and impressing their true meaning on the mind of auditors by their proper emphasis and the vital interpretation of gesture and his own natural elocution. Mr. Charles Dickens is an excellent reader. He uses little action, but he can make his features eloquent. He is far from monotonous, and throws an alternation of light and shade, so to speak, into his reading, by means of a rapid or slow utterance, according to the character or importance of the passages read. He, therefore, maintains the interest of his subject for two hours with comparative ease, and carries his audience with him by means of the variety which he imparts to his entertainment. Without any aid from costume, or any extravagance of motion, by the mere

Mr. Dickens reading "Little Dombey"

power of facial expression, he impersonates the different characters of his stories, and brings them ideally, but vividly, before the spectator's mind. Mr. Dickens has invented a new medium for amusing an English audience, and merits the gratitude of an intelligent public.

DEBARKATION OF ELEPHANTS AT CALCUTTA

Few of our readers are well acquainted with the laborious process of unshipping a cargo of elephants. Such a striking sight has been recently witnessed at Calcutta and has been sketched by an obliging Correspondent.

Two cargoes have been landed [January, 1858] since the previous mail left. One arrived in the ship *Tubal Cain*, consisting of twenty elephants; the other in the *Belgravia*, and numbered fifty elephants. The process of hoisting these most gigantic of existing quadrupeds from their berths on board ship, and getting them on shore, was a novel and curious sight. It took place at the Government dockyard, about half a mile below Fort William. Strange to say, there is no wharf at this dock-yard alongside of which the vessels could be brought, so that they had to be moored about fifty yards from the shore. They were, however, brought near the jetty, at the extremity of which is a large crane, and by means of this and the tackle on board ship, all the elephants were safely landed. The first party in the *Tubal Cain* were hoisted up from between decks, the hoisting tackle was connected with the crane-chains, and the crane was then turned slowly round, each elephant in succession being lowered and deposited on the bank of the river. This plan gave too much liberty to the elephants after reaching *terra firma*; for, as some of them chose to indulge in a roll and bath in the shallow water after their voyage, time was lost before the drivers could manage to lead them away. It was, therefore, found more convenient and expeditious to lower each elephant into a barge alongside the ship, and to land him afterwards by drawing the boat the short distance to the shore.

The fifty elephants in the *Belgravia* were all brought between decks. One of the largest was said to weigh 3 tons $2\frac{1}{2}$ cwt. There was no opposition to the process of hoisting on the part of the animals, for they had sagacity enough to understand that it was the means of quitting the ship. There was great excitement among the crowd on shore when the boatswain's whistle was heard directing the sailors at the capstan to hoist away, and presently the rough, inert-looking mass of the animal's spine and back was seen above the deck: then part of the head, with which the animal from time to time prevented himself from being struck against the sides of the hatchway as he swung round on either side; the small, sluggish eye, which seemed to be calmly surveying the scene; the active proboscis, forming by its constant movements a remarkable contrast with the rest of its passive frame; and, finally, after the crane tackle had been connected, the whole creature came into view, dangling in the air, and suspended by a couple of ropes which seemed like mere threads compared with the size of the animal which depended from them. He was then swung over the bulwarks, and lowered into the barge alongside.

No accident occurred during the disembarkation, but two elephants were drowned at Moulmein in embarking them.

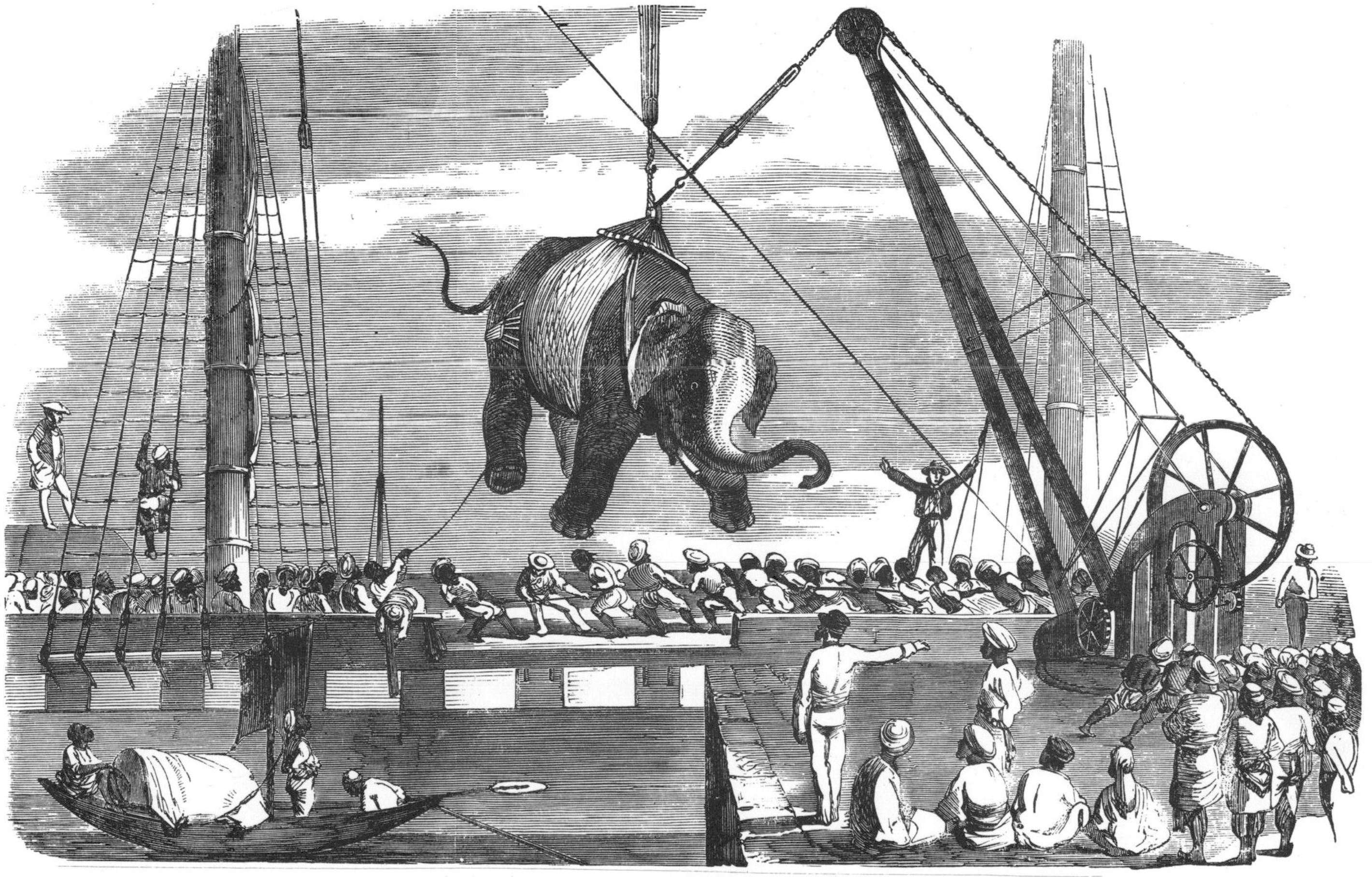

Unshipping elephants at Calcutta.

THE PRINCE IMPERIAL OF FRANCE

The portrait which we now present is from a photograph taken recently by Messrs. Miall (Frères), at the Tuileries, of the Prince on a toy horse. The Imperial Prince, who, it will be remembered, was enrolled in the 1st Regiment of Grenadier Guards a few days after his birth, and who has ever since drawn the pay of a private soldier, has just been promoted to the rank of corporal, due to a vacancy by reason of the transfer of Corporal Prugnot to the 3rd battalion of the 4th company. [August, 1858.]

ERUPTION OF MOUNT VESUVIUS

Naples, June 8, [1858].—The accompanying sketch of the present grand eruption of Vesuvius presents a view of the mouths which feed the great stream of lava still running down towards Resina. As a general view, there are few things grander than what one witnesses from St. Lucia—the two great streams of liquid lava flowing down on each side of a ridge on which stands the Observatory and Hermitage. That on the left, after running to a certain distance, falls into a gigantic ravine, called Fosso do Faraone, and thence courses on to Massa di Somma and several other towns and villages. That one on the right, issuing from the mouths represented in the Sketch, runs through the Piano delle Ginestre, and, falling over cascades, descends into the Fosso Grande, which is traced through cultivated grounds down to Resina. On no evening has the eruption been so fine as it was on Saturday evening. The fountains of the fiery deep seemed to have opened up with fresh vigour, and the work of destruction, a little above Resina, not more than an hour's distance, was going on at a rapid rate. The vines were scorching and lighting up like matches, while the tall trees shook like giants overcome with fear. There was a perfect calm around, and yet the trees waved backwards and forwards as though struck by a heavy wind. The peasantry were running about, some of them cutting down timber, and taking up poles from the very edge of the fire, for, with the sanguineness of hope, they had left it to the last moment;

The Mouths of the Great Stream of Lava on Vesuvius.

Meeting of the Metropolitan Charity School children at Crystal Palace.

most, however, stood by silent and overwhelmed with grief. The width of the living stream was about 800 palms. It was black on the surface for the most part, for a slight exposure to the air hardens and darkens the exterior. Over this vast black bed there ran, moreover, wide streams of liquid fire, so red as to dazzle the eye and so fluid as to appear like gullies. A house was embedded in the stream, and close by was a handsome villa, at the foot of which ran the red river, destroying all the grounds. Higher up was a house which fell at midday, and now could only be discovered by the massive white fragments intermingled with the black masses. A short distance higher, one could look downwards on the rolling streams of fire—for there were two of them—and upwards to the sources which fed them. The lava was running with the rapidity of a racehorse; it was running down in the form of cascades, of so pure and liquid a fire that it might have issued from a furnace; and so it continued, as far as the eye could reach, carrying with it ruin, poverty, and all but death—for no deaths have been reported as yet.

To exaggerate the grandeur of the scene would be impossible. There is still great activity upon the mountain; and the smoke, which is rising up from many points, promises a brilliant scene this evening.

CHARITY SCHOOL CHILDREN AT THE CRYSTAL PALACE

This very interesting assemblage took place on Wednesday [August 4, 1858]. The children of the various London Charity Schools, to the number of above five thousand (by a joint arrangement similar to that whereby they are annually brought together in St. Paul's Cathedral), were conveyed to the Crystal Palace by special trains, for the purpose of enjoying a whole day's recreation. They all reached Sydenham before ten in the morning; and after having been mustered and abundantly supplied with the "creature-comforts" hospitably provided by the Crystal Palace Company, they dispersed themselves at their pleasure over the building and its beautiful grounds, till they were reassembled, at three o'clock, in the great "Handel Orchestra" in the Central Transept, presenting a most striking and picturesque coup d'oeil, of which the accompanying Sketch will convey a more lively idea than can be given by a verbal description. They sang several of our fine old psalms—the Old Hundredth, "Martin Luther's Hymn," "St. Ann's," and some others, concluding with "God Save the Queen." There was no attempt at musical display: the voices were all in unison, accompanied by the organ; and the swell of these thousands of youthful voices had a natural sublimity which could not be reached by all the resources of art. They were again dispersed to resume their joyous sports in the grounds; and, after having evidently passed a happy and healthful day, both to body and mind, they were carefully conveyed to their homes.

Mr. Kean as *Benedick*—On Saturday Mr. C. Kean varied his tragic series by the revival of "Much Ado About Nothing". We have been accustomed to associate with the part of *Benedick* the fine figure and finished art of Charles Kemble, and cannot easily build it again in another body and with another manner. But in all the ideal Shakespearean characters there are more than one possible conception, and we need not, therefore, be surprised that Mr. Kean has been eminently successful in the embodiment of this great comic part, in a novel and appreciable form, very satisfactory to the taste of the judicious. The soliloquy in which he discovers that "the world must be peopled" was never better delivered. The smile that spreads over his face and remains there illuminating the countenance for a while, reminds us strongly of Mr. Edmund Kean: Mr. C. Kean has inherited it to a nicety, and it was pleasing to recall an old charm in the possession of its rightful heir.

CHOTA HAZIREE—THE LITTLE BREAKFAST

The sketch here engraved from a photograph taken in India, illustrates one of the familiar phases of Anglo-Oriental life. The "chota haziree" is a meal which is not habitual with persons in this country, although something akin to it prevails in France, and, we believe, in Spain. It may be called the *avant-courier* of the regular process of restoration which goes on during the day in India. Any one who desires to retain such health and activity as Europeans can by care and arrangement of their habits obtain in an Eastern climate, makes early rising the starting point of their system. At an hour somewhat about that at which the market-gardeners who supply London are making their way towards Covent-garden market, gentlemen and ladies in India are mounting their horses or getting into their carriages for the early ride or drive. On their return, the light refection which is portrayed in the Engraving—consisting of tea, toast, and occasionally fruit, succeeded in the case of the male sex by the inevitable cheroot or hookah—is partaken of in the lightest of dresses and in the airiest of verandahs, or housetops, as is the custom in the East. As the coolness of the morning has not yet passed away, and the frame is not yet suffering from lassitude, the dwellers in bungalows are enabled to enjoy their newspapers and books, or the gossip of the town or station. The "chota haziree" is often prolonged to such an hour as only gives time to take the regular daily bath, and to perform the rather more serious duties of the toilette, if the "convenances" of the occasion require it, in order to be ready for the next breakfast, at half-past ten or eleven. This is an elaborate and abundant *dejeûner à la fourchette* in which every possible dish, light and solid, is flanked, not only by tea and coffee, but by light wines, and the perennial bottle of pale ale. After the performance with knife and fork, spoon, cup, and glass, which this gastronomic display has stimulated, rest within doors, in large and lofty rooms, covered with cool matting—and in the hot season closed with "tattis", that is, matting on which water is kept constantly poured—and beneath the soothing influence of never-ceasing punkahs, is the order of the day until the hour of "tiffin." This luncheon is no less pronounced in every sense than the second breakfast; and is, in fact, a little more solidified, and would not be miscalled if it were denominated dinner, but that the appropriation of that title would interfere with the rights of the meal which is served up between seven and eight in the evening, and for which any appetite that exists has been gained by another ride or drive after sunset. This is the last regular refection of an Indian day, for we are told that suppers are not habitual, unless a ball or any other cause induces sitting up until after midnight.

THE IMPERIAL TRAIN ON THE ORLEANS RAILWAY

This luxurious train on the Orleans Railway, which was made a present to the Emperor [Napoleon III of France] by that company, is so complete that their Majesties might almost imagine themselves seated in a boudoir either at the Tuileries or at St. Cloud, and witnessing a never-ending panorama. The train consists of half a dozen carriages:—1st: The *salle-a-manger* and aides-de-camp carriage. 2nd: An open-roofed carriage, fitted with an ornamental gilt grating, for the convenience of smokers, or of those who wish to be in the open air. 3rd: The Imperial saloon. 4th: The sleeping-rooms. 5th: The carriage of the Prince Imperial, containing every convenience, and two sleeping-closets for the lady attendants. 6th: The baggage wagon.

The carriage of the aides-de-camp, provided with crimson velvet seats, serves also for the dining-room: it contains three dining-tables, placed down the centre, which are also adapted for whist-tables. There are two small compartments at the end of the carriage, one for the butler, the other a *cabinet de toilette* for the

"Chota haziree," or little breakfast in India.—From a Photograph by A. Williamson.

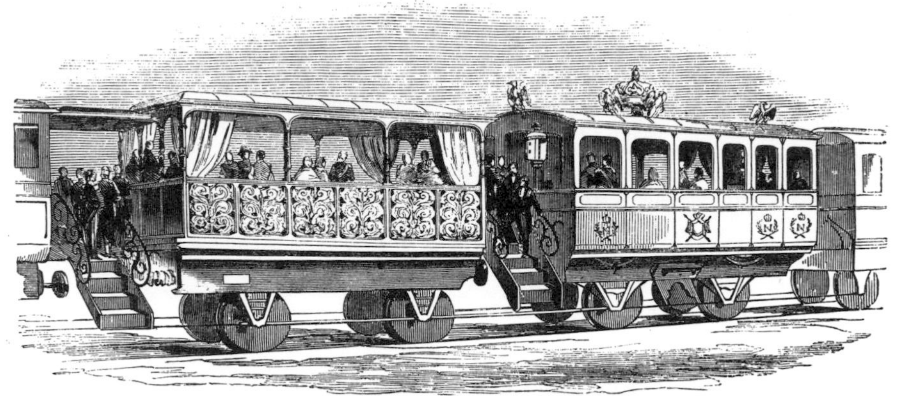

Open Saloon and Imperial Saloon on the Imperial Train.

The Saloon of Honour on the Imperial Train.

aides-de-camp. Water is laid on in all the carriages.

The open-roofed carriage is surrounded by a very elaborately-ornamented gilt grating, and hung with handsome curtains. Here his Majesty smokes an occasional cigarette.

The principal carriage of the train is the saloon of honour, which is occupied by the Emperor and Empress. It is surmounted by the Imperial crown and eagles, is in exquisite taste, and all the colours of the decorations blend with a harmony that is really charming. The covering of the couches (which are so contrived as to draw out in front and serve for beds if required) is in damasked green silk, welted throughout; the carpet is in mockadees; and the ceiling is richly decorated with gilt beadings, the white ground-work being covered with roses painted on the wood. The little table in rosewood placed between their Majesties in our Illustration is quite a curiosity: although occupying so small a space, it contains four tables.

All the carriages communicate with each other by carpeted passages, which can be closed from the weather, being lighted at night by lamps. A magnificent series of oak carvings separates the decorations of the ceiling from the walls of each carriage, and by their simplicity give a most chaste appearance to the *coup d'oeil* of each apartment.

NEW SUBMARINE BOAT

The boat is built in the shape of a fish: it is the invention of Mr. Lodner D. Phillips, of Chicago, and was patented there on the 9th of November [1852].

It has two double hatches, one on the top and one on the bottom, and may have side hatches. The upper hatch is sealed when the vessel is submerged: when the upper hatch is open the bottom one is shut, and *vice versa*. It has two sight-domes, which are used when the vessel is on the surface of the water; and has four interrupted keels to prevent it from turning over when submerged. When in deep water, lights with reflectors are placed opposite some of the bull's-eyes seen in the side; and, owing to the shape of the vessel, the bull's-eyes nearest the fore-part of the boat enable those within to see where they are going. Should the vessel run into anything it can be extricated without injury, having on its point or bow a thimble, or outer case, which is so constructed that by reversing the screw the boat would be backed, leaving the thimble. Having a glass tube properly marked, the exact depth from the surface is always shown. Fresh air is supplied as necessary from tanks containing many atmospheres compressed. The boat is sunk by admitting water into tanks or pipes, and raised by expelling the same. It can be kept stationary at any required depth of water, from an inch to two hundred feet. In this lies the secret which makes the boat effective. It has, likewise, a secret method of loading guns under water; but no doubt its greatest value will be in the many ways it can be employed in examining ships' bottoms, repairing and building docks, wharfs, &c., having patent tools for working through its side, likewise for pearl fisheries.

It may be propelled by hand-power or electro-magnetism, with a screw of Mr. Phillips's invention, fitted on a universal joint, by which a rudder is dispensed with. It is to carry twenty or thirty men. It is sixty feet long, by seven feet six inches in diameter. The first boat constructed on this novel principle was built at Michigan city, and publicly tried there with complete success. On both sides of the Atlantic the invention has attracted much attention, and been favourably mentioned by the press.

New Submarine Boat.

THE BROUSIL FAMILY

This interesting family group will require but a brief notice from us at present, having already appeared with distinguished success three times before her Majesty, as well as at the Crystal Palace, and in most of the large cities and towns of the kingdom. Though natives of Bohemia, it may be truly said that they have, through their several instruments, a language that can be understood everywhere—music capable of reaching the hearts as well as the ears of all classes in all nations.

The charm, too, of a quiet though cheerful demeanour, and of an unaffected enjoyment of the delight they afford to others, adds much to the agreeable effect of their performances. Bertha, their leader, when only three years and a half old, solicited her father to give her lessons on the violin, and made such progress that while yet a mere child she was able to take part in distinguished public performances. Moriz Mildner, first professor in the Conservatoire of Prague, became her further instructor; and her brother and sisters, Cecilia, Alags, Adolphe, and Albin, respectively four and a half, five and a half, seven, and eleven years old—began in turn to learn upon their little instruments; their elder sister, Antonia, aided with great natural skill and taste upon the pianoforte. Their father's birthday afforded an opportunity for surprising and gratifying him with a family concert, and gave Professor Mildner the idea of presenting them to the public. This led to their appearing before the Austrian Court at Tschl; and next at Salzburg, they appeared before Caroline, ex-Empress of Austria, who, struck with the resemblance of little Alags to Mozart, gave him the pet name of her little "Mozartl". M. Brousil and his children were now talked of throughout the Continent, and in due time visited its principal cities, being everywhere received with enthusiasm by the highest and most cultivated classes of society.

The Musical Brousil Family.

THE SHIP "BLEROIE CASTLE" IN A WHIRLWIND

The *Bleroie Castle* started from Gravesend on the 9th September last [1858], with troops for Kurrachee. On the 14th of October she came in contact with a waterspout, the particulars of which are given by the gentleman who made the accompanying sketch.—"We were in latitude 5° 55′ north, longitude 22° 57′ west: it was about half past three p.m., when the captain remarked that it looked very dark, and went on deck to see what it was. Then we heard the cries of 'Whirlwind!' and 'Whirlpool!', and on looking out I saw one on our port quarter, and another passed across us a little ahead of our bows. It was instantaneous but did us great mischief—carrying away our maintop gallant and royal masts, and the mizzentop gallantmast; and in a moment everything was in a dreadful state of wreck and confusion. It was nearly a dead calm at the time, and excessively hot; it rained tremendously for several hours afterwards.

The waterspout was about three feet in diameter; which, if it had fallen upon us would have filled us, and nothing could have prevented our going down."

MANNERS AND CUSTOMS OF THE CHINESE

Our special Artist and Correspondent recently [1859] visited Formosa, and has forwarded us the following descriptive details:—

Here, in this secluded spot of earth, mails are as yet things of the future; and if my pencil has too long lain dormant for you, the reason is now explained. This is a beautiful place, on the south-west coast of Formosa. One great advantage is that it scarcely ever rains; and, though tropically hot, the midday breezes do not fail to fan us from ten o'clock until sunset, making it one of the most delightful climates in the world. There is no cold weather here to speak of. From where I am writing I can see a chain of mountains, and I am told they average between 8000 and 10,000 feet in altitude; they are clothed to the very summits with trees, mostly camphor and other valuable timber. The island is rich in vegetable and mineral products, rattans, indigo, bamboo, camphor, sugar, rice, pineapples, &c. The interior has not been explored. On the other side of these mountains the country is in possession of the aborigines, and John Chinaman has a wholesome dread of these gentlemen.

This harbour has the most wonderful entrance you can imagine. A narrow channel between high rocks leaves scarcely room for two brigs abreast to pass in. The high rock near the village is supposed to be fortified—I say supposed, because a small wall and cardboard fort do not inspire one with much awe.

Thousands of a kind of palm grow on this hill, giving it a very tropical look. The rocks are a kind of coral, and most beautiful in their tints—a warm grey. They crumble very much; and last year, during the Swatow typhoon, an enormous mass fell into the sea, leaving a very shaky portion standing. The general appearance of the country reminds me much of Manilla, the bamboos especially.

The women here are all of the small-feet tribe, and are much given to "gorgeous array"; such scarlet and bright blue, orange and purple, I never saw; and yet they are mostly fishermen's wives, which shows a certain marital devotion on the part of their

The "Bleroie Castle" in a Whirlwind.—*(See preceding page.)*

husbands. Their hair is arranged in a most tasteful manner, and quite differently from our Canton friends, who are so much devoted to sombre-hued garments; they one and all wear artificial flowers in their hair, and to see them you would think them mandarins' wives at least. The houses, containing only one floor, are thatched generally with paddy, some of them being built of bamboo and mud, others of sun-dried bricks. The towns, however, are much cleaner than those of China. The bricks here are red, like those in Europe, not the blue-grey of the Canton brick. The streets are paved with small bricks, and a sewer runs on one side, in which pigs love to puddle.

Soon after I arrived here the mandarin of the village came on board, and, as I happened to be making a view of the rock, I thought if I took his phiz that I might make him more or less happy, so I proceeded immediately to transfer his jovial features to paper, and presented them to him with Celestial politeness. The other persons with him pronounced a favourable verdict and chewed betel vigorously. Then they took me ashore, and made me sit down in the public yamun, where my boy accompanied me, and the turbaned attendant brought us tea and betel nut and handed round the brass hubble-bubble, out of which I took three tiny whiffs. The mandarin then took me to a shop, where we sat down and ate pineapples with sugar, and after a little while to his private house, and asked me to paint him a face, which I did.

First Attempt to Launch the Great Eastern

Navigation Company's Steam-Ship.—(See next page.)

THE GREAT SHIP "GREAT EASTERN."

The *Great Eastern* is six times as large as our largest line-of-battle ship, and she can carry, when loaded, 22,500 tons, with accommodation for 4000 passengers and 10,000 troops. The deck is perfectly flush from stem to stern, a length of 696 feet, and breadth across the paddle-boxes 118 feet. All this immense length is double, and is also composed of a system of cells formed by plates and angle-irons. By this multiplication of rectilinear compartments, the ship is made almost as strong as if she were formed of solid iron, whilst, by the same system of construction, she is rendered as light, comparatively speaking, as a bamboo cane. There is a separate principle of life in every distinct portion, and she could not w ll be destroyed if even broken in two or three pieces, since the fragments, like those of a divided worm, would be able to sustain an independent existence.

THE CAB NS OF THE "GREAT EASTERN"

A suite of saloons of magnificent dimensions occupies the centre of the vessel, stretching down its length from about 180 feet from the head to about the same distance from the stern, and interrupted only by the engine-room. This suite of saloons is in two tiers, one above the other, light being admitted to the lower tier by the floors of the upper not extending the entire width of the saloons. The cabins lie all along both sides of the saloons. We have selected for our Illustration one of a group lying off the principal saloon. The end opposite the spectator is the ship's side, lined, of course, with wainscot; the port is represented as open, for the day is fine and warm; beneath the port is a couch or settee, covered with crimson velvet.

Family Saloon Cabin in the "Great Eastern."

THE "GREAT EASTERN" AT NEW YORK

Past the shores of Staten Island and on to the Narrows the *Great Eastern* continued her stately way, every minute increasing the

The Arrival of the "Great Eastern" at New York.—From a Sketch taken on the Jersey Side by E. Hall.

excitement and adding scores to the number of yachts, pleasure-boats and steamers swarming round. In vain the band of the *Great Eastern* played "Hail, Columbia!"; in vain the bands of the other steamers essayed "Rule Britannia"; music was drowned and shouted down with cheers. The "universal hat" went into the air—the "universal handkerchief" was waved, and the Americans, always "guessing," guessed for this time truly when they said no such ovation had ever been paid to any vessel in the world.

THE DISASTER TO THE "GREAT EASTERN"

Through the courtesy of a correspondent we are enabled to present our readers with an Illustration in connection with the breakdown of the Great Eastern in the recent gale.

Mr. Hayward, a passenger, has favoured us with a sketch of the grand saloon when the rolling of the vessel was at its worst; and a scene in which the ludicrous is more mixed with the painful and dangerous it would be difficult to conceive. We have received from Mr. Hayward, with his sketch, a lively account of the short but perilous voyage of the *Great Eastern*: "While all this was coming to pass, as serious a disaster or even worse, perhaps, was occurring in the grand saloon, where ladies and children principally, who had not ventured into the dining-saloon, were congregated. From side to side they were being swayed to and fro, along with the settees and sofas, tables and sideboards, sliding or rolling on the floor in an undistinguished mass. As the dining-room victims escaped the scene became worse. Some, being dashed against the iron balconies which gave way with the pressure, and falling on to the glass flooring at the sides, smashed it to atoms with fearful crashes. The iron columns became the temporary supports of clinging victims, and were loosened in their grasp, while three or four gentlemen were dashed with violence against the great mirror, and actually burst through it—the glass falling about them in slices, and inflicting cuts and bruises in all directions. The lower mirror was 'stove in' by a monster stove which had tumbled over at an early period, and was rushing about amongst us all with frightful rapidity; whilst the pianoforte was thrown down in the ladies' saloon, and began to play an entirely new tune, and to dance to its own sweet music. The lowing of three poor cows on the deck added to the horrors of the time, till at last they were swept down altogether, and the chief part of their house and its contents precipitated through the skylights, one poor animal hanging its head down and inquiring in a mournful manner what all the row was about. At last, to our astonishment, a swan—*rara avis in saloonis*—came flying down, and added to the picturesque but awful catastrophe.

All this fearful destruction and alarm continued day and night until we steamed off with a mended rudder. Let anyone who has seen the towering sides of the Great Eastern understand that the top platform of the paddleboxes actually dipped the water on each side several times, and they will, perhaps, have a slight notion of the extent of the slope of the saloon floor."

The Great Eastern continues to lie in Queenstown harbour. The Board of Trade have, it is understood, resolved to institute an official investigation into the disaster. [September 28, 1861.]

The Disaster to the "Great Eastern": State of her Grand Saloon during the Gale.

Inauguration of the Albert Viaduct at Saltash.

OPENING OF THE CORNWALL RAILWAY

The Saltash, or, as it is now called, the Albert, Viaduct, was opened on Monday week [May 2, 1859] by his Royal Highness the Prince Consort. This viaduct carries a railway across the estuary of the Tamar, which separates Devon from Cornwall, and the great breadth of which, together with its treacherous bottom, offered very serious obstacles to the engineer. Mr. Brunel is the engineer to whom is due the merit of having overcome these difficulties; and the Albert Viaduct is another example of his great mechanical genius. The railway itself, although only sixty miles long, presented unexampled difficulties, and in its construction has required seven tunnels and forty-three viaducts. The Albert Viaduct is on the tubular principle and is additionally supported by massive suspension chains. Furthermore, the principle of the bow-string girder is introduced, and a massive wrought-iron bow for each span gives increased rigidity to the whole structure. In forming the foundation for the side piers, Mr. Brunel had no difficulty, but to procure a firm basis for the pier in the centre of the river he had to overcome many. The water was seventy feet deep, and below it lay a stratum of mud and gravel of twenty feet thickness. To establish the foundation by means of a common coffer-dam would be of course impossible, but the difficulty was overcome by a novel application of the coffer-dam principle.

The two gigantic wrought-iron tubes were put together on the river bank and afterwards floated down to their places, and then raised as one piece. These are constructed of wrought-iron boiler plates; each span with its chain and ties weighs upwards of 1200 tons. When the tubes were raised to the requisite elevation the suspension-chains were attached to them, and the roadway was quickly constructed. The total length of the bridge, from side to side of the valley, is 2240 feet, 300 feet longer than the Britannia Tubular Bridge. The greatest width of the basement of the central support is only 30 feet, and the greatest height from the foundation to the summit is 260 feet. The quantity of iron used in the bridge is in all about 3850 tons, 2650 tons of wrought iron, and 1200 tons of cast iron. In the structure no less than 14,000 cubic feet of timber were used, and in the construction of the piers and stone columns no less than 459,000 cubic feet of masonry.

At about a quarter past twelve on May 2nd, the distant booming of a royal salute announced the arrival of the Royal train on the Devon side of the bridge, amidst the cheers of the spectators. His Royal Highness did not alight, but stood upon the steps of the Royal carriage and received the various deputations. After this the Royal train proceeded at a slow pace across the viaduct to the Cornwall side, whilst the battery stationed on the hill fired a Royal salute. As the train crossed the bridge the vibration and oscillating motion was plainly perceptible to those in the carriages, though, probably, the absolute deflection of the arches did not exceed one inch. As there are sharp curves at both ends of the bridge, which causes the line to assume a horseshoe form, an excellent view of it can be obtained in approaching it from either the Cornwall or Devon side. The train, therefore, after reaching Saltash station, continued on for about a quarter of a mile, to give the Royal party an opportunity of inspecting the bridge from one of the best points of view. On returning to Saltash, the Prince Consort alighted and minutely inspected the bridge and its works.

The Cornwall Railway was formally opened on the following day, and was thrown open for public traffic on Wednesday.

NEW GYMNASIUM AT OXFORD

The University of Oxford has just received an important addition towards the further practical development of physical education in the erection of a very extensive and commodious building devoted purposely to gymnastic exercises. It has been erected at the sole cost of one individual—Mr. M'Laren, who is not only a perfect master of his profession, and possessed of considerable scientific attainments bearing specially upon the science, but who occupies a high position in Oxford, gained by the time and attention he has bestowed on the physical training of the members of the University for several years past, and the untiring zeal and kindness of manner shown alike to all his pupils.

The building is situated in Albert-street and lies nearly in the centre of the University and City. Its appearance is most interesting, and far exceeds anything of the kind in this or any other country. Long rows of lofty windows give sufficient ventilation in summer, and, when in cold or damp weather these are closed, their place is efficiently supplied by a ventilating octagonal lantern rising from the dome-shaped centre roof, and fitted with swing sashes so adapted that they can be opened and shut with the greatest facility. A large centre space, open from the ground to the dome, allows every spot to be seen from every other, and not only gives accommodation for the apparatus for high climbing and swinging exercises, but affords facilities for the most complete control and supervision. One half of the upper floor is fitted up as a fencing school, while the corresponding portion contains modified exercises for young or delicate pupils. The area is entirely devoted to gymnastic exercises on a very extended scale; and, to ensure perfect safety, the floor is composed of a carefully-constructed padding, soft, thick, and elastic.

The physical condition of every pupil, child or adult, on his first entrance to the gymnasium, is carefully examined, so that his exercises may be adapted to that part which is defective.

The building is open daily from nine until four o'clock. Different exercises are meted out to different pupils in accordance with their age, habits and physical calibre. Mr. M'Laren appears to know what gymnastics truly mean—viz., the education of the body and the apportioning with skilful hand and experienced eye the quality and quantity of the exercises best suited to the special wants of each pupil. Here, too, may be seen that most interesting display—the human frame brought by skilful culture to its perfect attainable point of grace and strength; and in the afternoon, when the more advanced pupils are going through the various feats, it presents a scene so animated and striking that few turn from the visitors' gallery without a feeling of something more than interest in this well-contrived and ably-conducted institution.

THE CALLIOPE STEAM ORGAN

This musical instrument has been lately brought over from America by the inventor, Mr. Arthur S. Denny. This steam-organ consists of a framework of iron supporting two cylinders, upon which are arranged a series of brass tubes. Steam is conveyed into the cylinders, and from them admitted to the pipes, which produce the notes, opened by levers in connection with wires acted upon by ordinary pianoforte keys, or by pegs. The instrument is the softest-toned ever made, and is played upon at a pressure of 5 lb to the square inch. However, the force of steam may be increased to the extent of 150 pounds to the square inch; and such is the volume of sound given forth at this high pressure, that the instrument may be heard at a distance of twelve miles.

The Oxford Gymnasium—W. Wilkinson, Architect.

THE RECENT CONFLAGRATION IN SAN FRANCISCO

You will learn by this mail [May 3, 1861] that San Francisco is again in ruins; nor could the aspect of misery and desolation she now wears be under any circumstances more than equalled. Fire here has assailed its victim as does the intermittent fever of the country; for as the one waits, as it were, for returning strength and convalescence only to overwhelm with a relapse, so, in the midst of confidence and security, has this last conflagration swept everything before it, leaving San Francisco more helpless than before; regardless alike of iron or stone, vault or safe—heaping ruin on ruin—destroying life, property, confidence, and, I might almost say, hope.

The details are these:—A fire in a paint store, at eleven at night, with a hurricane to fan the oil and turpentine; flames burning with incredible rapidity in every direction, at once to windward and to leeward: these, travelling over the first few blocks of wooden buildings, gathering heat and power as they go, are borne on the brick and iron buildings in Montgomery-street—encircle them with flames—curl up their iron shutters—eat under their foundations, and leave them a wreck; and so to house after house—hotels, gambling-houses, banks, theatres, and stores—all (with scarcely an exception) fall; and in seven hours nothing remains of the business portion of the city but the ruins I have attempted to depict. It is difficult to say how many lives were lost—perhaps 20 in all.

The fire companies (which are here composed of gentlemen volunteers) behaved nobly, but were almost powerless: the blazing masses, even where approachable, sent back the water in hissing jets of steam. Those who held the hose-pipes were protected on their side by men who held wet blankets before them; and to their exertions and courage may be attributed the safety of such buildings as yet remain at the end of Long Wharf.

It was not until day broke, and the smoke in some degree had cleared away, that the full extent of the damage could be ascertained; and then it was discovered that the whole business portion of the city had been completely destroyed, and that, in seven hours, property had been scattered to the winds whose estimated value is fifteen millions of dollars.

Whether San Francisco will ever *entirely* recover from the blow, is, I think, doubtful. Under any circumstances, it will take time. Energy unlimited is here—such energy and elasticity as never were equalled in so large and so mixed a population. The Americans set us the example, and all follow it; even the Dutchman runs up his house in a day or two and no longer thinks of sleeping and smoking "upon it."

That San Francisco will eventually assume a *safer* position, I believe; contracts are already tendered for the construction of buildings of stone—the produce of the vicinity—at an expense one-third less than that which has hitherto been incurred for bricks.

The causes of these fires, and the direful effects they produce, may, I think, be traced to the general carelessness of those who live in the wooden portion of the city.

THE IMPREGNABLE IRON FORTRESS

About a month since [March 1860], the attention of the public was called to the defencelessness of the metropolitan port against the sudden attack of an enemy, by Mr. William John Hall, who on that occasion propounded his scheme for protecting the Thames and London against any such hostile approach. The public-spirited inventor of the Impregnable Iron Fortress, assisted by his engineer, Mr. William Bush, demonstrated upon that occasion the fearful risk to which the commercial community would be subjected in the event supposed, and challenged for this plan the most rigid scrutiny. Subsequently the large model and sectional drawings of the proposed fortress were exhibited at the Royal Society, where the details of the plan were submitted for the approbation of the Prince Consort and a large number of distinguished scientific visitors.

The cost of three such fortresses, upon the Nore Sand, the Goodwin and the Maplin, being under a million, is equivalent to something under three farthings in the pound, and therefore singularly economical.

There can be no doubt that the certainty of our being enabled to resist and repel an enemy is the very best security against hostile attack, and the fulcrum of defence could be nowhere placed to greater advantage than at the embouchure of our metropolitan river. The nature of the proposed fortification may be readily understood from the accompanying Engravings. The diameter of the structure at high-water mark will be 120 feet, and its height from that line about 130 feet—the total elevation being 240 feet. There are portholes for seventy cannon, twenty-one of which can always be brought to bear upon a given point. The internal space will

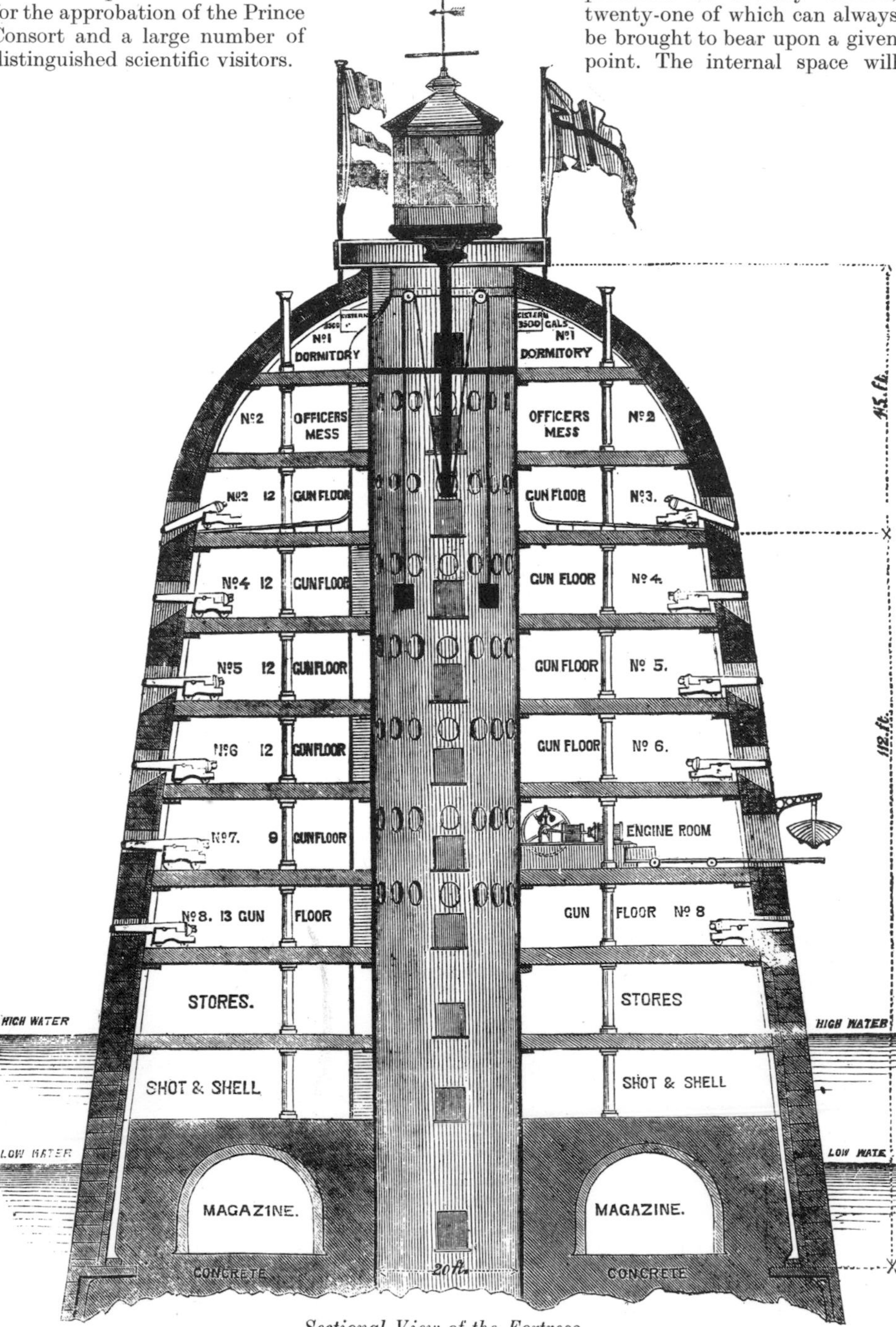

Sectional View of the Fortress.

Impregnable Iron Fortress for the Coast and River Defence of the United Kingdom.

accommodate a garrison of fifteen hundred, whilst, upon the assumption that one-third of that number will suffice for all ordinary purposes, Mr. Hall suggests the propriety and social policy of training a thousand destitute lads from our streets into useful members of society, as sailors, engineers, or mechanics. The ediface will have for its base an enormous caisson, sunk through the sand to the solid substratum, and filled with concrete, whilst the exterior wall will be composed of cast-iron blocks, each of five tons weight, so dovetailed and amalgamated by fused metal as to form a homogenous wall of iron, two feet in thickness, and absolutely impenetrable against all known projectiles.

The weight of the fortress will be, in iron, about 32,000 tons, making, with wood and concrete, a total weight of about 110,000 tons. Its magazines are to be formed in the solid concrete, and placed below low-water mark. It will be surmounted by a lighthouse, capable of being lowered into the capacious air-shaft, twenty feet in diameter from the base to the summit, and which will serve, among other important purposes, for pumping water by steam-power from an artesian well, and raising powder, shot, and shell from the magazines, and stores of all kinds, from the lower to the upper floors. The entire building will be heated by steam passing through the hollow columns supporting the several floors.

BRILL'S SWIMMING-BATH FOR LADIES

This magnificent establishment, which has recently been erected at Brighton, is the only sea-water swimming-bath for ladies in the kingdom, and, we believe, in Europe. The swimming-basin is of oblong form, 60 ft. in length by 25 ft. in breadth, 30 ft. from the floor to the ceiling. At one end is an elegant fountain, from which pours a continuous stream of fresh sea water, that flowing through passes off again to the ocean. The basin, which is lined with porcelain tiles, is $3\frac{1}{2}$ ft. deep by the fountain, increasing to $4\frac{1}{2}$ ft. in the deepest part. The bath is lighted by five large windows of ground plate-glass along one side, and down the other are ranged seventeen commodious dressing-rooms. The building having been designed specially for the purpose, at an expense of £7000, the fashionable visitors to the queen of watering-places have already bestowed their patronage. The water is always kept at the summer temperature of the sea by steam, and the woodwork throughout is of polished mahogany and pitch pine.

THE FIRST DAY OF OYSTERS

Our engraving represents a scene in a locality which still preserves the aspect of old London on a day which is still a small festival in its way. On the 5th of August oysters can be lawfully sold and eaten; and on the morning of that day these delicate testacea appear all over the town with a suddenness and abundance which prove an admirable organisation in the transmission from their beds on the coast, and their dissemination for retail sale. Old St. James's Day (July 15) was at one time the first day on which oysters were brought into the London market, and there was a notion that whoever ate oysters on that day would not want money throughout the year. At any rate, the custom of indulging in this luxury is largely observed on the occasion of their first coming to market, inclination and taste taking the place of superstition. It is said that £125,000 are yearly spent in London on oysters. The number sold in the streets is no less than 124,000,000 annually.

On Monday the legal opening of trade and traffic in oysters took place at Billingsgate. But seven vessels in all formed the oyster fleet, which in years past amounted at times to thirty-eight. The prices ruled very high, and natives were very scarce. The short supply is to be attributed to the fact that the day of Billingsgate as a "premier" oyster mart is past, the railways having obtained most part of the oyster conveyance.

"Una and the Lion" by the late John Thomas.

UNA AND THE LION

We here engrave one of the best works by the prolific, versatile and much-lamented sculptor, the late John Thomas. In this group, which has been executed in bronze for the International Exhibition, Una is naturally and appropriately posed, and the modelling of her figure sufficiently indicates the eminent position the artist would have taken if he had found more time, from the multifarious works, decorative, ornamental, and architectural, upon which he was engaged, to devote to the higher branches of his profession. It is not improbable that this subject was suggested to his inventive mind while engaged upon the enormous lions (30 ft. long) for the entrance piers of the Britannia Bridge over the Menai Straits. But why do not our artists, especially our painters—for no poet is more full of colour or more picturesque than Spenser—go more frequently for subject to that inexhaustible but unworked mine, "The Faërie Queene"? If Spenser had been a German poet, almost every public building throughout Germany would have been decorated with wall-paintings of the heroes, heroines, and adventures teeming in his allegorical and romantic poem. The episode of Una seeking her lost knight would afford many pictures beside the incident chosen by our sculptor. While she rests a lion rushes out from the thickest part of the wood and makes towards her with ravening mouth; but, as he drew near, awed by her virgin beauty, his ferocity disappears, and,

> Instead thereof he kissed her weary feet,
> And licked her lily hands with fawning
> tongue
> As he her wronged innocence did weet.
> O how can beauty master the most strong
> And simple truth subdue avenging wrong?

"The kingly beast upon her gazing stood", and thenceforward becomes her guardian and servant, whether she was waking or sleeping, till his noble breast was pierced by that fierce paynim, Sansloy. The "milk-white lamb" which accompanied the Royal virgin is well introduced: the "lowly ass, more white than snow", on which she rode was of course not necessary to point this situation, and has been judiciously excluded.

NORMAN'S NEW SWING CRADLE

This little arrangement, which is of the deepest interest to our fair readers, may be said to be a cradlelike cot which swings from head to foot, and not from side to side in the usual manner, the peculiarity consisting in the direction of the motion rather than in its form. There can be little doubt that the alteration in the direction of the motion here made is desirable; and to those who still retain the idea that it is advisable that a child should be rocked we would certainly recommend this cot, especially if the pillow be kept high and the rocking be not excessive, as in this case blood will not be thrown to the head. Mr. Norman's cradle may be said to be a swing with a cradle as a seat. As exhibited it is neat, and is draped in an aërial style. It has doubtless led many to covet it, if not to enter into the marriage state, with the hope of having such pretty furniture.

THE NATIONAL RIFLE ASSOCIATION

Inauguration by Her Majesty of the First Prize Meeting.

The first great trial of skill amongst the members of this association took place on Monday [July 2, 1860] on Wimbledon Common, her Majesty the Queen inaugurating the meeting by firing the first shot from a Whitworth rifle at a range of 400 yards. The fineness of the day attracted a vast number of persons to the spot, and at early hour in the afternoon the inclosure was well filled with company, who in the vicinity of the Queen's marquee increased to a dense crowd. There was a considerable attendance of ladies of distinction.

There were ten pairs of targets on the ground, each pair supported by a butt of earth, the latter divided by a space of eighty yards. The ranges varied from 200 to 1000 yards. At the lesser distances the targets are six feet by two feet, with a bull's-eye of eight inches; and at the greater ranges the targets are six feet square with a two feet centre and no bull's-eye.

Her Majesty and the Royal party were conducted from the reception-marquee along a raised platform, covered with crimson cloth, to the Royal shooting-tent, where Mr. Whitworth was presented to the Queen, and had the honour of explaining the mode in which her Majesty was to fire the first shot from one of his own rifles. A piece of scarlet cord attached to the trigger was handed to the Queen, who gently pulled it, and the Royal rifle-shot was fired. In an instant the red and white flag was shown by the marker, and "three points" were scored to the Queen of England. Loud cheering followed as her Majesty declared the prize meeting opened, and a salute of twenty-one guns announced the fact to the thousands who did not hear the few words spoken by her Majesty. A messenger from the butt arrived in a few moments with the diagram showing the exact spot struck by the bullet. It was exactly on the vertical line drawn through the centre of the bull's-eye, and one inch above the horizontal line.

The Royal party retraced their steps to the pavilion, and proceeded to examine a selection of guns and rifles of modern invention, before passing in the carriages along the whole line of firing-points, when they were loudly cheered by the volunteers and the great mass of the spectators who had now cleared all the boundaries, and were swarming over the common in thousands.

Her Majesty returned to Buckingham Palace by the same route as that by which the cortège had arrived.

Her Majesty Firing the First Shot at the National Rifle Prize Meeting.

The Prince of Wales landing at Quebec.—From

a Sketch by our Special Artist G. H. Andrews.

The Funeral of the late Prince Consort in the Chapel Royal of St. George's, Windsor.

THE COURT

December 14, 1861.—We are sorry to announce that the Prince Consort has been confined to his apartments for the last fortnight suffering from a feverish cold with pains in the limbs. The fever rather increased on Sunday last; but there were no unfavourable symptoms . . . .

December 21, 1861.—The transient notice we were able to give in our last Number of the indisposition under which the Prince Consort was suffering could not have prepared our readers in any degree for the most lamentable announcement, since made known all over Europe, of his Royal Highness's death on the evening of the day of our publication. No event of similar gravity has occurred since the premature death of the Princess Charlotte forty years ago, and it may be fairly said the national sympathy has never been more universally excited than at the present moment for our beloved Queen. Happily for the nation, her Majesty has up to this date borne her bereavement with a remarkable fortitude, and the latest bulletins describe the Queen to be in a state of calm resignation under the over-powering affliction.

DEATH OF THE PRINCE CONSORT

The death of His Royal Highness Prince Albert, on Saturday last [December 14, 1861], is the heaviest national calamity which has befallen this country for many years. Our gracious Queen! The hearts of her people bleed with hers. They share her agony of grief. They are overwhelmed with the same sense of desolation. Every family in the land is smitten with the awe and the sorrow which Death excites when he breaks into the domestic circle and snatches from it its chief pride and joy. For the moment there is no consolation. Even faith is stunned, and can only murmur forth in faltering accents, "Thy will be done."

Most of us can recall the joyous satisfaction we felt when the young Prince came hither from his father's Court to claim the fulfilment of what maiden love had promised. Royal marriages had so seldom in this country been a union of hearts as well as hands that this exception to the rule awakened the liveliest interest, and everything concurred to surround them with an atmosphere of affectionate sympathy, and to diffuse over the whole kingdom the gladness of hope. Nor from that day to the day of Prince Albert's death has that hope been dimmed or that sympathy impaired. The responsibilities of his exalted relationships were so calmly recognised, and their duties so faithfully discharged, that the public had come to regard him almost in the light of an institution, as confidently to be relied upon in its movements as it seemed to be necessary to complete national development. He marked out his own sphere with sagacious precision, and he filled it with propriety and consistency, and it is from him, and from him alone, that we derive our present notions of what is becoming to the position and character of a Prince Consort.

Brilliant as were the prospects of Prince Albert when he received the hand of our beloved Queen, to a thoughtful mind like his they must have presented not a few difficulties. From the domain of politics his activities and influence were jealously excluded, and his own self-respect, as well as his respect and affection for her Majesty, forbade his sinking down into a mere man of pleasure. In the work of government political etiquette and tradition prevented him from taking any part. However, he described a wide realm of usefulness in which he might become leader without exposing himself to party suspicions and without trespassing beyond constitutional limits. There was no reason why he should not become the patron of social reform; why he should not give himself to philanthropy, or bring his efforts and influence to bear upon raising the educational tone of the people; why he should not apply the stimulus of his favour and his example to scientific research. Accordingly, having mapped out for himself a broad area of duties, he zealously discharged them. He has done more than can be computed to elevate the taste of his adopted country—to give its intellect a useful direction—to trace a channel for its fertilising energy, and to open a new and beneficent sphere for the utilisation of leisure, means, and talent.

His name will ever be identified in the recollection of the public with the Great International Exhibition of 1851. Whether the original conception of that magnificent enterprise was due to his genius, or whether he adopted it, little matters: he made it his own by the enthusiasm with which he welcomed it, the zeal and perseverance with which he laboured to realise it, the unbounded affection with which he watched over its growth and helped it on to maturity. If by that competitive display of manufacturing art an emulative spirit was kindled in the bosom of this country prompting to higher aims and conducing to better results, the change is mainly due to the exertions and influence of the late Prince Consort.

We never know the full value of our blessings until we lose them. It would be impossible to estimate, even now, the immense advantage which the departed Prince conferred upon this country in his capacity as husband of our most gracious Sovereign and father of her children. To what extent his sagacious counsels may have helped to shape her Majesty's constitutional course, his suggestions and reflections may have soothed her anxieties, his loving sympathy may have relieved her from the pressure of responsibility, we have no adequate means of knowing; nor can we measure with any approach to precision the influence he may have exercised in forming the characters, directing the education, and developing the powers of his now orphaned children. But that we justly, albeit unconsciously, attributed to him his full share in the performance of these duties, and rated that share at a high value, may be inferred from the spontaneous outburst of our solicitude on behalf of the Royal widow and her family. The directness and strength of this national solicitude and sympathy testify to the unspeakable worth which the nation set upon the Prince Consort.

THE FUNERAL OF HIS LATE ROYAL HIGHNESS THE PRINCE CONSORT

On Monday December 23 [1861] the remains of the late Prince Consort were interred in the last resting-place of England's Sovereigns—the Chapel Royal of St. George's, Windsor. By the express desire of his Royal Highness the funeral was of the plainest and most private character; but the chief men of the State were assembled to do honour to his obsequies, and by every sign of sorrow and mourning the nation at large manifested its sense of the loss which it had sustained.

The Royal borough of Windsor at an early hour assumed the character of a garrison town owing to the number of soldiers arriving from London and Woolwich to take part in the mournful ceremonial of the day. Business was entirely suspended, and the groups of inhabitants who dotted the streets were exclusively occupied in discussing what every one appeared to think an individual loss.

At sunrise, when the union-jack was displayed at half-staff from the summit of the Round Tower, five-minute guns were fired from the end of the Long Walk by a battery of the Royal Artillery, and this was continued during the morning until the Royal remains left the Castle, when the firing was increased to minute time.

St. George's Chapel presented very much the same aspect as upon the recent occasion of the interment of the remains of the Duchess of Kent. A gradually rising platform led from the Castle-yard into the nave, along the sides and centre of which a stage had been erected upon a uniform level with the choir. This stage, as well as its approaches, and the floor of the chapel itself, were covered with black cloth; a simple white line marking the course of the bier from the west end of the nave to the entrance of the Royal vault.

The escort of Life Guards and the guard of honour of the Grenadier Guards, with colours draped, entered the Castle-yard at eleven o'clock and took up their respective positions.

At half past eleven o'clock the distinguished personages invited to be present in the chapel were conducted by the Lord Chamberlain's officers to their places in the choir.

Precisely at noon the mournful cavalcade moved from the castle to the chapel, the artillery firing minute guns and the troops presenting arms with the colours lowered. . . . The coffin was brought immediately over the Royal vault at twenty minutes to one o'clock, and, the mourners having taken their places, the Dean of Windsor read the usual lessons. Then the machinery supporting the bier was set in motion, and the coffin gradually descended into the vault, amidst a dead silence, broken only by the suppressed emotion of some of the mourners.

The Prince of Wales returned to the vault before leaving the chapel, and caused to be placed upon the coffin, three chaplets of flowers, the last tribute of affection to her Royal Consort from his widowed mother, who had forwarded them from Osborne that morning.

Society of Friends' Soup Kitchen in Manchester.

RELIEF FOR THE COTTON OPERATIVES OF LANCASHIRE

Great and sudden events, particularly those which are calamitous, impel men to avow their brotherhood. It was remarked, while muffled bells were tolling the dirge of the lamented Prince Consort last December [1861] England to-day feels as one family. Again is the great heart of this nation stirred with noble sympathy towards noble sufferers. Dead, indeed, should we be if, in full view of the sacrifices all classes depending on the cotton manufacture are called upon to endure in order that the nation may maintain a policy with respect to the disrupted States of America which a sense of honour obliges us to adopt, we failed to hold forth the hand of help as well as present the tribute of praise.

Of the 355,000 operatives in Lancashire usually employed in spinning and weaving cotton, only 40,000 are now working full time. The mills cannot be put to work until cotton is forthcoming, and the appearance of that substance does not depend upon us, but on the continuance of the blockade of Confederate ports. A calm consideration of the results of this tremendous disturbance fills the discerning mind with dismay. Lancashire's cry of distress has penetrated to the farthest extremities of the empire, and touched the hearts of all upon whose ears it has fallen. The tokens of a true sympathy press in from all quarters, and pour upon our shores the substantial evidences of their deep commiseration.

A soup-kitchen was opened in Manchester on April 8th [1862] and has been in constant operation since [until November]. The first engraving represents the boiling house, where excellent quality soup is made and sold at one penny a quart, less than the cost of the material, without calculating the expenses of labour or plant. A large proportion of tickets in exchange for which soup is given are purchased by the various relief societies for gratuitous distribution, in addition to bread and meat. At present 1000 gallons a day can be made, and that quantity could be largely increased at a small outlay.

THE PRESIDENT ELECT OF THE UNITED STATES

Abraham Lincoln, recently elected by the people of the United States of America to the Presidential chair, is a man whose career in life will furnish one of those richly illustrative chapters of history of which nations may well be proud. That he was born in obscurity; that his baptism was one of poverty; that he was early thrown upon his own resources; that he rapidly stepped from one occupation to another, from the merest manual toil to the highest intellectual pursuits, mastering all with incredible ease; that by sheer force of mind, will and character, unaided by any great military conflict, or by any revolutionary ferment, he fought his way from one of the lowest positions of life to the very highest to which an American can aspire, reflects glory not merely on the man who has achieved this marvellous success, but upon the country whose social and political institutions made it possible. We do not pretend that President Lincoln owes nothing to opportunity; but America may justly boast that when character and opportunity meet she puts no insuperable barrier in the path of any of her citizens to the topmost place of authority and honour.

It is worthy of note that Mr. Lincoln is a type—a rare one, no doubt—of a considerable class of his countrymen. Self-reliant, observant, keen to discover every opening in the pathway of life, prompt to take advantage of it, believing that his qualifications to enter any sphere constitute a patent right to occupy it, full of energy, of indomitable will, patient, industrious, unswervingly persistent—in all these attributes the new President represents the distinctive character of the best class of his fellow-citizens. There are many cast in the same mould, although, undoubtedly, he is *primus inter pares.* "Excelsior" is their motto; to toil upwards is the rule of their life. What they become is held to depend upon what they are and what they can do. They look for their resources chiefly within themselves. They know that they must win position—that it will not be made for them. They may often over-estimate their capabilities, miss their footing, mistake their way; but it is of such men that great nations are made.

In the rapidity of his ascent from obscurity to greatness the newly-elected President strikingly resembles the country he is called to govern. From the Declaration of Independence to the present day the progress of the United States of America has outrun even the wildest anticipations. The handful of people who, less than a century ago, constituted a neglected and oppressed colony of England have germinated into a great nation—a mighty federation of republics. America owes much of her present eminence to the profound sagacity of her early statesmen. Nothing but a wise combination of State autonomies with federal unity, which their genius devised, and which their successors have faithfully developed, could have given free play to such an endless variety of popular characteristics, and, at the same time, welded together into one consistent whole such a multiplicity of different and sometimes conflicting interests. It must be remembered that all the nations of Europe have contributed to swell the population of the United States,—that the States differ widely from each other, not merely in geographical position, climate, and natural productions; but in social structure, industrial interests, and even religious views. To leave to every State its own social and political individuality, and yet to unite the whole in one grand federation, having a common army and navy, a common diplomacy, a common system of customs, a common coinage, and a common Legislature and Executive for federal purposes, was a happy conception, the profound practical wisdom of which has been shown by experience.

THE THREAT OF CIVIL WAR IN AMERICA

Everything tends to point to a struggle of the most energetic and unyielding description when once it has actually begun. Notwithstanding some inequalities of strength, we know enough of the spirit of all Americans, when their blood is up and their impulsive feelings thoroughly enlisted in a cause, to be sure that conquest, in the strict sense of the

Fight at Hainsville, on the Upper Potomac—Advance of the Wisconsin men (Federalists) on the secessionist Position.

term, of the seceding States is just an impossibility. It may happen that the power of the North may be so far predominant after a time as to enable its forces to devastate the territory of its adversaries, although even that is not by any means a proximate event. It may be that ere long a slave insurrection will be added to the difficulties which the South will have to encounter, and who shall say what may be the consequences of such a thing? But that the revolting communities will ever be brought by coercive measures into the federation which we have hitherto known as the United States is about as likely as the return to their allegiance to England of her then colonies in North America was after the Declaration of Independence. Unless some miracle of compromise be performed, the world must henceforth expect to see two moderate Republics established on that continent where for many years it has been accustomed to contemplate the growth of a nation which bade fair to be stupendous in its greatness. [May 4, 1861.]

ESTIMATED STRENGTH OF THE NORTHERN AND SOUTHERN ARMIES

In another letter by the *Times* Special Correspondent, written on the 19th ult., he estimates the effective strength of General M'Dowell's army at 30,000 infantry, with about sixty field guns, and ten squadrons of cavalry. He reckons General M'Clellan's corps in Western Virginia at 35,000 men, and General Patterson's division at 22,000. The reserve at Washington he estimates at 16,000 men, the troops in Maryland at 7400 men, and the corps lying at Fortress Monroe and Hampton at 11,000.

The strength of the Southern army under General Beauregard at Manassas Junction was, he says, estimated at 60,000 men. The rest of the Southern army he reckons at 18,000 or 20,000 men at Norfolk, and 8000 to 9000 at Aquia Creek, besides General Johnson's corps of some 10,000 men. [August 10, 1861.]

SKIRMISH BETWEEN THE FEDERAL AND THE SECESSIONIST TROOPS ON THE UPPER POTOMAC

Our Special Artist in America, writing from the Federal Camp, on the 7th ult., says he managed to pay a flying visit to Patterson's division at Martinsburg, getting up in time to witness his gallant and successful dash at the Confederate troops, on the 2nd ult., at Hainsville, on the Upper Potomac. In reference to this brisk encounter he has forwarded a Sketch showing the advance of the Wisconsin men through the wheatfields, after fording the river, to attack the enemy's position. Their behaviour (he says), considering it was the first time they were under fire, was admirable: they went on very steadily, poured in two or three volleys, and then, making a rush with bowie-knife and revolver, sent the Disunionists flying towards Winchester, leaving behind them many dead, wounded, and

Naval Engagement in Hampton Roads: the Confederate iron-plated steamer Merrimac (or Virginia) running into the Federal Sloop Cumberland.—From a Sketch by T. Nast.

Federal Cavalry Scouts entering the Depot at Manassas Junction.

prisoners. The building burning in the distance is a barn in which they had planted some guns. A few shells sent into it by the Federal artillery soon dislodged them, and completed the discomfiture of their already wavering troops. [August 10, 1861.]

THE CONFEDERATE ACCOUNT OF THE NAVAL FIGHT IN HAMPTON ROADS

In the Confederate Congress, on the 10th ult., the following communication was received from the Executive, in response to the resolution of Mr. Lyons calling for the report of the naval battle in Hampton Roads. It will be observed that the Merrimac is throughout called the Virginia, having been renamed by the Confederates:—

Confederate States' Steam-battery Virginia, off Sewall's Point, March 8.

"Flag Officer [F. Forrest],—In consequence of the wound of Flag-officer Buchanan, it becomes my duty to report that the Virginia left the yard this morning at eleven o'clock, steamed down the river past our batteries, and over to Newport News, where we engaged the frigates Cumberland and Congress and the batteries ashore, and also two large steam-frigates, and a sailing-frigate and several small steamers armed with heavy rifled guns. We sank the Cumberland, and drove the Congress ashore, where she hauled down her colours and hoisted the white flag; but she fired upon us with the white flag flying, wounding Lieutenant Minor and some of our men. We again opened fire upon her, and she is now in flames. The shoal water prevented our reaching the other frigates. This, with approaching night, we think, saved them from destruction.

Our loss is two killed and eight wounded. Two of our guns have the muzzles shot off; the prow was twisted, and armour somewhat damaged; the anchor and all flagstaffs shot away, and the smoke-stack and steam-pipe were riddled. The bearing of officers and men was all that could be wished; and, in fact, it could not have been otherwise, after the noble and daring conduct of the flag officer, whose wound is deeply regretted by all on board. Enclosed I send the surgeons' report of the casualties.

I have the honour to be, Sir, very respectfully,

Your obedient servant,

CATESBY AP. R. JONES, Ex. and Ord. Officer."

[April 5, 1862.]

FEDERAL CAVALRY ENTERING MANASSAS JUNCTION DEPOT

Our Special Artist has forwarded to us an Illustration of the Federal cavalry scouts entering the Dépôt at Manassas Junction, on the 10th ult.

The first into Manassas was a party of cavalry scouting in advance of the Federal columns. The dépôt was found to be on fire, all kinds of stores smouldering in heaps or lying strewed about in the greatest possible confusion. There were great numbers of muskets, pistols, and bowieknives—the latter with "Yankee-slayer" engraved in large letters on the blades—all kinds of wearing apparel and officers' trunks, and military stores of every description. The station was surrounded by earthworks and fascine batteries. All the guns had been removed, except here and there one which had tumbled into a ditch.

Here, as at Centreville, there were some sham wooden cannons. [April 12, 1862.]

SERIOUS RIOTS IN NEW YORK

The attempt to enforce the conscription in New York has either provoked, or been made the excuse for, formidable riots. That city was for three days in the hands of a mob, which commenced with stopping the draughting, destroying the building in which it was going on, and assaulting the officers.

Balloting began on Saturday, the 11th ult., and during that day the names of more than 2000 conscripts were drawn. On the morning of the 13th a mob assembled in front of the Provost Marshal's office, broke into it, destroyed the ballot-boxes, and fired the building, which, with the adjoining houses, was completely destroyed, as the firemen refused to attempt to extinguish the flames. The mob, which is said to have consisted of about 15,000 persons, and to have been headed by a Virginian named Andrews and some three hundred other leaders, afterwards dispersed in strong bodies throughout the city, and committed atrocious outrages.

The Riots in New York: the mob lynching a Negro in Clarkson-Street.

The disturbances spread to Staten Island, and some negroes' houses were burned in Brooklyn; but few or no further murders of blacks were committed, as the negroes had fled from the city. On the 15th the riots continued, business was again suspended, and there were several fresh collisions between the troops and mob in the upper part of New York.

New York papers of the 18th state that the riots had almost entirely subsided on the previous day. The wards where the greatest excitement had prevailed were filled with large forces of military, who patrolled the streets entirely unmolested by the populace. The Republican press argue that the riots in New York are really part and parcel of the Southern rebellion, while the Democratic press assert the obnoxious conditions of the draught to be the sole cause. But Americans would gladly escape the principal blame and lay it on the Irish. [August 1, 1863.]

THE MOB SACKING AND BURNING THE COLOURED ORPHAN ASYLUM

The disturbances on Monday, July 13—the first day of the outbreak in New York—culminated in an outrage which fitly crowned the day's excesses. The Coloured Orphan Asylum, a large plain building situated in Fifth-avenue, was fired about five o'clock in the afternoon. The infuriated mob, eager for any outrage, were turned that way by the simple suggestion that the building was full of coloured children. A few policemen who attempted to make a stand were instantly overpowered, several being severely or fatally injured. While this was going on a few of the less evil-disposed gave notice to the inmates to quit the building. The sight of the helpless creatures stayed for a moment even the insensate mob; but the orphans were no sooner out than the work of demolition commenced. First the main building was gutted and then set on fire. While it was burning the large wing adjoining, used as a dormitory, was stripped inside and out. The

The Riots in New York: Destruction of the Coloured Orphan Asylum.

Family Worship in a Plantation in South Carolina.

fire-engines were there in great numbers, but were not permitted to work, except upon the adjacent buildings. Eyewitnesses of the dastardly outrage state that they saw scores of half-intoxicated Irishwomen, staggering along under burdens of bedding and clothing, shrieking as they reeled along, "Hooray for Jeff. Davis!" "Death to the Naygurs!"

A NEGRO HANGED

Towards night, one negro got into difficulty with a white man; loud words followed, and the crowd set upon the black man. He retreated a little way, and finally drew a pistol and discharged its contents into the crowd. The ball took effect in the breast of one of the assailants, who fell forward as if killed. The negro, terrified at the act, took to his legs and ran with all possible speed towards Hudson-street, the affray having taken place in Cornelia-street. He was overtaken and severely beaten. He was then stripped of all his clothes except the shirt, and a rope was loudly demanded. One was procured from a store near by—a stout clothes-line—and it was attached to the negro's neck. The other end was then slung over a tree, and he was drawn up several feet. Some of them then set his shirt on fire, and the sight presented was a frightful one. At last orders were given to have the body cut down; and this was done.

SLAVES AT WORSHIP ON A PLANTATION IN SOUTH CAROLINA

In the character of the negro as developed in the Slave States of America the two most marked features are his capacity for strong attachment and fidelity to his master when kindly treated and his susceptibility to religious influences. This latter quality is carried in many cases into the region of fanaticism; but a deep, simple, and fervent piety characterises a large portion of the slave population, especially those advanced in years.

The Illustration is from a sketch made in a rude chapel erected for the slaves on a cotton plantation near Port Royal (South Carolina), now [December 5, 1863] in the possession of the Federal forces.

The "incumbent" was an intelligent old house servant, a slave. He could read, but not write; and his extempore sermons, although sometimes marred by his predilection for high-sounding phrases and long words (not always appropriate), were characterised by strong good sense and a certain rude native eloquence, often rising to the dignity of pathos, and admirably adapted to the comprehension and temperament of his audience. The Methodist persuasion is the one which finds most favour among the slaves in the Southern as well as among the free negroes in the Northern States.

ILLUSTRATIONS OF THE WAR IN AMERICA

A blockade-runner has brought us some sketches from our Special Artist in Charleston, one is engraved on the next page. Respecting this Engraving—"The Assault on Fort Wagner on the night of July 18"—our Special Artist and Correspondent writes as follows:—

"I returned from the south-west just in time to witness this most formidable of all attempts made by the enemy on the defences of Charleston. You are already doubtless aware that the Federals succeeded a fortnight since in effecting a lodgment of their forces on the islands forming the approaches to the city. A temporary success enabled them to throw up works in front of Fort Wagner, and to commence an advance on the last-named stronghold. In conjunction with their iron fleet, which took up an enfilading position seawards, they maintained a heavy fire of mortars, 11-inch and 15-inch guns, on the devoted sandworks during the whole day

Assault on Fort Wagner, Charleston Harbour, on the Night of July 18—the rush of the Garrison to the Parapet.

preceding the assault. At a little after eight in the evening the Yankees attacked with three brigades, believing that a bombardment of twelve hours' duration from ordnance of hitherto unheard-of calibre would have demoralised or driven the garrison out. They could not have had less than 8000 men engaged, some of whom reached the parapet and died there; yet, with only 1500 to oppose them, they were eventually driven back with a loss equal to the entire force of the Confederates in the fort. The period chosen for my illustration is the moment when the last shell fired from the fleet burst over the battery; and the troops, illuminated by the glare, are seen rushing to the parapet to repel the assault. Some of the enemy have already reached the crest of the work, but only to pay for their temerity by falling where they stand.

"The horrible scene that met the eye the morning after the attack beggars description. All through the night we could hear the screams and groans of the wounded lying within a few yards of us; but as a continual fire was kept up by the advanced pickets it was impossible to do anything for them without running great risk of being shot. Early in the morning, however, the Federals sent a flag of truce asking for a cessation of hostilities, that they might bury their dead. The first demand was granted, but they were told they could not be permitted to come within the lines of the Confederates, and that the latter would perform the last offices for the fallen enemy. In the ditch they lay piled, negroes and whites, four and five deep on each other; there could not have been less than 250 in the moat, some partially submerged; and, altogether, over 600 were buried by the Southerners." [September 26, 1863.]

A RAILWAY INCIDENT

(*From our Special Correspondent.*) I left Charleston with some of the regiments ordered to report to General Johnston in view of the immense operations about commencing in the south-west. The campaign in the valley of the Mississippi will, I believe, decide the duration of the war; and the battles that will be fought there, under the respective leaderships of General Johnston and General Grant (Federal), will I think, be on a much larger scale than those of Virginia.

The incident illustrated in the Engraving on the next page will give you an idea of the perils of travelling on a used-up military railroad. Three times the cars ran off the line, injuring many of the men, and on one of these occasions the carriage in which I was got smashed all to pieces, and for some time I was unaware of what had taken place until I shook myself together, and then I found that my arm was badly bruised. We can hear heavy firing in the direction of Vicksburg. The place still holds out bravely, with a loss altogether, so says a prisoner, of nearly 20,000 men. The dead are lying unburied between the besieged and besiegers. The town is completely invested, and we only get intelligence by an occasional courier, who runs the gauntlet of the Yankee lines. [August 8, 1863.]

The war news, important as it is, containing notice of the surrender of General Lee, pales before the painful interest of the intelligence brought by the Nova Scotia on Wednesday. President Lincoln has been shot dead in a theatre at Washington, and Mr. Seward stabbed, it is feared mortally, while lying on a sick bed. The murderer of Mr. Lincoln—Wilkes Booth, the brother of the well-known actor Edwin Booth, and himself an actor—has been arrested; but his accomplice, who made the attack on Mr. Seward, has for the time escaped. The whole of New York is draped in black, and there is general mourning throughout the country.

In accordance with the requirements of the Constitution, Mr. Andrew Johnson, the Vice-President, was, on Saturday, sworn in as President. He said:—"The duties are at present mine—I shall perform them; the consequences are with God. Gentlemen, I shall lean upon you; I feel I shall need your support. I am deeply impressed with the solemnity of the occasion and the responsibility of the duties of the office I am assuming." Mr. Johnson appeared remarkably well, and his manner created a favourable impression. The new President has announced that he will make no changes in the Cabinet. [April 29, 1865.]

WAR NEWS—SURRENDER OF GENERAL LEE

The taking of Petersburg and Richmond was quickly followed by the surrender of General Lee. On the 9th inst. he yielded up his whole force (estimated at 25,000 men), to General Grant. The two Generals had been in communication from the 7th as to the terms. Grant pointed out that nothing but surrender was left. Lee, while not agreeing with this, thought it best to stop further effusion of blood, and asked for terms. The terms granted were generous.

The Northern newspapers assert that Lee's troops had, for the most part, deserted him before his surrender. He will, it is said, do all in his power to promote peace.

The Federal armies are closing in on Johnston's force, which is the only Confederate army east of the Mississippi. Johnston had evacuated Raleigh, and gone, it was said, to Greensborough. It is not likely, however, that he would be able to hold out there or anywhere else. The report of Federal successes in Alabama is confirmed, and the siege of Mobile is rapidly progressing.

President Lincoln, in a speech which he made at Washington, said that recent successes gave hopes of a righteous and speedy peace. Reconstruction would be fraught with great difficulties, which would be increased by any differences of opinion among loyal people. It was "immaterial whether the rebellious States were considered in or out of the Union;" and "all should join in the acts necessary to restore proper practical relations between the rebellious States and the Union."

The general tone of the Northern press is very conciliatory. The *New York Times*, however, recommends "the extreme sentence of the law" against Jefferson Davis. The *Tribune*, on the contrary, advises that the utmost moderation should be exercised towards the Southern leaders.

Several members of the Virginia Legislature, with the assent of the Federal authorities, who promised safe-conducts to the Governor and members of the State Legislature, had issued a summons for an extraordinary session to learn and consider the terms upon which Virginia may be received back into the Union.

Secretary Stanton, after consultation with Grant, has decided to stop all draughting and recruiting; to curtail all purchases of arms, ammunition, and supplies; to reduce the expenses of the military establishments and the number of general and staff officers to the actual necessities of the situation; and to remove all military restrictions.

Train with Reinforcements for General Johnston running off the Track in the Forests of Mississippi.

THE CURRENT PARISIAN CRAZE

The Parisians are always going mad about something, and the prevailing lunacy in fashionable society just now runs upon the practice of an egregious little art, called "Le Decalcomanie." Duchesses and demimondians, ambassadresses and actresses, all are determined decalcomaniacs. There are also "Le Decalcographie" and "La Decalcochrome", but the "manie" is the favourite. It is first cousin to the pleasing, but nearly extinct, art of "Potichomanie", which was so long a source of amusement to those who had nothing better to do, and enabled ladies to cut their pretty fingers and cover themselves with sticky strips of paper in the attempt to make good glass look like bad china.

"La Decalcomanie"

"La Decalcomanie" may be described as a method of spoiling tea-cups and saucers. You choose a nice white saucer, cup, or plate, or a snuff-box, or a fire-screen, or anything else with a nice, smooth, white surface, and stick a sheet of paper covered with some coloured design upon it by means of a thick varnish. Then you wash away the paper with a wet flannel. The coloured design remains, and your art of decalcomanie is accomplished. When you grow tired of spoiling your crockery—which becomes inexpressibly hideous under the decalcomaniacal process—you may varnish down the designs on the back of your hands, or on your nose, by way of a change. The "great sensation" in the thing lies in the amount of lamentable failures you are drawn into, and the number of francs you spend in the purchase of a box of materials, complete, for practising the delightful mystery. I don't bear the comely lady shopkeeper, and her comelier daughter in the Passage de l'Opera, any ill will for having extracted from me the sum of eighteen francs fifteen sous for a cardboard box full of sticky stuff and coloured patterns, but the next time I invest in decalcomanie I'm a Dutchman—that's all!

The "Monocle" or "Restoscope"

Another New Year's toy may be mentioned, but it is a cheaper and more sensible one. This is the "Monocle" or "Restoscope," which, by means of a single lens, produces all the phenomena of binocular vision when applied to a single *carte de visite*. The roundness and relief given, and the minutiae of texture and detail revealed in album portraits by the "monocle" are truly marvellous.

The photographers are all working as hard as mill-horses; for the visiting-cards left or sent by post on New-Year's Day—and their name is legion—are considered incomplete unless they are accompanied by a portrait of the sender. By-the-way, sundry recent advertisements in English papers enlightened us as to a curious system growing up among the ladies and gentlemen advertising for governesses of requiring by return a *carte de visite* portrait of the candidates for the post they offer. If there be any virtue in physiognomy, it becomes at once facile to tell what

Accident on the East India Railway last October.

ACCIDENT ON THE EAST INDIA RAILWAY

We give an Engraving of an accident which took place on October 1st [1862] on the East India Railway, near the station of Ahmoodpore, between Burdwan and Rampore Hant. In consequence of a heavy flood the small nullah which runs under the bridge was swollen to a great depth, the rush of water scouring out the foundations and occasioning the falling in of the arches. The driver of the first down-train on October 24, the morning after the accident, first perceived an unevenness in the line when two or three hundred yards off. He also saw a coolie kneeling close to the rails and holding up his hands. He immediately shut off his steam, put on the break, and, with his fireman, jumped off, calling to the guard as the break-van passed him to do the same. Fortunately the train consisted of only goods-waggons and a break-van, and no life was lost.

Patent Folding Furniture by Mannstein of Vienna.

kind of a temper your possible governess possesses: whether she will govern her pupils by the law of kindness or snub them and rap their knuckles. Shade of John Caspar Lavater!‡ has it come to this? [January, 1863.]

‡ John Caspar Lavater, an eighteenth century theologian, mystic and physiognomist.

MANNSTEIN'S PATENT FOLDING FURNITURE

A most interesting collection of patent furniture by Herr Mannstein, of Vienna, is to be seen at the International Exhibition [1863]. The figure in our Engraving has his hands resting on the ends of a bedstead which is so constructed that it can be formed into a child's crib of 2 ft. in length by 15 in. in breadth, or a bedstead of 6 ft. in length by 3 ft. in breadth, or to any intermediate size, and its construction is such as to combine great strength with this convenience. In principle of action it is similar to the lazy tongs; hence the height of the lattice-work around decreases as the bedstead is enlarged.

Mr. Coxwell's High Level Balloon at Crystal Palace

To the left of this is a whatnot consisting of four circular trays, so formed that by withdrawing a bolt and applying pressure all are collected together on the level of the third, which is about the usual height of a table. Upon this group of discs a circular top fits, similar to that of an ordinary loo-table, and thus a table or whatnot is formed at the option of the owner.

At the back of the Illustration two wardrobes are shown which are designed to act as packing-cases for six dining-room chairs, two armchairs, a sofa, and a loo-table, and it is difficult to say which purpose they best fulfil. The furniture to be inclosed in the two wardrobes is so made as to fold and divide into parts.

At the right-hand side of our figure an elongated invalid-chair is shown which is capable of being arranged as an ordinary easy-chair and of being extended into a camp-bedstead, and for travelling of assuming the form of the strong packing-case shown.

In Vienna the whatnot and loo-table combined sell for £7; but owing to the expense of transit they are £10 when delivered in London. The bedstead is £7 5s. in London; the folding easy-chair, £3; and the two wardrobes with furniture complete are only £40, in walnut wood, as delivered in our capital.

First Despatch of Mail-Bags through the Pneumatic Tube.

OPENING OF THE PNEUMATIC DESPATCH MAIL SERVICE

A company was registered in 1859 for the establishment in the metropolis of lines of pneumatic tube for the more speedy and convenient circulation of despatches and parcels, and an Act of Parliament received the Royal assent in the same year empowering the company to open streets and lay down tubes for the purpose. The directors, having satisfied themselves and the shareholders of the complete mechanical success of the company's system of transmission, by experiments upon a short line of tube at Battersea, and of its economy and peculiar application to the purposes in view, determined on laying down a permanent tube of thirty inches gauge between the Euston station and the North-western District Post-office, Eversholt-street. This tube, with the stations, machinery, and appliances, is completed, and is found to work most efficiently. The length of the tube is not considerable, reaching a distance of only a third of a mile. The transmission of the first batch of mailbags through it took place yesterday week [February 20, 1863]. Several of the principal officials from the Post Office were present during a part of the operations. The whole of the works were in the most admirable order, and, on the arrival of the first mail-train at 9.45 a.m., the mail-bags, thirty-five in number, were placed in the cars by 9.47. The long chamber was then exhausted, and the train containing the first mails ever dispatched by the agency of the atmosphere were blown through the tube to the station at Eversholt-street, reaching their destination at 9.48. The success of the experiment has been so decided that the company will commence the Holborn extension at once, and intend proceeding as rapidly as possible with the main work and all its ramifications.

HOME AND ABROAD

At last the streets are fairly assuming a foreignised and provincialised appearance. Our own country folks are as easy to make out in their peregrinations as our visitors from the Rhine, the Seine, and the Danube. They keep together in bodies, apparently apprehensive of the dreadful consequences of losing each other, and of being pounced upon by some dreadful ogre of a metropolitan rogue, who would infallibly witch the sovereigns out of their breeches pockets, in spite of the whole blue-coated force from A to Z. The foreigners keep also in small parties, and go "maundering" about, calling a halt every few minutes to retreat into a door-way, and have a noisy consultation over the map of London. The first thing the Frenchmen do—almost before they go to the [International] Exhibition—is to plunge down into the Thames Tunnel. I could never make out whether the practice is founded upon an intense natural love of tunnel engineerings in the abstract, or whether it is not to the genius of their countryman, Sir Isambard Brunel, that the homage is paid. I suspect the latter to be the true charm which collects a bearded group in the bows of every *Waterman* as she leaves the Hungerford pier. It is curious to observe with what gusto foreigners of all countries, from Italy to Norway, take to English porter. I dined the other day at the *table d'hôte* of a Leicester-square hotel, along with some forty or fifty ladies and gentlemen from over the water. Just four people had wine, light French wine; the rest paid their respects and that in the heartiest and most frank style, to ale and porter, appearing, indeed, to enjoy the coarser liquor more than I ever saw Frenchmen do the delicious product of their own vineyards. In France, be it observed, beer is never drunk with meals. You cannot get a bottle of the light foaming Lyons, or the tart bitter Strasbourg beer, to wash down your *fricandeau* or your *civet de lièvre*. Rich and poor use either wine or water—doing, however, it must be confessed, little justice to the former. It is curious to observe how little value for their own consumption, the French set upon their wines. They do not appear to be worthy of the grapes which nature has bestowed upon them. It is rare to see a Frenchman sit over his bottle after dinner; and if he does, it is often—a terrible instance of heterodox taste—over a bottle of champagne. Here, however, as I have said, the *portare beer* finds great favour in their eyes; the performances in the way of swilling it which I have seen being sufficient to conciliate the respectful admiration of Barclay and Perkins themselves.

THE MARRIAGE OF THE PRINCE OF WALES AND PRINCESS ALEXANDRA OF DENMARK

The joy-bells ring out, clear and silver-voiced, and their clangour ascends to the Empyrean, mingled with countless exclamations of delight, with countless prayers for the future and lasting happiness of Albert Edward Prince of Wales and his young bride. In a thousand churches last Sabbath were devotional aspirations uttered to Him who disposes of Kings and Princes as of slaves and swineherds; to the King of Kings, before whom sceptre and crown must tumble down, and be made equal in the earth with the poor crooked scythe and spade, fervent orisons from myriads of hearts went forth for blessings to be vouchsafed to this union; for this marriage to be in spirit and in truth one of affection, to be ripened in time into a bond of mutual confidence and esteem. "God bless the Prince of Wales!" "God bless Princess Alexandra!" Inscriptions such as these have blazed in gas or scintillated in many-coloured lamps, or have been 'broidered on banners, or intertwined with festoons of flowers all over the land this fortnight past; but the blessings invoked find a deeper echo in the people's hearts.

Those who care little for pageantry and raree shows—those who are poor, and sick, and unhappy—those who can never hope to bask in the sunshine of Alexandra's face—can still pray, and are still praying, for Heaven's blessings on her marriage—the blessings without which the bridal contract is null and void and the Office a mockery, the blessing in whose absence the orange blossoms wither and the bride's veil turns to sable crape.

Loyalty in this country is a Great Fact; and, like all other facts, it is a résumé of subordinate and ascertained truths. We are not an imaginative people; we are not frivolous; we are not volatile; nor was it with sudden and unthinking rashness that we became fervently loyal. We went, as we have always gone, upon Facts. At this distance of time it is easy to account for the unpopularity of many of our Sovereigns. We have the Facts before us. We know now that they were

The newly-married pair leaving Windsor for Osborne.

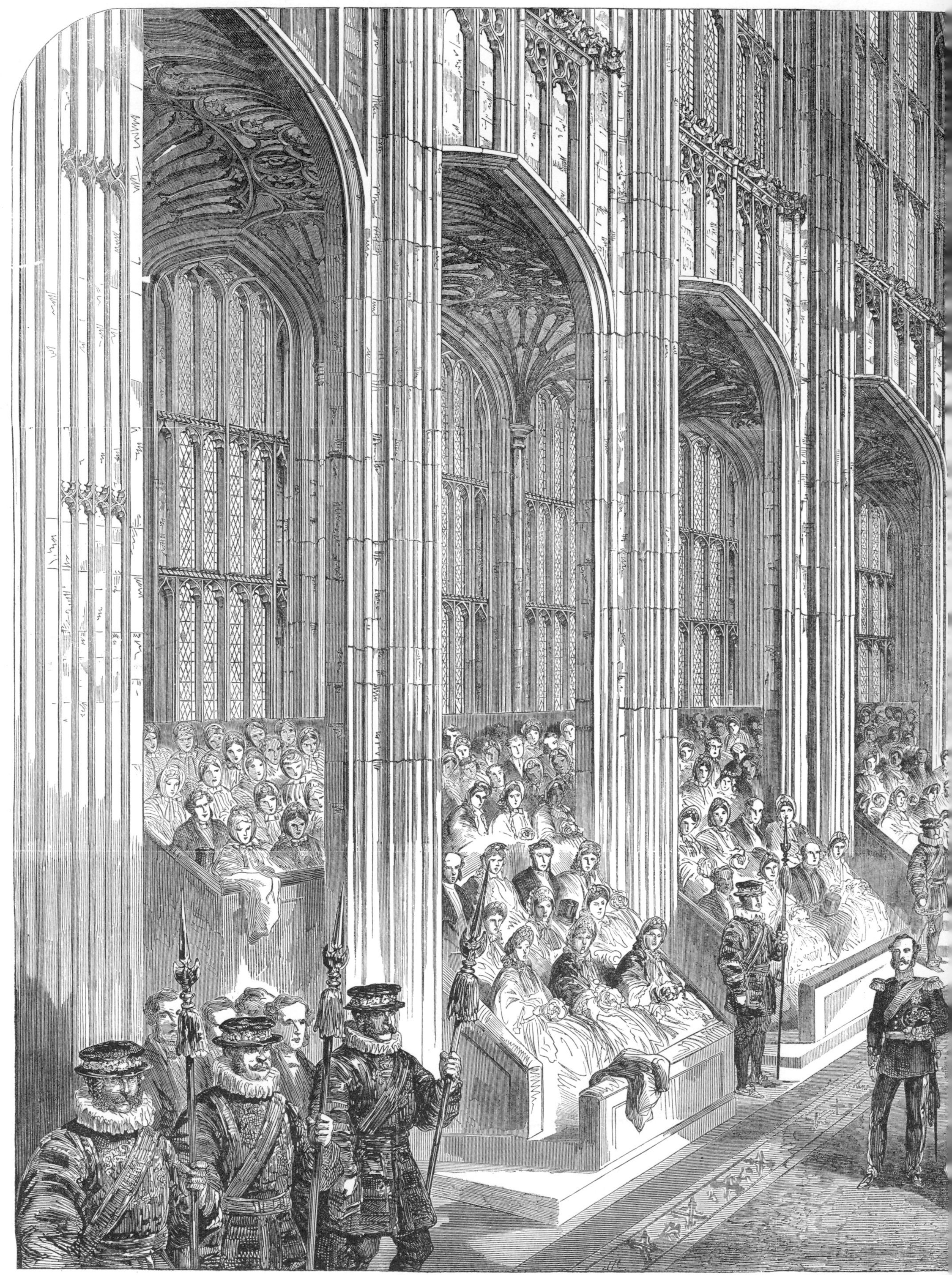

The Royal Marriage

in St. George's Chapel.

cruel, or wicked, or vicious rulers, and that the outward devotion and homage that surrounded them seldom went beyond mere hypocrisy and lip service; and we are now equally enabled to call facts to justify us for the profound and devoted feeling of loyalty entertained by the people of England for their gracious Sovereign and her family. Those facts are plain and palpable; they shine forth in our Queen's own virtue, integrity, and benevolence; in the example she has set, by her own domestic life, to the wives and mothers of England; in the pattern she has shown to foreign Courts in making her own the purest in Christendom. With truths undeniable as these to rest upon, Loyalty at once becomes easy of comprehension; nor are we, it is to be hoped, over-sanguine in looking for the continuance and perpetuation of that loyal feeling towards the Heir Apparent to the Throne and his bride. The young Princess of Wales comes to us with all the credentials that youth, innocence, and beauty can give. The Prince bears recommendations as weighty: the weightier, perhaps, that he has been amongst us from his infancy. Stalwart and gallant, travelled and accomplished, trained under the auspices of the tenderest of Mothers and the wisest, the best of Fathers, what can we—what should we—look forward to, in the union of the illustrious and amiable pair, but a Spring of love and gaiety, a Summer time of splendour and power, a Golden Evening when lives spent in wisdom and goodness shall culminate in reverence and honour. [March 10, 1863.]

THE WEDDING

With white shoulder-knots and collar of the Order of the Garter over his bright General's uniform, the Prince of Wales looked a noble and gallant, as he is a handsome, bridegroom. The Princess looked beautiful; but she was evidently in a state of extreme nervous agitation; her eyes were downcast, and it was easy to perceive the tremulous motion of the large bouquet of orange-flowers she carried. Her dress, of ample but inordinate dimension, was of white tulle over white silk, richly decked with orange-blossoms; a wreath of the same pretty components encircled her head, and mingled with her soft brown hair, which was not so entirely *coiffé à la Chinoise* as on Saturday, but had sufficient abandon given to it to permit one of those long, pendent curls called a *repentir* to fall on her neck. For all ornament she wore the superb parure of pearls and diamonds presented to her by the bridegroom. Her train, which was of great length, was of white silk.

THE OXFORD AND CAMBRIDGE BOAT-RACE

Our Engraving represents the somewhat rough landing of the Oxford crew after their gallant and successful match on the 28th ult. [March, 1863]. Upon nearing the shore their boat was found to have made so much water as to be in a sinking state, and the order "Sauve qui peut!" being given by the coxswain, who himself set the example of obeying it, the winning crew left their boat and scrambled through the water to land, amid the hearty congratulations of their friends.

The winning Oxford Crew Coming Ashore.

The Oxford Commemoration: the Procession of Boats.

OXFORD COMMEMORATION

On Tuesday morning [June 16, 1863] their Royal Highnesses the Prince and Princess of Wales, attended by their suites, left Marlborough House for the Paddington station, and travelled by the Great Western Railway to the Fulham station, en route for Oxford, to attend the Commemoration—one of the most brilliant festivals ever held on the banks of the Isis. Oxford was gaily decorated, the streets were crowded, and it is scarcely necessary to say that the Prince and Princess were greeted with a hearty welcome. The august visitors proceeded at three o'clock to the Sheldonian Theatre, where the Prince received from Lord Derby, the Chancellor of the University, his diploma of D.C.L. The same degree was conferred upon Prince Louis of Hesse, and on the chief officers of the households of the Prince and Princess of Wales—namely, Earl Spencer, the Earl of Mount-Edgcumbe, Lord Harris, and Lieutenant-General Knollys. In the course of the afternoon the Royal party went to Trinity College, entering by the grand garden gates, which have not before been opened since George III passed through them.

Wednesday was the great Commemoration Day. The Sheldonian Theatre was again crowded to excess, and again there were the noisy demonstrations of the undergraduates. Each recipient of the D.C.L. was vociferously cheered as he was presented to the Chancellor, and so also were the more distinguished of the visitors, without much distinction of party; but the loudest cheers of all were reserved, as on the previous day, for the Prince and Princess—cheers being called for and given in their honour, again and again, all through the proceedings. There was afterwards a boat-race, a banquet at Exeter College; and a grand ball given by the members of Christchurch wound up the day.

Earlier on Wednesday evening the time-honoured procession of boats took place on the Isis. The river presented a most beautiful sight. The various college barges moved along the bank, their tops covered with gaily-dressed ladies. The University barge, adorned with flags and flowers, was an object of general attraction. On the opposite side of the river large stands were erected, and filled with ladies. The Prince and Princess arrived at the barge in a boat constructed for the occasion. Mr. Hoare, the famous University "stroke", occupied that position in the Royal boat. After rowing past the barges the Royal boat returned to the University barge, when the Prince and Princess disembarked. The roof of this was covered with a distinguished company. Two picked crews then pulled a short race past the Royal barge, very few of the spectators caring which won, though all must have admired the skill and strength with which they rowed. Then came the procession of the boats, and Trinity, as at the head of the river, sweeping proudly up in its "eight", which came flying over the water as silently and as quickly as a bird, stopped in its own length before the Royal barge, that the boats of all other colleges might do homage to their supremacy and past year's triumph over them. This they did in the usual manner as they came in long procession, tossing their oars in honour of Trinity, and then waving their hats and cheering in honour of the Princess, who seemed deeply amused and interested in the whole proceeding. This over, the whole long file of boats swept under Folly Bridge, and, turning there, came back again in procession two and two abreast. All again tossed their oars as they passed the Princess. Again the Royal visitors took to their boat, the band played "God Save the Queen", and the prettiest of the Commemoration sights was over.

On Thursday, the Prince and Princess, in spite of their fatigues through the week, prolonged till an early hour at the Christchurch ball, were early astir. They drove off to Blenheim Palace, and breakfasted with the Duke and Duchess of Marlborough; on their return they paid short visits to the chief colleges and the objects of the greatest interest at Oxford, attended by the Dean and their suite. A public luncheon was given at two o'clock at Christchurch, at which the Prince and Princess were present; and at 3.30, after taking an affectionate farewell of the Dean and Mrs. Liddell, the Royal pair drove to the railway-station, up St. Aldgate's and down Queen-street, along both of which flags were flying and the houses decked out with wreaths, carpets, and artificial flowers round the windows.

Garret at No. 10 Hollybush-place.

THE DWELLINGS OF THE POOR IN BETHNAL GREEN

That public attention has at least [October, 1863] been directed to the condition of the poorer neighbourhoods of Bethnal-green is attributable to the evidence of the medical officer who, at an inquest held on the body of a child, declared that death had been caused by "blood-poisoning," through the impure state of the dwellings in a certain locality. That a wide and populous district has for years been subject to all the foulest influences which accompany a state of extreme filth and squalor may be due to the fact that private moneyed interests have had little to fear from parochial authority, even when they have not been represented by the same individuals.

The disgusting details which have lately been revealed to that portion of the public who have only heard of Bethnal-green as a low neighbourhood where the weavers live, somewhere in the far east of London, have been the steady growth of years. Those whose duty it has been to point out their inevitable consequences have treated them with indifference, or have suffered themselves to hope that some more powerful authority would eventually compel the alterations which they have faintly suggested. But "threatened men live long;" and even now the owners of the putrid sites in the purlieus of Friars-mount, in Thorold-square, in Twig-folly, and other centres of pestilence may well believe that neither board, nor commission, nor sanitary officer will trouble them if they can only let inquiry itself die, and so contrive to hush up the whole matter until the passing excitement is directed to some new object.

Anybody whose acquaintance with Bethnal-green commenced more than a quarter of a century ago will remember that some of those names of streets and rows which now seem to have such a grimly sarcastic meaning expressed not inaptly the places to which they originally referred. Hollybush-place, Green-street, Pleasant-place, and other neighbourhoods, which now consist of ruinous tenements, reeking with abominations, were outlying, decent cottages, standing on or near plots of garden ground, where the inmates reared prize tulips and rare dahlias in their scanty leisure, and where some of the last of the old French refugees dozed away the evenings of their lives in pretty summer-houses, amidst flower-beds gay with virginia stocks and creeping plants.

At this time, and before the present main road was formed to supersede the old Bethnal-green-road, which lies nearer to Cambridge-heath, this district was but a sort of country extension of Spitalfields; for Spitalfields had begun to assume the appearance that it exhibits now that its worst features have been exceeded by the wretched maze of streets and alleys which have built all greenness, except that belonging to rottenness, out of Bethnal. It may be remarked that the worst parts of Bethnal-green are not those inhabited by weavers, and that wherever the weaver *is* found his personal cleanliness and the tidiness of his poor room offer a striking contrast to those of many of his neighbours. His work requires a "long light," or leaden casement, so that he most frequently occupies garrets originally designed for his trade. Poor, suffering, nearly starved, and living in a house which shares with the rest the evils of bad or no drainage and insufficient water supply, his business requires at least some amount of personal cleanliness, or the delicate fabrics on which he is employed could never come out unsullied from the touch of coarser hands.

Skirting the station of the Great Eastern Railway in Shoreditch, and traversing Club-row—the Sunday resort of pigeon and bird fanciers—the earnest visitor has only to cross the road and turn up Nicholas-row, to find himself in as foul a neighbourhood as can be discovered in the civilised world, and amongst a population depressed almost to the last stage of human endurance. Should he have started with an impression that report had exaggerated the misery of these dwellings he will, if he have the heart—and, let us add, the stomach—to inspect them, prove that no allowable strength of language could do more than adequately express the condition of the dens which surround Friars-mount. Let the traveller penetrate further, and he will enter on a maze of streets each of which is a social crime, and each of which contains tributary hovels many degrees worse than itself. The miserable rooms are underlet and teeming with inhabitants to an almost inconceivable extent. The water for some fourteen or fifteen

Room occupied by a military tailor at No. 10 Hollybush-place.

houses is frequently supplied from one tap in a dirty corner, where it runs for only a short time every day; and the places are mostly undrained. Add to this the decay of vegetable matter, the occasional evidence of the presence of pigs from adjacent houses which have back-yards (these have none), and the sickly odour which belongs always to human beings living in such a state, and the result will represent a score of places extending over Bethnal-green parish for more than a mile in length and half a mile in breadth. There is nothing picturesque in such misery; it is but one painful and monotonous round of vice, filth, and poverty, huddled in dark cellars, ruined garrets, bare and blackened rooms, teeming with disease and death, and without the means, even if there were the inclination, for the most ordinary observations of decency or cleanliness.

This foul district must be purged, or our sanitary legislation is ineffectual, and all the wonderful sanitary schemes of which we have heard, and for which we shall all have to pay so much, are but costly failures.

CIVIC FESTIVITIES—Such of our readers as are familiar with civic festivities will remember that the Fruiterers' Company have annually presented to the Lord Mayor certain bushels of early apples, and have been entertained by his Lordship at the Mansion House. This year the fruit-offering has been increased to a remarkably fine dessert, and the Lord Mayor in the liberal spirit which has distinguished his Mayoralty, extended the invitations to 170 guests.

A LITANY OF GRATITUDE AT CHRISTMAS-TIDE

Christmas again! And England is, happily, at peace with all the civilised world; her condition is prosperous, and there is accumulation of evidence that the country is thriving that must force upon the least patriotic the conviction that we have much to be thankful for at this Christmas-time. And we honestly believe that when the English people gather, on Friday next, to inaugurate the season of festival, as their forefathers have done for ages, by a solemn recognition of the religious character of the feast, all this will come to their hearts and form a Christmas litany of gratitude.

By a time-honoured custom, at this period of the year the journalist is permitted to relinquish his ordinary themes, and for a few days to assimilate his tone to that of the rest of the world; and we would at this time dwell upon the subject of charity. In the days which will precede Christmas Day there are ample and abundant opportunities of preparing a happy Friday for many who, if no such forethought be taken, will spend but a wretched one. Let us, therefore, recall to the recollection of all who have money, food, coals, clothes at their disposal—and who is there that has not something to spare?—that a gift which appears to them a small one will become great in the eyes of the destitute. We believe that myriads of kind things are left undone because persons in comfortable circumstances have no idea of the exceeding smallness of the resources of the poor, and of the proportionate value of aid which the benevolent often withhold because it seems so small. There is scarcely a coin, an article of clothing, or a present of any other necessary, that will not become an important element in the Christmas Day of the needy. Surely every one who reads these words can bestow a half-crown, or a garment, or half a sack of coals, or a child's dinner? We are sure that we shall be thanked for the suggestion when those who may carry it out have been thanked by the eyes of the receivers of such gifts.

Our aim is to point out facts to those who do not know how much good they can effect. They have but to look around them; or, if they are unable to perceive an object of kindness, let them ask their minister or their medical man to tell them of one. And for other persons whose money is ready enough, but whose time is still more precious, there are the magistrates' poor-boxes. Next to examining a case one's-self, there is no better way of giving alms than through the excellent magistrates, who have such effectual means of ascertaining that charity is not given to those who do not need it. If the Christmas litany contain a recital of things for which gratitude is due to the Author of all Good, can such gratitude be better shown than by helping the poor to believe that Christmas is not all selfish holiday, but a solemn memory for those who enjoy the numberless comforts of a happy home. [December 19, 1863.]

UNDERGROUND WORKS IN THE EUSTON ROAD

Our Engraving represents a section of the underground works at the junction of Tottenham-court-road and Hampstead-road with Euston-road. The view is taken from beneath the north-west corner of Tottenham-court-road looking towards the east along the line of Euston-road. It will serve to show what extensive subterranean works are being constructed in different parts of London, yet which make no show on the surface, and the very existence of which is probably unknown to a very large portion of the inhabitants residing in the neighbourhood or daily walking over the site. We have chosen this particular locality because it is a point where the lines of a number of different works intersect each other.

There is, first, immediately under the surface of the road, a double set of mains and pipes for supplying the district with water and gas. Beneath these passes, transversely, the iron tube belonging to the Pneumatic Dispatch Company, through which parcels are constantly being conveyed backwards and forwards, and occasionally the mailbags also, between the General Post Office and this district. Under this tube, is the tunnel for the Metropolitan (or, as it is more generally called, the Underground) Railway, through which trains are constantly passing and repassing.

The pneumatic Dispatch Company's tube cuts through the crown of this tunnel. On each side of it run large sewers which form part of the London Main-Drainage works. Beneath all is a longitudinal section of the proposed Hampstead, Midland, North-Western, and Charing-cross Railway.

Underground works at the Junction of Hampstead-road, and Tottenham-court-road.

COCOANUT TREE AT SION, ISLEWORTH

It is chiefly to the liberality and to the interest taken in such matters by our nobility that horticulture is indebted for its extra-ordinary development, for they furnish scientific men with opportunities to set the harsh climate of our northern island at defiance, and, in the artificially created tropical climate of their great glass houses, set before us, in luxuriant growth, all the wonders of vegetable creation. Those, therefore, who may not have had opportunities for travelling may see the plants of far-off lands grow, flower, and bear fruit, almost as well as those who have; for it is only in very rare instances that our eminent horticulturists have failed in fruiting the plants of other climates. The subject of our Illustration is an example of the skill and energy displayed in this department of science; for it is to Mr. Smith, of Isleworth, who has the management of the grounds and conservatories of his Grace the Duke of Northumberland at Sion, that the merit is due of producing the first cocoanut ever grown in Europe. There is now at Sion a cocoanut tree, in luxuriant condition, bearing numerous flowers, both male and female, and fruit which is rapidly increasing in size. The first formed is now nearly ten inches in diameter, and bids fair to become a nut of large size.

This success has been brought about entirely by the ingenuity with which Mr. Smith contrived to manipulate the pollen, and bring about, by purely artificial means, such results as are produced by wind or birds when the tree is growing in its native soil.